PRINCIPLES OF

PSYCHOLOGICAL

MEASUREMENT

THE CENTURY PSYCHOLOGY SERIES

Richard M. Elliott, Gardner Lindzey & Kenneth MacCorquodale

Editors

G. C. Helmstadter

Arizona State University

PRINCIPLES OF PSYCHOLOGICAL MEASUREMENT

 New York

Appleton-Century-Crofts

Division of Meredith Publishing Company

Copyright ©1964 by
MEREDITH PUBLISHING COMPANY

6114·–2

Library of Congress Card Number: 64-13199

PRINTED IN THE UNITED STATES OF AMERICA

E43470

To my mentors, who, because they were effective teachers, may find their ideas expressed in this volume; and to my students in whose future work I hope to see the effects of my own small contributions.

Preface

EVER SINCE my first years of teaching a basic course in measurement to psychology students, I have felt the need for a text which concentrates on the underlying principles of testing rather than on the instruments themselves. Perhaps because those students I found in my classes differed so markedly in their ultimate goals — some wished to become behavioral scientists who would need to measure human behavior in their research studies; some hoped to aid their fellow man through personnel, guidance, or clinical work and desired to use measurement to better understand those with whom they worked; others simply wanted to be able to correctly interpret standardized tests and to be able to construct their own achievement exams so as to facilitate their task of classroom teaching; still others aspired to become specialists in the field of measurement and felt a need to dig deeply into theory as well as practical application — differed so much in what they expected, that I became acutely aware of the fact that the only common ground for all the separate applications of testing was to be found in the logic of measurement and in the body of empirical findings which was accruing through many years of extensive investigation of the measurement process.

I also discovered that, even with a single set of principles, sufficient flexibility to meet the varying interests of classes whose composition changed from term to term could be achieved if the tests themselves were used (different ones in each different class) as vehicles for illustrating the principles rather than as major objects of concentrated study.

The purpose of this volume, then, is to summarize, for the student, the logic and the major principles of measurement as they are known in the light of today's knowledge. The teacher who uses this text is thus afforded an opportunity to meet the particular interests of his specific classes and to make his own special contribution through the selection of whatever current, published, or self-constructed instruments he finds of greatest value for demonstrating the application of these principles.

This book differs from others in the field in one other important aspect — it assumes that the student has some fundamental knowledge of elementary descriptive statistics. In psychological measurement, as in all other fields of both pure and applied science, it is becoming increasingly difficult to grasp modern concepts without some facility with the application of mathematics. Thus, it is my firm conviction that much is lost when the concepts of measurement cannot be presented in the terms and context in which they were originally developed.

Fortunately, instruction in basic statistics is moving downward in our educational structure. Once taught only at the graduate level, statistics is now required in many undergraduate curriculums; it is being taught in advanced high schools throughout the country; and, in some experimental situations, the basic concepts are now presented at the elementary school level. This means that a great number of today's students, and most of tomorrow's, will have had some exposure to the necessary fundamental statistical concepts before they engage in the study of measurement. For those who find their way into a course in measurement without prior exposure to statistics, there are now available some effective self-helps in the area. The instructional programs prepared by Teaching Machines Incorporated and by Gorow are just two of the many which might be mentioned. Or, the instructor who wishes to refresh his students in basic statistical concepts can do so as the need arises.

The experienced teacher of measurement will also note several other innovations. For example, the classical criteria for evaluating a test — standardization, objectivity, reliability, and validity, have been presented in a unifying framework of error types. Expectancy tables are presented as a form of norms, since, after all, they represent ways of giving meaning to raw scores and not a special type of validity data independent of the information summarized by a test-criterion correlation coefficient. Finally, factorial validity has been classified along with other forms of content validity rather than listed as a type of empirical validity. Although factorial validity does involve the gathering of data, it logically is primarily concerned with an analysis of the content of a test rather than the relationship between a test and some non-test behavior which the measure is supposed to predict.

In the writer's experience, each one of these breaks with tradition has been of great benefit in helping to achieve the kind of broad, basic understanding of the process of measuring behavioral traits which every instructor in this area hopes to bring about in his students.

G. C. H.

Contents

CONTENTS   xv

List of Tables

List of Figures

PRINCIPLES OF
PSYCHOLOGICAL
MEASUREMENT

1

General Nature of Testing

INTRODUCTION

WITH THE POSSIBLE EXCEPTION of psychoanalysis, probably no other application of the study of human behavior has become so widely known to the general public as that of testing; and the reader himself will be quite well aware of the growing influence that the results of "mental measurement" are exerting on the lives of the members of our society.

It was recently estimated, for example, that during a single school year some four million people took tests administered by only five of the agencies that give tests on a nationwide basis. And, this figure includes neither the tests given locally in the schools and classrooms all over the country to evaluate educational progress, nor those administered by the military services to aid in the placement of inductees into various training programs, nor those offered by such agencies as the U. S. Employment Service in vocational guidance work. Furthermore, it excludes selection and employment tests given by many institutions and companies as part of an application for admission or employment and the tests used in clinics and hospitals as aids in the diagnosis and description of behavior disorders.

It would seem safe to say, therefore, that the life of every person reading this book is, at some time, going to be influenced by a test score. Certainly, when something becomes as important as testing now is in our society, it is well worth learning about.

As is often the case when the general public has an acquaintance with a relatively technical application of some science, there are many prevalent misconceptions about the nature of tests and testing. At one extreme are those who have complete faith in all tests, ignoring the limitations of such devices, and failing to differentiate between good and poor instruments. To them, once a test score is obtained, the future behavior of the individual measured can be foretold with exactitude, and there is little hope for the individual to alter his destiny. At the other extreme are the individuals who, having seen a poor test or having discovered that even a good test is not perfect, throw up their hands in horror at the very thought of testing—completely ignoring the evidence that in many, many situations a good test provides us with the very best information available on which to base a decision. Also, at this extreme, are those whose philosophical view of life somehow leads them to view tests as an invasion of human privacy or a coercion toward conformity.

To the person who fully understands the history and the logic behind the development and use of tests and who is acquainted with the results of the vast amount of empirical evidence gathered about questions raised with respect to testing, none of the above positions are tenable. In this and the following chapters, it is hoped that the reader will gain some insight into the whys and wherefores of testing; that he will understand enough of the principles of testing and be sufficiently familiar with the major experimental and empirical findings to be able to make an intelligent evaluation and use of published tests and to approach the development of tests of his own for classroom or other uses with a reasonable knowledge of the methods and tools available for this purpose.

Origins of Testing

If the writings of Aristotle and Plato were to be interpreted in the light of today's knowledge, the origins of testing might be set as far back as the third or fourth century B.C. To be sure, many devices have been employed down through the ages which serve the same purposes for which tests are used today. Nevertheless, the earliest antecedents having any direct bearing on mental measurement as we know it are to be found in the 19th century A.D.

Beginning around 1830 three relatively distinct developments in the fields of psychology and mathematics appeared which later gave considerable impetus to mental measurement. And, even today, traces of these distinct influences are discernible in the various approaches to the construction and use of tests. In France, through the influence of such men as Pineal, Esquirol, Itard, Seguin, Charcot, and Ribot, there arose considerable interest in the study of individuals who deviated from the normal pattern. At about the same time Weber, Fechner, and Wundt in Germany were establishing an interest in the experimental study of normal adult human behavior. Finally, during the same period, but in the field of mathematics, Laplace and Gauss demonstrated the usefulness of the normal curve (expressed previously in 1733 by de Moivre) as a mathematical tool—although it remained for Quetelet in 1846 to apply it to the measurement of human characteristics.

Should an attempt be made to select the man who might be called the "father of mental testing," the names of Sir Francis Galton (1822–1911), James McKeen Cattell (1860–1944), and Alfred Binet (1857–1911) would each find vigorous supporters.

Galton, profoundly influenced by the work of Sir Charles Darwin (whose *Origin of the Species* appeared in 1859), became intensely interested in the inheritance of mental traits and in 1869 published his famous book, *Hereditary Genius*. Fourteen years later a book entitled *Inquiries into Human Faculty and its Development,* which presents what might be called the beginnings of the scientific study of individual differences and of mental tests, was published. By 1886 Galton had established his famous anthropometric laboratory devoted to the measurement of physical and sensori-motor characteristics of human beings, and had worked out the concept of statistical correlations (though its mathematical formulation must be attributed to Karl Pearson, 1857–1936). Thus, the use of statistical methods as the major mathematical tool for the scientific study of individual differences and the evaluation of mental tests was inaugurated. Carried on in England by such men as Karl Pearson, Charles Spearman, Cyril Burt, and Geoffrey Thompson, and in America by T. L. Kelley, L. L. Thurstone, J. P. Guilford, and their students, the use of statistical inference and other quantitative concepts has become an integral part of today's development and application of mental measurement.

While Galton gave testing its scientific start in England, it was James McKeen Cattell who brought testing to the United States, still flavored with the experimental aura of Wundt's laboratory, and added to it a typical American pragmatism. As a graduate student in Wundt's laboratory at Leipzig, Cattell learned the importance of rigorous control in making observations of behavior, but rebelled against the classical concept that the major goal in psychology was to form generalizations about the normal human adult mind. Noting that deviations from these generalizations (in those days considered to be troublesome errors interfering with the work) did not completely disappear even when the most rigid of experimental controls were applied, Cattell preferred to think of such differences in performance as real variables worthy of scientific study. Thus, in spite of objections from Wundt, Cattell's doctoral dissertation was a study of individual differences in reaction time.

A few years later, having had his interest in the study of individual differences furthered through contact with Galton in England, Cattell established psychological laboratories at the University of Pennsylvania and at Columbia. In these laboratories, considerable attention was given to the development and refinement of mental tests—a designation first used by Cattell (1890) .

The mental tests used by Cattell in the 1880's, however, were not like those known today. Working in a time when the epistemological views of John Locke and British empiricism (which held that all knowledge came through experience) had not yet waned, and when the prevalent psychological theory held that complex mental life was but a combination of the simpler sensory experiences, it was only natural that early attempts at mental measurement should be concerned with sensory capacities and other simpler functions. Thus, among the "tests" given to all entering freshmen at Pennsylvania and Columbia one finds measures of reaction time, visual and auditory acuity, sensitivity to pain, and the like.

As almost any student of psychology today would anticipate, an empirical study of the relationship between scores on such tests and later scholastic achievement in college was disheartening. Wissler (1901), for example, reported that no significant relationships were found between the results of such tests given to freshmen at Columbia University and their course grades. Thus, while the essential mathematical refinements of measurement came from Galton and his followers in England, and the awareness of the importance of rigid control in making observations coupled with the concept of individual differences as a legitimate topic for psychologists to study was brought to America from Germany by Cattell, it remained for Binet in France to provide the content necessary to make tests the useful instruments we know today.

Alfred Binet was an experimental psychologist who worked in the traditional French climate where the major interest was in studying individuals, and particularly individuals who deviated from the normal. Thus, early in his training, Binet became interested in the investigation of retarded children. In 1896, after many years of carefully studying differences in the behavior of retarded, normal, and advanced children, Binet and a colleague, Victor Henri, described a series of tests of the "more complex" mental processes which they hoped to try out. In the years to follow, many experimental types of tests were examined to determine whether or not children in higher age or school grade groups did better than younger children, and whether or not the results agreed in general with teachers' judgments of the children's educational potential.

As these studies progressed, it became more and more apparent that the direct approach to measuring general ability was more profitable than the measurement of the simpler functions. And so it was in 1904, when Binet was included on a commission appointed by the minister of public instruction in Paris to study the problem of educating retarded children, that he and Th. Simon developed their first formal scale for the direct measurement of more complex abilities. Thus, although Binet's earlier work had suggested that his, as contrasted with Cattell's type of test, was the more promising, the success of the Binet-Simon Scale in 1905 and its subsequent revisions of 1908 and 1911 was required to establish testing on a firm basis. Once gaining a solid foothold, however, and given additional impetus through the development and use of group tests in the army during the First World War, mental measurement has steadily grown to become, at least in this country, an accepted part of today's life.

Use of Tests

Now that the reader has seen how important tests have become in our daily lives and has noted the main roots of psychological measurement in the history of psychology, he may be wondering more specifically about the major purposes or uses of tests in our present society. Cronbach (1949) has classified all applications of mental measurement under three main headings: *prognosis, diagnosis,* and *research.*

The first of these purposes, that of prognosis or prediction, is the one most obvious to the layman. Almost always, when psychological tests are mentioned, the so-called IQ tests given to children in school to predict their academic performance come to mind. Certainly, they offer the classical example of a situation in which observations in a standardized situation are made for the specific purpose of predicting future behavior.

Closely related is the application of tests in a selection situation. Here, an employer administers a test for the purpose of selecting those who will be hired; or an admissions officer at a college or university makes use of test scores to decide who should be allowed to enter. Though less obviously a problem of prediction, some thought about the nature of the implication when one person rather than another is hired or admitted to school will make it apparent that a prediction is involved. Every time a few candidates are selected from a large number of applicants, a prediction is made that those chosen will succeed and that those turned down would have failed, or at least not have performed as well as those selected. This is true whether or not the decision is made with the use of test results or by other means.

One other application of testing not often subsumed under the heading of prediction needs to be mentioned. This is the evaluation of accomplishment in a classroom or training situation. At first, the reader may be tempted to comment that this type of measurement does not involve prediction at all, but rather description—description of an individual's performance in some specific learning situation. However, if one asks why such a description of a person is desired, the relationship to prediction becomes clear. Whenever a grade is assigned, a prediction is made as to the individual's quality of performance in some future situation which depends upon the knowledge or training received, be it in the classroom or on the job.

Thus, whether tests are used to predict future academic performance, to select individuals for employment or admission, or to evaluate the extent to which an individual has profited from some learning situation, their function is that of making a prediction of future performance.

The second major use of tests listed by Cronbach is that of diagnosis. Actually, as will be shown later, diagnosis is really an elaborate form of prediction. However, this form of prediction is sufficiently distinct from what is usually meant by the term, so that there is considerable justification in listing diagnosis as a special class of uses of psychological measurement.

The diagnostic use of tests may be distinguished from the predictive use of such instruments first of all on the basis of the type of measurement involved. In prediction, the emphasis is primarily on differences between performances of individuals or between the performance of one individual and some standard; in diagnosis, on the other hand, considerable attention is paid to the analysis and description of the various characteristics or performances from task to task within one individual. The types of test score interpretation which must be used in these two different situations correspond roughly to what Cattell (1944) has called *ipsative* and *normative* measurement. In normative measurement, which is the type appropriate in the predictive use of tests, test performances are intepreted in terms of the performances of other individuals in the same situation. In ipsative measurement, however, the interpretation of the performance in the test situation depends upon the performance of the same individual in other test situations.

A second major difference between the diagnostic and predictive use of tests involves the extent to which there is concern for finding causal relationships. In making predictions of academic success or in selecting employees it is not necessary to single out and find the causes of success. All that is needed is an empirically observed relationship between some observable behavior exhibited prior to the criterion situation (the situation to which a prediction is made) and some measure of later success. In diagnosis, on the other hand, it is the prime purpose of the test to isolate those characteristics which are responsible for the difficulties being diagnosed.

An example which may serve to illustrate these differences between the diagnostic and predictive use of tests is that of John who receives a low score on a test used in admitting students to college. If previous follow-up studies of students have shown that a high degree of relationship exists between scores on the test and subsequent performance in college, this is all that is needed to make a prediction about John's grade point were he to be admitted to college. Suppose, however, that John were admitted to college, and it turned out that he failed. With no more information than the one test score, we have no knowledge of *why* he failed. It could have been because he had little scholastic aptitude, because he was deficient in knowledge of subject matter taught in high school, or because he was an extremely poor reader. Any one (or combination) of these could have caused both the low score on the admissions test and his failure in further studies. To make a diagnosis of John's difficulties, that is, to determine which of the above is responsible for his failure, requires a comparison of scores obtained by John on several tests. If, for example, it were judged from an interview and a talk with John's parents that he was studying hard, and it was further found that his scores on an untimed test of aptitude and on certain subject matter tests were high, while scores on a reading test were low, a tentative diagnosis would be that John's troubles were chiefly the result of his poor reading.

This same example might be used to show why it was mentioned earlier that diagnosis is actually an elaborate form of prediction. To see the reasoning behind such a statement, it is necessary to answer only the question of why one bothers to make a diagnosis in the first place. Why are we not content with just the empirical relationships between test scores and grades and the prediction that John will have difficulty in college? What reason is there for wanting to make a statement that poor reading is the cause of John's trouble? An additional hint as to the reason that diagnosis can be thought of as a form of prediction is obtained if it is recalled that the diagnosis made in the example was but a tentative one.

The answer to the above questions is, of course, that a diagnosis is made because there is some hope of remedying the situation, and further, the correct one from among the several possible causes is sought because the action to be taken to improve the situation will depend upon the outcome of the diagnosis. This means, then, that a diagnosis is but a prediction that if a certain action were to be taken, the difficulties would vanish. In attributing John's difficulties to poor reading a prediction is made that if John were to improve his reading, he would find that he could succeed in college. If John were sent to a reading clinic, his reading improved, and then he returned to college and was successful, then our prediction would be verified and our diagnosis confirmed.

It certainly takes no great deal of imagination to suppose that a test, as a sample of human behavior in a standardized and controlled situation, might be useful for research purposes in a science of human behavior. And, this is the case.

The use of tests for research purposes, however, is not as great as for prediction and diagnosis. And, there is good reason for this. When used for research purposes, tests must usually be considered as completely valid measures of certain human characteristics. While no good researcher is naive enough to believe that tests are infallible, he must treat test scores in his experiment as accurate quantifications of real and useful variables. For, only by treating tests in this way can they be used as control variables, as descriptions of human characteristics, or to verify hypotheses about relationships among behaviors.

Classifications of Tests

Finally, before turning to the logic of testing, it might be worthwhile to take a look at the various ways in which modern tests are classified. Not only will this provide an overview of the wide variety of tests which are now available, but it will also serve to familiarize the reader with a number of common terms used in describing tests.

Before the different types of tests are discussed, it should be mentioned that classification systems per se are not right or wrong but useful or useless. Not every expert in the field of measurement would classify tests in the same way. In general, however, the classifications presented here have been useful for a number of people working in the area.

One major dimension along which tests have been classified is that of the nature of the trait which it was designed to measure. Perhaps the broadest classification in this respect is that which divides tests into what Cronbach (1960) has called measures of *typical behavior* and measures of *maximum performance*. In trying to measure such things as attitudes, interests, and personality characteristics an attempt is made to get some index of an individual's usual or typical behavior as he goes about his daily life. In such measures, the examinee is not urged to put his best foot forward, but to report how he would normally behave in some situation. There are no right or wrong answers except as they are truly representative of the individual; and, instead of one key, there may be several, each representative of different sets of typical behaviors found within a human population.

In measures of maximum performance, on the other hand, an attempt is made to determine just how well a person can perform in a given situation. Here, it is hoped that the individual will do his best and the examinee's responses are compared with a key, prepared by experts, which distinguishes between correct and incorrect answers.

Traditionally, measures of maximum performance have been separated into three subclasses: tests of aptitude, of ability, and of achievement. As more and more has been learned about the correlates of and influences upon test performance, however, it has become increasingly difficult to ascertain the extent to which such devices measure "innate capacity" as contrasted with environmental influences. Thus, in the light of today's knowledge, it is inappropriate to think of tests of aptitude, ability, and achievement as discrete classes of tests distinguished by whether they measure innate ability, the influence of environment, or a combination of both. There remains, on the other hand, a continuum of the extent to which performance on a test is modifiable by experience. Thus, aptitude tests can be thought of as those which measure functions that improve little with practice; ability tests as those which show some relationship to general environmental enrichment; and achievement tests as those designed specifically to measure the degree of accomplishment in some particular educational or training experience.

As is always the case, when a classification system is based on a continuous rather than a discrete variable (in this case modifiability) there will be many tests which are difficult to place in one group rather than another. And, there will always be some disagreement as to whether a particular test is aptitude or ability, or is ability or achievement. Nonetheless, there are some areas upon which almost universal agreement has been reached. Thus, for example, it is common practice to speak of musical aptitude and clerical aptitude, because performance on these tests changes little even with practice; of scholastic ability and mechanical ability, because scores on these tests can be improved to a limited extent; and classroom achievement tests, for these measure what has been learned. Always, the basis for distinguishing among the classes is the extent to which the trait measured is modifiable by environmental experience.

In addition to a classification of tests according to what kind of a trait they measure, a second major dimension of classification has been developed according to *how* the trait is measured. Thus, tests are sometimes described as individual vs. group; objective vs. subjective; paper and pencil vs. performance; language vs. non-language; and as power vs. speed.

As the name implies, individual tests are those which must be given to only one person at a time. Such tests, most commonly, are those which require the manipulation of apparatus or in which the examiner seeks to make observations other than those easily recorded by the examinee as he responds to each question. Group tests on the other hand, are presented in a format which permits each individual to record his own response and, of course, which is relatively inexpensive to produce in quantities. The classical example of an individual test is the famous Stanford-revision of the Binet; and any of the tests commonly used as entrance examinations to colleges and universities throughout the country, such as the College Entrance Examination Board Tests, the College Ability Test, and so forth, serve as examples of a group test.

A classification of tests as objective or subjective depends upon the way in which the test is scored. If a test is set up in such a way that every person who scores the test, no matter when he scores it, will get the same score for a given individual, the test is completely objective. On the other hand, if some judgment in the evaluation of the response is left to the person doing the scoring, then the test is called subjective. It should be noted that the objectivity-subjectivity dimension for labeling tests is really a continuous one, and not dichotomous as is sometimes assumed. A matching or multiple-choice test in which the examinee selects from a list of possible answers the one which he thinks is correct, and for which a stencil key can be cut, is (because of clerical errors in scoring) highly, but not completely, objective; a short answer test in which the examinee must fill in a blank with a word or phrase, or a mathematics test in which some credit is allowed for partially correct answers (for example, correct procedure but a minor arithmetical error) is somewhat more subjective; and a test composed of general discussion and essay type questions represents an extreme of subjectivity.

The terms used in classifying tests as paper and pencil vs. performance need no explanation. A typical apparatus test is one of mechanical ability which requires the examinee to assemble certain objects such as a bicycle bell, a lock, etc. (see Figure 1); a paper and pencil form of mechanical ability test (see Figure 2) might be one in which tools are to be matched with the materials on which they are used.

FIGURE 1: The Minnesota Mechanical Assembly Test
Reproduced through the courtesy of C. H. Stoelting Company.

Nonlanguage tests are those which, in contrast to most tests, use no written or spoken word in either the directions or the test questions themselves. All instructions are presented by demonstration and pantomime, and answers often involve performance on an apparatus though paper and pencil tests are sometimes used. Such tests are used primarily for measuring aptitudes or abilities of illiterates, or for those speaking foreign tongues.

Once again, in attempting to classify tests as speed vs. power, it is necessary to think of the characteristic involved as really being continuous, with most tests falling near the middle of the scale rather than at either extreme. A pure speed test is one composed of items so easy that every one who tries them will answer them correctly. Thus, the score obtained is entirely dependent upon how many items the examinee reaches in the time limit allowed. In a pure power test, on the other hand, every examinee is permitted to try every single item and his score depends entirely on how many questions he can answer or problems he can solve without regard to the rate at which he works. A classical example of a pure speed test is the Minnesota Clerical Aptitude test in which the task is to examine a long list of pairs of names and pairs of numbers and to indicate which of the pairs contains identical numbers or names (see Figure 3). Obviously, with sufficient time, everyone would be

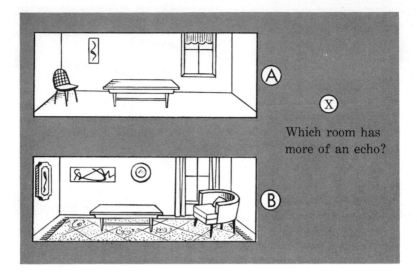

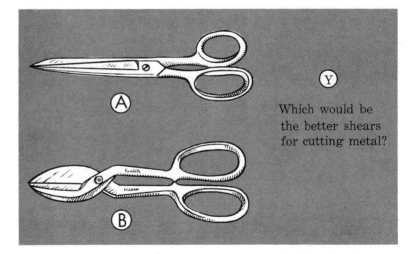

FIGURE 2: Sample Items from the Bennett Mechanical Comprehension Test

able to get every item correct. Thus, a severe time limit is imposed and scores are almost entirely dependent upon how far an individual gets without making careless errors. A vocabulary test, on the other hand, in which no time limit is imposed would represent a pure power test.

INSTRUCTIONS

On the inside pages there are two tests. One of the tests consists of pairs of names and the other of pairs of numbers. If the two names or the two numbers of a pair are *exactly the same* make a check mark (√) on the line between them; if they are *different,* make no mark on that line. When the examiner says "Stop!" draw a line under the last pair at which you have looked.

Samples done correctly of pairs of *Numbers*

79542 ____ 79524

5794367 _√_ 5794367

Samples done correctly of pairs of *Names*

John C. Linder ____ John C. Lender

Investors Syndicate _√_ Investors Syndicate

Now try the samples below.

66273894 ____ 66273984

527384578 ____ 527384578

New York World ____ New York World

Cargill Grain Co. ____ Cargil Grain Co.

This is a test for Speed and Accuracy.
Work as fast as you can without making mistakes.

FIGURE 3: Sample Items from the Minnesota Vocational Test for Clerical Workers

Source: D. Paterson and H. Longstaff, *Minnesota Vocational Test for Clerical Workers*. Reproduced by permission of The Psychological Corporation. Copyright 1933. All rights reserved.

Finally, a third major basis for the classification of psychological tests results from the recent utility theory (Cronbach & Gleser, 1957) as contrasted with the more traditional measurement theory approach to testing. Considering the function of testing to provide information on the basis of which personnel decisions can be improved, it is reasonable to classify tests according to the use to which they are put—that is, by the type of personnel decision for which they provide the most useful information. Thus, more and more commonly, one hears of placement tests, classification tests, and selection tests.

While at first such a system of describing tests seems somewhat artificial, it is perhaps the most important from a practical point of view. For, although a test of mechanical ability might be used for any one of the three types of decisions, it is becoming more and more apparent to those in the field of psychometrics that different approaches to the construction and evaluation of tests are needed depending upon the use to be made of the instrument. Thus, the same test which is extremely valuable in improving guidance or psychotherapy decisions (a classification situation) may not be the most desirable test where the problem is one of selection or one of placement.

Although other schemes for classification of psychological tests are possible (for example, tests can be grouped according to whether they are conventional, situational, or projective) those ways presented above are the ones which are most commonly used in describing tests at the present time, and which are of greatest help in untangling the maze of labels used in naming published tests.

LOGIC OF TESTING

Nature of Mental Traits[1]

In the preceding section it was noted that a psychological test can be thought of as a way of obtaining a sample of human behavior under controlled conditions. This is an extremely gen-

[1] The material of this section summarizes part of an important discussion of construct validity presented by Cronbach and Meehl (1955). Students whose primary interest is in testing per se would do well to refer to the original article.

eral statement which needs some clarification. To be sure, when a test is administered, a sample of human behavior is obtained. But this sample is always taken with respect to some very specific characteristic or trait. And, when a scoring system is applied to the test, the observations made are quantified so as to resemble a measure of some existing, real, underlying variable which is often referred to as a mental trait.

But just what is this "thing" called a mental trait—this "thing" which is being measured? Certainly it is not something that can be seen, heard, touched, smelled, or tasted. And if it is not something that can be known through one's senses, what justification is there for saying a mental trait, for example, that of intelligence, exists?

If a physicist were to be asked to indicate what gravitation was —really, he would probably either mention something about the force of attraction between two bodies or he would directly describe some empirical observations. Should the term force be used in describing the nature of gravity, it would be necessary to inquire as to what force is; and, if the physicist were pushed far enough he would ultimately retreat to the description of observable phenomena.

Exactly the same situation is true in the measurement of behaviorial characteristics. If a psychologist is to avoid specifying the nature of intelligence in terms which themselves need to be explained, he must ultimately resort to the description of certain observations. Thus, in the final analysis, a mental trait is nothing other than a convenient handle for specifying a particular set of observations; or, if the psychologist wishes to go beyond a mere label and summarize a great mass of observed data, a theoretical concept. Such things, then, as mechanical ability, musical talent, clerical aptitude, and even intelligence are to be considered as *postulated* attributes of people—attributes which are *assumed* to be reflected in observable behavior.

Although the original conception of some mental trait arises as an explanation for some particular set of data, almost never is the concept evolved restricted to one group of observations. The problem with which a psychologist is faced in defining a mental trait, therefore, is not just that of developing a concept which accounts for present observables (that is, facts and empirical laws of which knowledge already exists) , but also forming the concept in such a way that it provides implications for new observables which might be found. This latter is essential because the psychologist is always interested in using his concepts in situations other than his laboratory. A counsellor, for example, must rely on definitions of mental traits which have some generality. Otherwise, when sitting with a test score and a client before him, he would be unable to forecast behavior in diverse or even unique situations for which the relationship between test score and later behavior is not at present known.

Formally, a concept which meets the requirements of accounting for present knowledge and providing implications about new observables, is known as a *construct*. Mental traits, as hypothetical constructs, always carry with them what might be called associated meanings. Thus, every time a test score which purportedly is a measure of some mental trait (that is, some construct) is interpreted, certain properties are added to this construct. For example, in interpreting a test score it is implied that a person who possesses a given amount of this attribute will, with some specified probability, act in manner X when placed in situation Y. More concretely, when a test score is interpreted, assertions such as "a person with an IQ of 125 has a probability of .80 of getting a B in English at the State University," are made. This assertion and others like it give additional meaning to the original construct.

Thus, in the context of testing, the definition of a mental trait—that is, the specification of what it is that a test is measuring —must consider all the known relationships of test scores to other things *and* to that which is asserted about people who achieve certain test scores. It is apparent, then, that in formulating a concept of a mental trait, such questions as those following must be considered. Is the trait stable or does it fluctuate from time to time within an individual? What is the distribution of the trait in the human population? To what extent is the trait influenced by heredity, and to what extent by environment? What are the laws governing the development of the trait as the person matures? If the concept is to be accurate, all these must be answered.

Obviously, not all answers to these questions will be alike. Thus, one psychologist might define a trait which he calls intelligence in such a way that it is constant, and then explain observed changes in test scores with age as a result of changes in motivation, or as the effects of an irrelevant portion of the test which measures a trait that is influenced by learning; a second psychologist, however, might postulate a trait of intelligence as one which *does* change with maturity or environmental enrichment. Consequently, the early literature of mental testing is full of controversy as to whether this or that definition of some mental trait is correct. The modern point of view is that the hypothetical construct defining a mental trait is not to be thought of as right or wrong, but useful or useless for explaining present knowledge and suggesting new relationships to be empirically verified.

Two important things for a beginner in the area of testing to realize are:

1. It is not possible to have, until all the data about humans and their behavior is in, a completely satisfactory and universal definition of a mental trait such as intelligence.
2. Before a test designed to provide a measure of some psychological trait can be evaluated it will be necessary not only to know the something about the test and the author's concept of the trait, but to subscribe to it as well.

Although no existing theoretical network suffices to account for all existing knowledge about any trait, sketches for many traits have been constructed. Otherwise it would not be possible to say anything intelligible about mental traits, only to simply list a series of observed empirical relationships. Since psychologists are still in the process of discovering laws of human behavior, all of their concepts will have some vagueness about them. They are, nonetheless, often quite useful.

The importance of knowing the author's construct when evaluating and/or accepting a measurement of some trait can be illustrated by recalling the two possible concepts of intelligence mentioned above. An appropriate measure of intelligence for the psychologist who postulates a constant trait would not vary with age if motivation could be held constant experimentally or corrected statistically; nor would it change with alterations in environmental enrichment. On the other hand, a measure which failed to change with age with motivation controlled, or which failed to reflect changes in the learning environment would be the one which was considered inadequate if the second psychologist's hypothetical construct of intelligence were accepted.

In summary, then, mental traits are to be thought of as hypothetical constructs formulated to varying degrees of precision on the basis of present knowledge of observable relationships. As such, the resulting traits are of necessity somewhat vague, and therefore, when considering tests or other devices as instruments for measuring individuals with respect to these traits, it is essential to fully understand the particular construct as presently formed.

Nature of Measurement

In the measurement of physical quantities such as height, weight, and time, a scale value of zero is meaningful and it can be reasonably assumed that the interval between equal points at various places along the scale represents equal amounts of the quantity being measured. Unfortunately, this is not so in mental measurement. A score of zero on a test of intelligence does not mean a complete lack of mental ability. Nor can it be said that a gain in score from 10 to 20 items correct on some achievement test represents the same increase in performance as does a gain from 70 to 80 items correct. Thus, psychologists, even more than workers in other fields, have had to concern themselves with the logical basis of measurement.

S. S. Stevens (1951) who has done much work in this area, points out that, in its broadest sense, measurement is the process of assigning numbers to objects according to certain agreed upon rules. Exactly what rules are used in any particular situation depends upon the type of comparisons which can be made with the objects to which numbers are to be assigned. Strictly speaking, it is not permissible to use rules which allow those manipulations with numbers which cannot also be performed by comparing the objects themselves.

Generally, one of four sets of rules is used. Measurements which follow these different sets of rules are referred to as measurements on four different types of scales, each of which represents a different level of quantification of the variable in question.

The simplest form of quantification involves nothing more than the assignment of numerical labels to individual objects or classes of objects and is referred to as measurement on a *nominal scale*. An example of this type of measurement would be the arbitrary assignment of numbers to various occupational groups. The only rule enforced is that all individuals in the same occupation are to be assigned the same number, and no two individuals having different occupations can be given the same number. When this sort of quantification is adopted, the only type of mathematical operation which is permitted is that of counting—for example, determining the number or proportion of individuals in each occupation. As long as there is some way of setting up different classes of objects, a nominal scale can be achieved.

At the other extreme, is measurement on a *ratio scale,* where the values assigned to objects behave like real numbers and thus can appropriately be used in all mathematical operations except those exclusive to imaginaries. This type of measurement, frequently available in the physical sciences, is never achieved in the measurement of behavioral traits. Ratio scales require an absolute zero (that is, zero on the scale must represent complete absence of the characteristic involved) as well as equal units of measure throughout the scale (for example, the difference between 2 and 3 on the scale must represent the same degree of difference in the characteristic involved as a difference in scale values of 16 and 17).

In between these extreme levels of quantification are found the two types of scales most frequently encountered in psychological measurement: the *interval scale* and the *ordinal scale*. Unlike ratio scales, interval scales do not demand an absolute zero; they do, however, require equality of units along the scale.

Perhaps the best way to illustrate the limitations imposed when interval or ordinal scales must be used rather than ratio scales, is to draw an analogy as to what the result would be like were similar restrictions placed on the measurement of a familiar characteristic like height. Measurement on an interval scale places one in the position he would be in if it were necessary to measure the heights of a group of individuals from some arbitrary zero point (such as the top of a table) rather than the floor. Thus it might be noted that person *A* was 36 inches higher than the table and that person *B* stood 18 inches above the same table. Certainly it would be possible to say that person *A*, for whom the distance from the tabletop to the top of his head was 36 inches, was taller than person *B*, for whom the same distance was only 18 inches. And, with only the one restriction, it could be said that the difference between the heights of these two individuals and those of persons yielding similar measurements of 40 and 22 inches was the same. But, it could *not* be said that the person who was 36 inches higher than the table was twice as tall as the person who was 18 inches higher than the table. (If the table were 30 inches high, the actual heights would be 66 and 48 inches respectively.) Thus, when measurement is made without an absolute zero (that is, it only achieves an interval scale) it is not legitimate to multiply or divide the values recorded as measurements. These arithmetical operations can be performed, of course—the numbers themselves will not complain. The only difficulty is that some of the in- ferences drawn and conclusions made as a result of such procedures are likely to be misleading.

Fortunately, even interval scale measurements are very use- ful in assessing behavioral characteristics, for they do permit the use of most statistical indexes (such as the mean, standard devia- tion, and correlation) which are used in this area.[2] The real problem is that most of the raw data recorded as a numerical description of a behavioral trait seldom reaches even this level of measurement. Most scores have only the properties of an ordinal scale.

The analogy of the measurement of heights from tabletops can be carried one step further to illustrate the additional re- strictions imposed when only ordinal measurement is possible. Suppose the measurement of height above the table could not be found with a ruler, but only by piling books on top of the table and counting how many books high an individual was. This would be measurement on an ordinal scale. Just as it is extremely difficult (if not impossible) to get items on a psychological test which are of exactly the same difficulty, it would probably be difficult to find books all of which were of the same thickness. And, it should be obvious that if the books were put in order from thickest at the bottom to thinnest at the top, that a difference in two books of height near the tabletop would not be the same

---

[2] One commonly used statistic which is not legitimate, even with an in- terval scale, is the *coefficient of variation*.

as a difference in two books near the top of the pile. Similarly, in testing, the gain from a score of 30 to 40 items correct does not necessarily reflect the same change in underlying performance or ability as does an increase in score from 90 to 100 items correct.

If it is not possible to make statements about the equality of numerically similar difference at various points along the scale, it is not legitimate to perform even the simple arithmetical operations of addition and subtraction. As a matter of fact, strictly speaking, the only statements which can be made are those which indicate the rank order position of individuals such as person A is tallest, person B is next tallest, person C is shortest. And, even these statements may be incorrect unless exactly the same books are used in exactly the same order with every person described. This latter clearly indicates the advantage of structured measurement procedures over the informal interview and other similar approaches, when the object is to obtain a numerical description of the extent to which a person possesses some characteristic.

It should be apparent that since the highly restricted conditions just described are imposed on most measurements of behavioral characteristics, the use of many common mathematical procedures or the direct interpretation of scores can lead to serious errors. Under these circumstances, there appear to be three alternatives:

The first alternative is to simply restrict oneself to the use of those statistical procedures developed especially for use with ranked data, such as the median, Kendall's tau, and others. The second possibility is that of assuming (because of some empirical evidence or logical deduction) that the underlying trait is normally distributed in the population, and using procedures described by Guilford (1954) to convert the ordinal information to an interval scale. By far the most common procedure, however, is to recognize the fact that measures of behavioral characteristics are relative, and not absolute quantities. This means that the "raw" values originally recorded are never interpreted directly. Rather, a conversion to some form of "derived" score which relates the performance of an individual to that of a whole group of persons is first made. Then, and then only, by very carefully defining exactly what is meant by a zero point and a unit of measure considered to be equal throughout the scale, can the usual mathematical procedures be used and interpretations be made without misunderstandings. Exactly what these procedures are will be discussed in the next chapter under the topic of standardization.

Logical Steps in Using Tests

Knowing that mental traits are hypothetical constructs devised to explain various observations, it seems reasonable to ask something about the logic of the process by which such measures of mental traits will be put to use.

Actually, the whole of testing has grown up as a scientific solution to the problem that led the ancients toward gazing into the crystal ball—to see, to guess, to predict what might happen in the future. After years of looking at refracted light in spherical chunks of silicon, of getting stiff necks gazing at the stars, and of drinking gallons of tea, people finally came to the conclusion that the most profitable—at least for the customer—way to look into the future is to make predictions on the basis of what has happened in the past in similar circumstances.

And, actually, this is the basic assumption of science. Insofar as two things are similar, what happens in one instance will also happen in another. Think for a moment about the prediction you would make as to what would happen if a person holding a piece of chalk were to release it. You would, of course, predict that it would fall to the floor. But why? By what reasoning did you arrive at such a prediction? It would certainly seem that the only logical explanation is that time after time after time in the past, when the support for some object was removed, it fell toward the earth. To base an answer on the law of gravity is not satisfactory because it does not go far enough. One must ask, from where did the law of gravity come? Once again, the answer must be that the law of gravity is but a formalized description of a general class of events which have been observed in the past.

Exactly the same thing happens in a testing situation. After seeing hundreds of persons receive low scores on an aptitude test and then fail in some future activity, while those persons who received high scores were succeeding, one might predict that the next time someone gets a low score he, too, will fail; and when some new person comes along who gets a high score, his success will be predicted. The prediction of behavior from tests, then, involves this procedure:

1. The assignment of the individual to some group of persons about which some information of success and failure is known.
2. Predicting that what has happened in the past to the individuals composing the group will also happen to the new person.

Now this is certainly nothing new. It is done by everyone almost every day, in fact every time a judgment is made about an individual. For example, when the remark is made, "What a character he is," there is a recognition of similarities between this individual and others who have been designated as "characters," and there is the prediction that there will be similarities between this person's future behavior and that of others so classified in the past—even if the similarity is only in that the behavior will be nonconventional.

The whole of testing, then, is nothing more than a refinement of this everyday process—the process of classifying individuals accurately on the basis of their past behavior and of making accurate estimates of the probability of the occurrence of some specified future behavior for those in a given class. Typically, then, the process requires two assessments separated by a time interval and a study of the relation between them. On the basis of the first assessment, so-called *predictor categories* are set up (and predictor categories can refer to score intervals when the trait used as a predictor variable is considered to be a continuous one). The second assessment sets up what are called *criterion categories*. The problem is to estimate, on the basis of past experience, what an individual's criterion category will be once knowing his predictor category.

The relative-frequency concept of probability provides the mathematical basis for predicting human behavior in this way. Although the beginning student in testing is not expected to know all the mathematics involved, there are some very important logical points of which he must be aware if he is to properly understand this process of prediction.

First, with regard to the classification, it should be noted that the classes used for predictor categories need not always be, though certainly they are most commonly, based on similar behaviors of individuals in the group. The class *can* be defined in terms of behaviors of a single individual in a set of similar circumstances or situations observed over a period of time. This point is best illustrated through an example similar to that presented by Meehl (1954) in his discussion of inference from class membership.

Suppose the task were to predict whether or not some person, say person Y would make a grade of A in an advanced chemistry course, say Chemistry X. The information available for making a prediction most commonly would be that of a sort presented in Table 1, showing the relationship between scores on an aptitude

TABLE 1: Information for Making Predictions on the Basis of the Past Behavior of Others

Group	Aptitude Score	Person	Grade in Chem. X	Relative Frequency
1	Very high	a	A	3/5
		b	A	
		c	A	
		d	B	
		e	B	
2	High	f	A	2/5
		g	A	
		h	B	
		i	B	
		j	C	
3	Average	k	B	0/5
		l	C	
		m	C	
		n	C	
		o	C	

– – – – – – – – – – etc. – – – – – – – – – –

test and later success in Chemistry X. With this type of information, the procedure would be to first give person Y the aptitude test, then to note into which class or group he fell, and finally to make a prediction on the basis of the relative frequency with which other persons in the class have received A's in the past. Thus, if person Y received a score which placed him in Group 1, a prediction would probably be made that he would get an A; if his score placed him in Group 3 or lower, the prediction would be that he would not get an A.

On the other hand, it could be that the past information on the basis of which a prediction is to be made is a case history of individual Y describing his performance in several situations. Thus, the data might be something like that presented in Table 2. With this kind of information, the procedure would be to de-

TABLE 2: Information for Making Predictions on the Basis of Observations of One Individual in Several Situations

	Situation 1 Lecture			Situation 2 Recitation				Situation 3 Laboratory	
Class	i	ii	iii	iv	v	vi	vii	viii	ix
Grade	A	B	A	A	B	A	C	C	B
Relative Frequency	2/3			2/4				0/2	

termine whether or not Chemistry X was a lecture, a recitation, or a laboratory course, and to make a prediction about the grade person Y will receive on the basis of the relative frequency of his performance in similar situations in the past.

If both kinds of information were available, then the two tables could be combined, and if further relevant (that is criterion-related) data were available, then the table could be elaborated even further. The more knowledge gained about what variables are predictive of the criterion performance, and the more information available about the individual, the more refined the classification system will be and the more accurately a class description will define the individual members assigned to it. Unfortunately, as the classification system becomes more and more elaborate in this way, it will be more and more difficult to find enough persons or repetitions of the situation to form a stable relative frequency on the basis of which a prediction can be made. Thus, for example, when giving an individual test, it might be noted that some person received a score of 79 in spite of having been in a highly excited state because of an automobile accident she had had just before the exam. While this additional information permits a more accurate description of the examinee by assigning her to a class of persons getting a score of 79 while in a highly excited state, this additional refinement can be of value only if we have some observations as to the future behavior of persons who get a score of 79 while in a highly emotional state as compared with persons not in such a state when they receive a score of 79.

In summary, then, it should be apparent that, teachers, counsellors, and clinical psychologists who insist that they are interested only in the individual and not in groups of persons, can still be making use of actuarial tables based on relative frequencies when making predictions on the basis of test results.

The second major point concerning the relative frequency concept of probability as it is applied to the prediction of human behavior involves a distinction pointed out by Meehl (1954) between a statement about the person for whom a prediction is made and a statement about our prediction.

Consider for a moment the statement that "student X has one chance in six of graduating from the state university." Strictly speaking, phrased in this way, the statement is incorrect. What is meant is this: Student X will not graduate from the state university, and if I make this same statement about all students classified in the same way as student X, five out of six of the statements will be correct. Obviously, student X will or will not graduate. Thus, his probability of success is either zero or one. The probability of 1/6 is a statement not about the person but about a set of predictions which might be made.

This seemingly pedantic distinction is of real and practical importance because the statement about the individual and the statement about the prediction must be empirically confirmed in two different ways. To verify the statement about student X, it is necessary only to wait and see whether four years hence student X receives a diploma. To confirm the statement about the prediction, a large number of persons classified in the same manner as student X must be observed to see what happens to them with respect to graduation.

Failure to make this distinction has led a great number of persons involved in the use of test scores to believe that all predictions (even those which from their appearance seem to be predictions about individual, concrete events or individual persons) actually have an implicit reference to a classification system of some sort and thus to conclude that all meaningful predictions are actuarial. (A prediction is meaningful only if it can somehow be confirmed.)

Until around 1950, then, it was felt that the *only* logical basis for any prediction was that just described—that which is based on relative class frequency. Meehl, in his lectures around 1949 and in his 1954 book, pointed this distinction out and suggested another possible logic of prediction. It is this latter which will be considered next.

Meehl developed this second logic of prediction after a considerable amount of introspection about what he was doing as a clinician when in a therapy session with a patient. What he noticed was that whenever he was reading over information about a patient or listening to his client in a therapy session, he was continually formulating and reformulating a concept as to what the patient was *really* like. Each concept was based on prior observation of the patient and of materials gathered about the client, but was not a formal consequence of these. In addition, Meehl noticed that when he had formulated a concept of what the patient was like, this concept suggested ways in which the person might behave under certain circumstances (if the present concept were correct).

Actually, this process is a form of prediction very similar to that used by the scientist. Time after time a researcher is confronted with a mass of observational data and must ask himself what must be the state of things in order to account for all these observations. And, almost always, when the scientist has invented a state of things to explain the results of past observations, his concept will suggest further things which one should be able to observe. Then, and only then, does he resort to formal logic and to statistics to specify and test the implications of his postulated conception of nature.

What the clinician, or the counsellor, or the teacher, or other user of test scores does, then, is to develop, on the basis of a combination of his observations and some crudely formulated psychological laws, a conception of the inner state or structure of the person at hand, and on the basis of this concept, predict what the individual will do in certain circumstances. This is in direct contrast to the actuarial case where a finite (although possibly very large) set of facts is known about the individual, and the particular combination of facts defines a subclass of the population of individuals for which certain relative frequencies have been determined. To arrive at a prediction for an individual, in the actuarial sense, it is necessary only to apply the calculus of probability in a straightforward fashion and arrive at a number which determines automatically what the prediction will be.

However, if the prediction comes as a consequence of some sort of structural-dynamic hypothesis concerning the personality of the particular individual, the situation is different. Unlike the actuarial case, the hypothesis formulated is not in any sense deducible from the facts which support it. The initial formulation of the hypothesis about what the person is really like represents a genuinely creative act with which the person predicting actuarially, as such, has no concern. Thus, in this second logic of prediction there is a stage at which someone must have thought up a hypothesis which was supported by the facts but was not a formal consequence of them. Again, this is in direct contrast to the actuarial logic of prediction where the frequency for a subclass *is* a formal consequence of the application of the principles of probability to a set of data. These and other important differences between the two basically different logics for using test results are summarized in Table 3.

What Meehl has done, then, through his analysis of the logic of clinical activity is to show that prediction about people on the basis of tests or other types of observation, need *not* be actuarial

—even though statistical predictions can be made about individuals. In doing this, Meehl has annihilated the argument of Sarbin (1944) which led to the statement believed by so many others that it was irrational to expect anyone using the clinical approach to improve upon strict actuarial methods since, after all, the clinician was really only making crude actuarial predictions.

TABLE 3: Difference Between the Statistical and the Clinical Logics of Using Test Results

Statistical	Clinical
1. Based on *intensive* study of a few traits	1. Based on *extensive* information about one person
2. All information must be of class membership sort	2. Any form of data can be used
3. Prediction is based on the calculus of probability	3. Prediction based on knowledge of behavior theory
4. Prediction, as a formal consequence of the observation, can be set up to be done by a clerk	4. Prediction, as a creative act, must be done by a highly skilled person
5. Cannot make use of rare (contingency) events	5. Can incorporate contingency events into the prediction

Having shown that there is no real reason to assume that explicitly formulated mathematical rules are better suited than the clinician's, or counsellor's, or teacher's creativity for making predictions, Meehl points out that it is an open question which has an empirical answer as to whether clinical or statistical prediction produces the best results.

For an answer to this latter question it is necessary to examine studies which compare the relative success frequencies of the two methods. This, too, Meehl has done. Out of nineteen studies for which the results were not ambiguous, ten failed to find a difference between the two methods, nine found differences in favor of actuarial prediction, and not one indicated that the clinical approach to prediction was superior. The inescapable conclusion is that, with our present meager state of knowledge and when appropriate data is available, statistical prediction is to be preferred. Thus, until sufficient knowledge about human beings is available to formulate more accurate descriptions of behavior, teachers, counsellors, and clinical psychologists are urged to spend their valuable time in therapy rather than in prediction and diagnosis. There are, of course, situations in which adequate data for actuarial prediction simply is not available. Under these circumstances clinical prediction is the only alternative. Knowing that greater efficiency can be achieved by a clerk with an actuarial table, however, should motivate workers to obtain appropriate information to make statistical prediction possible. In the meantime, they can only take some consolation in knowing that *half the time* they will be doing no worse than if they had further information.

Knowing, now, some of the logic of testing, it should be apparent that even with the best possible psychological measuring instruments, errors will be made. It simply is not possible to note that a person's scores show high verbal ability, high reasoning ability, and musical talent, to combine this with the information that he has enough money to go to college, and to come up with the unmistakable conclusion that the individual should spend his life as a lawyer for a shady music concern.

But this does not mean that tests are no good. The baby shouldn't be thrown out with the bath. Research has shown that carefully developed tests—even those achieving only the crudest form of a measuring scale—often provide the best information available as a guide in making a decision. What should be done, rather, is to learn what sorts of error can occur; to develop procedures for estimating this error; and, insofar as possible, to utilize methods of test construction and administration which minimize these errors. Finally, when using tests, every effort should be made to obtain data for an actuarial table and to make predictions and diagnoses—even for the individual—on a statistical basis.

2

Evaluation of Tests – Standardization

CRITERIA FOR JUDGING TESTS

IT IS OBVIOUS THAT classroom teachers, measurement specialists, and research workers who develop their own measuring devices must all be concerned with how to determine whether any instrument which they prepare is a good one. But others, too,—administrators who use tests for selection and promotion of personnel, counsellors and clinical psychologists who are concerned with the adjustment of an individual, and those researchers who are fortunate enough to find ready-made tests as measures of psychological variables in which they are interested—will also need to make decisions as to whether testing is appropriate for a particular situation and then to select from among those tests which are available, the one which is most likely to provide the desired information. This and the next four chapters, therefore, are devoted to providing the reader with a basic framework for making intelligent judgments about the usefulness of tests by pointing out the kinds of things which need to be considered when selecting a test, and by describing the technical criteria which have been developed to indicate whether or not it is a good measuring device.

Basic Considerations

It seems almost too obvious to mention that a test of high level scholastic ability is not appropriate as a selection instrument for truck drivers or that a test designed specifically for use with children should not be used with adults. Yet, time after time, in everyday situations, tests have been used which are completely inappropriate for the group involved or for the problem at hand. Thus, the initial consideration in choosing a test is the purpose for which it is to be used.

Since the function of a test is to provide the best possible information on the basis of which a decision about some problem can be made, it is apparent that the first step should be to carefully specify what questions need to be answered and about whom. Similarly, it is necessary to clearly delineate the outcomes of the various alternative choices of the decision maker and to assign values to these outcomes. Only when this has been done, is it possible to accurately ascertain the effectiveness of testing as contrasted with other kinds of information or to determine which of several alternative tests will be most useful in the given situation.

A second basic consideration in choosing a test is its feasibility. Although certain kinds of information might be extremely valuable in helping to make a correct decision, the cost of obtaining the data, either in dollars and cents or in terms of human values, may far exceed the cost of an inaccurate decision.

It is not difficult to list many of the practical kinds of things which need to be considered. For example, purchase price is obviously important. Almost always, the user of tests is operating within a budget, self-imposed or otherwise, and a highly expensive test must be worth the price in terms of yield. Sometimes it just is not possible to purchase the best instrument available, and because of price, a less desirable test must be used. The time involved in taking the test is another important factor. An employer must consider how many man-hours are lost to production or other work when employees take tests while on the job; in school or military training situations where regular class meetings exist, not only the total time, but the extent to which time limits on the test or its parts fit in with the classroom schedule becomes an important consideration.

The ease of administration and scoring, the possibility that the test content will offend some examinees, and whether comparable forms are available (this latter especially in education where it is necessary to be certain that those tested have not had previous experience with the items, or in research where a measure both before and after the application of some experimental variable is desired) are all additional aspects which need to be given some thought when choosing a test.

Finally, but far from least in importance, a major basis for selecting a test is whether or not it is a good measuring instrument, or, at least, whether the test is the best which can be obtained with the funds available. While the first two basic considerations mentioned are largely a matter of common sense, judging whether a test is a good measuring instrument requires some technical knowledge. Thus, in the pages to follow, considerable time will be spent describing the various ways of assessing tests with respect to the adequacy with which they serve as measuring instruments. To begin with, however, some attempt will be made to provide a background for the study of these techniques by describing the various kinds of errors which occur in the measurement of behavorial characteristics.

A Classification of Errors[1]

Interpretive Errors.   It has already been noted that original measurements of behavioral characteristics lack both an absolute zero point and any guarantee that the units are equal throughout the range of the scale. Because of these conditions, the test score achieved by any one person has no meaning until it is interpreted in terms of the performance of other individuals. Unless the test user has a clear understanding as to exactly which "other indi-

---

[1] The classification of errors of measurement used in this section was suggested by Mursell (1947).

viduals" are used for this interpretation and precisely how the
one person's score is related to the performance of the group, he
is likely to attribute an inappropriate meaning to the score. Such
misinterpretations are called interpretive errors.

Interpretive errors, then, are those which result from a
misunderstanding as to one of two things: first, with what sort
of group the individual is being compared, and second, the way in
which the comparison between the individual and the group performance is expressed. For example, it would make a considerable
difference in the interpretation of the results if the score obtained
by a high school senior is compared with that of high school freshmen rather than college freshmen. Similarly, the prediction made
and the action taken would be quite different for a reported score
of 70 if it were an Intelligence Quotient than would be the case if
the number 70 were a ranking indicating that proportion of the
others who took the test who got a lower score than the individual
in question.

In testing, this problem of interpretive errors is taken care
of through a process called *standardization*. By standardization
is meant, simply, that the test has been given to a well-defined
group (for example, college sophomores, female clerical workers,
applicants for admission to medical school, and so forth) and
that careful records have been kept as to the scores which the
specified group or groups have made. These records are the norms.
Norms may be provided for many groups even for one test, and
may be defined in such terms as occupations, geographical region,
sex, age, school grade, or any combination of these, the idea
being to provide data such that it is possible to make a comparison
of an individual's score with that of an appropriate group.

Generally speaking there are two kinds of groups with which
it is appropriate to compare an individual. The first, quite obviously, is a group to which the individual already belongs. Certainly, no reader of this text would be proud to know that he had
achieved the highest score among a group composed of twenty
third-grade children and himself; nor would he be likely to be
particularly discouraged because he was the lowest on an intelligence test given to himself, Galileo, Newton, Galton, and Ein-

stein; nor would he be particularly disturbed to discover his scores on a personality rating were completely different from those of Australian bushmen. None of these comparisons are likely to be relevant to the interests of the college student.

Sometimes, however, the most important comparison is not with a group to which an individual already belongs, but rather with a group to which he aspires. For example, if a college sophomore is interested in becoming a physician, it is of greater significance to compare his scholastic ability test scores with those of successful medical students than it is to compare them with college sophomores as a whole (or even with applicants to medical school).

The final problem with respect to interpretive errors—that of expressing the relationship between an individual's score and those of the normative group—involves the translation of raw scores into mental age scores, intelligence quotients, percentile ranks, standard scores, or other types of derived scores. Procedures for the development and computation of such scores as well as the advantages and disadvantages of the various possibilities will be discussed at length under the topic of standardization, and therefore need only be mentioned here.

Variable Errors. A second sort of error which may occur in psychological measurement is termed variable error. Variable errors are those arising from accidents and inaccuracies due to many causes. For example, if you were to measure the length of a table with ruler today, tomorrow, and the next day, or if several different persons each were to measure the length of the table today slightly different results would be obtained in each case. Exactly the same thing happens in testing, only here the errors are likely to be much greater than normally occur in the measurement of physical quantities. During a timed test a pencil breaks, a fire engine goes by outside the window, the test administrator gives incorrect directions, each causing those taking the test to receive slightly different scores for this testing from those they would receive under slightly different circumstances. All of these things result in chance inaccuracies called variable errors. These errors are referred to as variable errors because the amount of error varies from one person to the next and also because the amount of error is different for a given person each time he is measured.

In testing, the relative freedom from errors of this sort is spoken of as *degree of reliability*. As was the case with respect to relating the score obtained by an individual to that of a group, there are many approaches to the problem of estimating test reliability, each with its own special advantages and precautions. These, together with suggestions for decreasing variable errors in testing, will be presented in Chapter 3.

Personal Errors. When reading an automobile speedometer from his respective position in the car, each passenger is likely to come up with slightly different results—even though the instrument itself is keeping a perfectly accurate record of the rate of travel. Similarly, any two different persons observing exactly the same responses are likely to record different scores, because they can see the performance only from their own position or bias. Or, the same person examining the same responses on two different occasions is likely to vary somewhat in his reaction because he sees things differently each time.

Many studies have indicated that two readers of a given examination paper will often arrive at vastly different results. The same thing has been shown to be true even when the same person grades the same papers when the grading is done independently on two different occasions. Since such fluctuation in scores is directly attributable to the person who is doing the grading, they are called personal errors.

Because the personal bias of the person making the observations (that is, scoring the responses) fluctuates from time to time and from paper to paper, the resulting personal errors are, strictly speaking, but a special class of variable errors. Personal errors are, however, of sufficient magnitude to require special attention when measuring behavioral characteristics and therefore deserve a special label.

In the field of testing the term *objectivity* is used to designate that test characteristic related to personal errors. Just how personal errors are reduced and tests are evaluated by this criterion will be discussed later in this chapter under that heading.

Constant Errors. The final type of error which will be discussed arises from the fact that most measurements of behavioral characteristics are indirect. It is neither possible nor desirable to open a person's skull, look inside, or put a chunk of grey matter on a balance and say that this is the amount of his mechanical ability. Rather, a measure is obtained on something (a test) which, it is hoped, is related to the trait or characteristic about which it is desired to have information.

Indirect measurement, of course, is not unique to the assessment of behavioral characteristics. The same thing is done when one uses a thermometer. It is not the height of the mercury column per se which is desired. The height of the mercury column is useful only because it shows a very high degree of relationship to the amount of heat in whatever is being investigated. The major difference between this example and the problem in behavioral measurement is that in the latter, the relationship between the indirect index—the test score—and the underlying trait of interest is not nearly as perfect as it is with physical quantities.

It is not difficult to imagine that scores on a paper and pencil test which measures (indirectly, of course) mechanical ability will depend to a certain extent upon one's accomplishment in reading. To the extent that the resulting measures reflect differences in reading ability rather than differences in mechanical ability, error is introduced. This error is called constant error (in contrast with the variable error previously discussed) because the amount of error will be the same for every person who takes the test and the same for a given person no matter when or how many times the measurement is made. That is, if the test measures reading to a slight extent, it measures reading in this degree for everyone who takes the test and to this degree every time the test is taken.

In testing, the problem of constant error is the problem of *validity*. It is always necessary to have some evidence that indicates the extent to which the indirect measurement is actually a valid indicator of the trait under investigation. It is necessary to know whether a test really measures what we think it does, or more precisely, whether we can make the kinds of inferences from the test scores, which we think we can.

The Criteria

In the previous section it was noted that each of the four kinds of error described was associated with a different test characteristic. In turn, each of these characteristics represents a separate criterion for evaluating a test. Thus, to answer the question of whether a test is a good measuring device it is necessary to examine the following four things:

1. *Standardization*—the quality of which determines the extent to which interpretive errors have been avoided.
2. *Reliability*—an indication of the relative freedom from variable error.
3. *Objectivity*—the degree of which reflects the extent to which personal errors have been avoided.
4. *Validity*—an indication that the test measures what we think it measures, and therefore is not influenced by constant error.

It is important to note that a test is not necessarily a good one just because it is free from *one* of these types of errors. A test which is well standardized may still be highly unreliable, lacking in objectivity, and completely invalid. Similarly, a highly reliable test may not have been well standardized, or even if it were both well standardized and highly reliable, it could be completely useless for some specific purpose because of a lack of validity.

On the other hand, lack of objectivity will always be reflected in a lack of reliability. That is, a test cannot be reliable unless it can be scored with a reasonable amount of objectivity. In a like manner, validity requires some minimally satisfactory degree of objectivity, reliability, and standardization. If a test has been shown to be valid for a particular purpose (that is, for a particular way of making inferences from the test scores), it may be used in the way indicated without further question—although improvement with respect to the other characteristics would generally increase the validity (that is, make the test even more useful than it was). A test which lacks validity, however, is completely useless no matter how objective, how reliable in other ways, or how well standardized it may be.

Ideally, then, a test could be judged solely in terms of its validity. Unfortunately, no single bit of validity evidence tells the entire story (though lack of it may), and in many instances, for practical reasons, validity evidence is almost entirely lacking. In these circumstances, one evaluates the test with respect to the other characteristics and assumes (or just hopes) that the test is also valid. Finally, a test which shows some degree of validity in spite of a lack of objectivity, reliability, and adequate standardization, is a highly promising one; for additional refinement with respect to these latter characteristics is likely to result in a substantial increase in validity.

STANDARDIZATION

In the discussion of interpretive errors it was pointed out that the observation normally recorded in a testing situation, the raw score, whether it represents the number of items correct, the time required to complete a given task, or whatever, indicates little of general significance until it is compared with the scores obtained by members of some standardization group. Not representing an absolute scale with a zero point and equal units of measurement, the raw scores must be transformed to relative scores of some sort. The following sections, therefore, will present the various basic approaches to the solution of this problem of expressing an individual score in terms of its relative position among a group of scores.

The Frequency Distribution

To make a comparison of an individual score with those obtained by individuals in a standardization group, it is first necessary to summarize the group performance. For the most part this is done by constructing a frequency distribution of the raw scores by the usual procedures taught in elementary descriptive statistics. Although not always the case, the distribution generally found in the measurement of human characteristics (or in the measurement of the quality of human products) is close to that expressed by the Gaussian or normal curve.[2] The three notable exceptions to this general statement are situations where (1) the test in question is either too difficult or too easy for the group involved; (2) part of the group measured has had training or has been preselected with respect to the trait concerned while another part of the group has not; and (3) the trait under consideration is one in which social conformity may play a part in determining the results.

In the first instance, a skewed distribution is likely to be found. If the test is too easy there will be a piling up of scores at the high end of the scale, and if the test is too difficult there will be a piling up of scores at the low end of the scale. By making the assumption that the underlying ability or trait is normally distributed, it is possible to *normalize* the distribution when obtaining the derived scores necessary for interpreting the results. Generally, however, it is considered far more acceptable to revise the test in the light of item analysis data (see Chapter 7) to make the difficulty level more appropriate for those involved.

When part of the group has been preselected or has had some special training, a bimodal distribution is likely to result. Should this situation arise, considerable thought should be given to the reasons for combining both types of persons in one standardization group. In most instances it is best to eliminate one or the other or to make a separate set of norms for each of the two groups.

A classical example of a measure which reflects pressure toward social conformity is the speed with which drivers travel past a stop sign. The vast majority of persons will stop; thus there is a great piling of scores at the zero point of the scale. Some persons—a surprising number—will slow down, perhaps even shift into low gear, but not quite stop. Others, but fewer in number, will slow down considerably but not make any pretense of stop-

[2] Although Keats (1951) has suggested, as a result of an empirical study of large numbers of test scores obtained in Australia, that a closer fit can usually be obtained if the Beta rather than the Normal distribution is used, the difference seems to be so small as to have little practical importance.

ping. Still fewer will not even bother to slow down, and once in a while, in the middle of the night, a driver will race through the stop sign at a speed far exceeding the posted limit. Should such observations be cast in a frequency distribution, the result would be a highly skewed or *J*-shaped curve.

Similarly, in the measurement of certain attitudinal and personality traits, for example, honesty in monetary matters, one is likely to find that a markedly skewed distribution will occur. Since this is what is expected in these circumstances, no attempt to transform the raw data to achieve other distributions should be made. As a matter of fact, since the underlying trait is conceived as having this special distribution, any measuring instrument which tends to yield a normal distribution would be highly questionable.

Types of Derived Scores

Once the performance of the standardization group has been summarized by plotting a frequency distribution, by computing descriptive indexes such as the mean and standard deviation, or by some other procedure, the next task is that of somehow relating each raw score that it is possible to obtain to the scores of the group as a whole. This will have been accomplished when a so-called *table of norms* like those shown in Figure 4 has been set up. Such a table enables the user of the test to "read in" a meaningless raw score and convert it directly to some form of derived score which does make sense without further interpretation.

Age and Grade Scales. From the earliest days of mental testing, one solution to the problem of interpreting raw scores has been that of developing so-called age scales. Scales of this sort relate the performance on a test to the chronological age of individuals in the standardization group. This can be done by finding either the average score obtained by persons at each age level to be included in the norms or by determining the average age of persons receiving each of the possible different scores on the test. With either procedure, the result is a table through which raw scores on the test may be converted to "ages."

Age Norms*					Percentile Norms*			
Raw Score	M.A. Yrs. Mos.	Raw Score	M.A. Yrs. Mos.		Raw Score	Percentile Equipment for Grade		
						9	10	11	12

Raw Score	M.A. Yrs. Mos.	Raw Score	M.A. Yrs. Mos.	Raw Score	9	10	11	12
60	17-6	30	13-0					
				45	52	36	28	18
59	17-3	29	12-11	44	49	34	26	16
58	17-0	28	12-10	43	47	32	25	15
57	16-10	27	12-9	42	45	30	24	14
56	16-9	26	12-8	41	42	28	22	13
55	16-7	25	12-7	40	40	26	21	12
				39	38	25	19	11
54	16-6	24	12-6	38	35	23	18	10
53	16-3	23	12-4	37	33	21	16	9
52	16-0	22	12-3	36	31	19	14	8
51	15-9	21	12-2	35	29	18	13	7
50	15-6	20	12-1	34	27	17	12	6
				33	25	15	11	6
49	15-4	19	12-0	32	24	14	10	5
48	15-3	18	11-11	31	23	13	9	5
47	15-2	17	11-10	30	22	12	8	4
46	15-1	16	11-9	29	21	11	7	3
45	15-0	15	11-7	28	20	10	7	3

Standard Score Norms*

STA-NINE	Test 1 M Para. Mean.	Test 2 Word Mean.	Test 3 Spelling	Test 4 Language	Test 5 Arith. Reas.	Test 6 Arith. Comp.	Test 1J Para. Mean.	Test 2J Word Mean.	Test 2J* Word Mean.	STA-NINE
9	49-50	38	-50	67-74	44-45	40-42	48-50	38	38	9
8	47-48	37	48-49	63-66	43	38-39	46-47	37	37	8
7	45-46	36	45-47	58-62	41-42	36-37	44-45	36	36	7
6	42-44	34-35	42-44	52-57	38-40	34-35	42-43	34-35	34-35	6
5	38-41	31-33	37-41	44-51	34-37	31-33	39-41	31-33	31-33	5
4	33-37	26-30	32-36	36-43	29-33	28-30	36-38	26-30	27-30	4
3	27-32	20-25	25-31	26-35	23-28	24-27	32-35	20-25	21-26	3
2	18-26	14-19	17-24	13-25 below	17-22	19-23	28-31	14-19	15-20	2
1	0-17	0-13	0-16	13	0-16	0-18	0-27	0-13	0-14	1

FIGURE 4: Sample Norms Tables Using Various Types of Derived Scores

SOURCE: The Age and Percentile Norms are from the *Henmon-Nelson Tests of Mental Ability;* T. Lamke and M. Nelson, *Examiner's Manual.* Reprinted by permission of the publishers, Houghton Mifflin Company. The Standard Score Norms are for the *Stanford Achievement Test,* Elementary Battery Form M; Reading Reinforced, Form J Grade 4, Pinelas County, Florida, and are reproduced with the permission of Harcourt, Brace and World, Inc.

The primary advantage of such a procedure is that the results are immediately meaningful to even the person who is the most unsophisticated with respect to testing. Also, this type of derived score is very readily obtained, requiring only knowledge of the ages of the persons in the standardization group and the procedure for finding an arithmetical mean. On the other hand, such a procedure is completely meaningless unless the trait under consideration is highly related to age, at least within the range of scores under consideration. It would be meaningless, for example, to interpret a measure of cynicism on an age scale simply because one does not anticipate a regular increase in cynicism with age among most people. For this reason, age scales are usually used only with measures of general or scholastic ability or with achievement tests. Often in these situations, the age which is read out for any given score is called a mental age, and when such a derived score is divided by the individual's chronological age (and multiplied by 100), the result is frequently termed an intelligence quotient.

In many school situations, grade, rather than age, scales are used. Grade norms are obtained in exactly the same way that age norms are found—except that the child's grade level rather than his chronological age is used. To derive an accurate picture of how these scores are obtained one need only reread the preceding two paragraphs inserting the words school grade (or just grade) for chronological age (or just age).

Percentile Ranks.   More recently, and probably today most commonly, percentile ranks are used. The percentile rank corresponding to any given raw score is the percentage of persons in the standardization group who receive the given or lower score. Thus, a percentile rank of 75 indicates that 75 percent of the standardization group got the corresponding raw score or lower, and that 25 percent got a higher score; a percentile rank of 16 would mean that 84 percent of the standardization group got a higher score and 16 percent got the same or lower score, etc.

Percentile ranks are quite easily obtained from a frequency distribution of raw scores. As an instructive example, suppose the following scores were received by ten individuals in a class quiz: 21, 25, 23, 23, 21, 24, 23, 24, 24, 23. The first step is to list the raw scores in order from lowest to highest and to determine the frequency with which each was obtained. This has been done in the first two columns of Table 4. Next, starting with the

TABLE 4: Computational Example for Determining Percentile Ranks

Col. No.	1	2	3	4	5
Row No. j	Raw Score	Frequency f_j	Cum.Freq. cum f_j	Mid-point Cum.Freq. cum $f_{j-1} + \frac{1}{2}f_j$	Percentile Rank
5	25	1	10	9.5	95
4	24	3	9	7.5	75
3	23	4	6	4.0	40
2	22	0	2	2.0	20
1	21	2	2	1.0	10

lowest score, a cumulative frequency must be obtained. The cumulative frequency for any given raw score is the number of persons who receive the given score or a lower score. This is readily determined by adding the frequency reported for each row to the cumulative frequency in the row just below it. At this point the reader may, understandably, jump to the conclusion that all that remains is to divide by the total number of cases involved to get a proportion and to multiply this proportion by 100 to convert it to a percentage. Were he to do this, however, a percentile rank for the upper boundary of the score interval would be obtained.[3]

The percentile rank desired, however, is that for the midpoint of the score interval. To accomplish this, it is first necessary to assume that half of the cases falling in the score interval fall above the midpoint of the interval and half of the cases below the midpoint. Then it is apparent that the cumulative frequency to the midpoint of any interval will be the cumulative frequency reported for the interval immediately below plus *half* the frequency in the interval itself. In our example this is recorded in Column 4. Finally, the percentile rank computed for the mid-

[3] Such a percentage is called a *cumulative percent*. Even though it is not a true percentile rank, it may be similarly interpreted.

point of the score interval is obtained by dividing this frequency of Column 4 by the total number of individuals in the group and multiplying the quotient by 100 to convert it to a percentage. The final result is reported in Column 5 of the table.

Sometimes, when the data involve a large number of class intervals and the cumulative frequencies for each are known, it may be more convenient to determine percentile ranks by formula. Written so as to promote understanding of the relationships involved and translation from percentile rank to raw score as well as from raw score to percentile rank, the formula can be expressed as follows:

Score Scale Frequency Scale

(1)
$$\frac{S_{P_r} - L}{h} = \frac{\dfrac{N(P_r)}{100} - LCF}{f},$$

where:

S_{P_r} = raw score equivalent to a percentile rank of P_r
L = lower boundary of the raw score interval
h = length of raw score class interval
N = total number of persons included in the group
P_r = percentile rank corresponding to the raw score S_{P_r}
LCF = cumulative frequency at the lower boundary of the interval in which S_{P_r} falls
f = frequency in the interval in which S_{P_r} falls.

Suppose, for example, it was desired to find the percentile rank of a raw score of 24 among the ten scores given above.

Then, $S_{P_r} = 24$; and from the information in columns 1 and 3 of Table 4 it is apparent that:

$$L = 23.5; h = 1; N = 10; LCF = 6; \text{and } f = 3.$$

Substituting these values in the formula above,

$$\frac{24 - 23.5}{1} = \frac{\dfrac{10(P_r)}{100} - 6}{3}$$

and thus, $P_r = 75$.

This same formula can be used to obtain the percentile or raw score equivalent to a given percentile rank. Thus, if it were desired to set a cutting score at the 80th percentile, $P_r = 80$ and the raw score equivalent would be found by solving equation (1) for S_{P_r}.

More and more, especially when the normative sample is of very large size and when punched-card systems are used for computing and/or record keeping, cumulative percents are being used in place of percentile ranks. Cumulative percents are, actually, the percentile ranks of the upper class boundaries (rather than the midpoints of class intervals) and are much more readily computed than the true percentile ranks. To obtain the cumulative percents for any raw score it is necessary only to divide the cumulative frequencies as reported in column 3 of Table 4 by N (the number of persons included in the normative group) and to multiply the quotient by 100.

The major advantages of presenting normative data in terms of percentile ranks or cumulative percents are the ease with which they can be computed and the fact that they can be readily interpreted exactly even when the distribution is skewed or bimodal. This latter advantage, however, may be a false one, since, except in very special circumstances, tests are constructed so as to avoid distributions which are not normal or nearly so. Furthermore, as test users and the general public become more and more sophisticated, other types of relative scores will become more familiar and just as easily understood.

Against these apparent advantages, there are two major limitations of percentile ranks. First, when percentile ranks are used, small differences in raw scores near the middle of the distribution are magnified, and large differences in raw scores near the extreme of the distribution are reduced. For example, in one set of data obtained on an ability test given to college freshmen, the change in raw scores from 25 to 35 items correct results in an increase in percentile rank from 01 to only 04, while a change in raw score from 55 to 65 (near the mean of the distribution) is represented by a change in percentile rank from 39 to 63. The reason for this, of course, is that differences in raw score represent distances along the axis of a frequency distribution while differences in percentile ranks or cumulative percents are represented by differences in area under the curve. Thus, in Figure 5, the two equal intervals along the base line include vastly different areas under the curve.

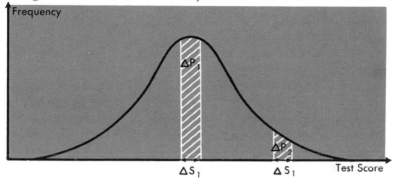

FIGURE 5: Changes in Percentile Ranks at Two Different Places in the Distribution for a Given Change in Raw Test Score

Growing out of this fact that percentile ranks and cumulative percents are not linear transformations of the raw scores, is the second major disadvantage of their use: they cannot be legitimately used in further statistical computation. Thus, if it were desired to note the percentile rank of the average of some subgroup of scores, the results could *not* be found by adding the percentile ranks and dividing by the number in the group. For example, if the four percentile ranks mentioned in the preceding paragraph (01, 04, 39, and 63) were averaged, the result would be 27, while if the raw scores (25, 35, 55, and 65) were averaged first and then the percentile rank of the average raw score looked up, the correct value would be found to be only 17. Thus, if percentile ranks are used in arithmetical computations, conclusions may be drawn which are quite misleading.

Standard Scores. A procedure which is much to be preferred to either age scores or percentile ranks is that which locates an individual score in relation to the group performance by indicating the number of standard deviation units above or below the group mean that this individual score falls. A derived score expressed in this way is called a standard score. A standard score, therefore, may be obtained by the following formula:

$$(2) \qquad z = \frac{X_i - \overline{X}}{s_x},$$

where:

z = the standard score
X_i = the raw score
$\overline{X}$ = the mean of the raw scores obtained by the standardization group
s_x = the standard deviation of the raw scores obtained by the standardization group

Using the same ten raw scores given in the discussion of percentile ranks, the mean and standard deviation are found to be 23.1 and 1.22 respectively. Thus, the standard score corresponding to a raw score of 24 is found by taking

$$z = \frac{24 - 23.1}{1.22}$$

$$= .74.$$

A raw score of 24, then, is located just .74 standard deviation units above the mean. That is, if we were to use the standard deviation of 1.22 as our unit of measure, we would find the raw score of 24 located just .74 of this unit to the right of the group average which is 23.1. Any positive standard score is above the mean; any negative standard score is below the mean. The magnitude of the standard score indicates how far above or below the mean the given raw score lies.

Using the formula given above, standard scores are obtained which, when taken as a group, have a mean of zero and a standard deviation of one. Thus, nearly half of the scores used will be negative, and the range of scores will generally be from only − 4 to + 4.

In some situations, the use of negative numbers and decimal points as required by this type of standard score is awkward. Thus, another form of standard scale is sometimes used. The

Navy, for example, has developed for its aptitude battery a so-called T score which has a mean of 50 and a standard deviation of 10, but still represents a standard score. To convert raw scores to this form of standard score, the following formula can be used:

$$(3) \qquad T = 50 + (10)\left(\frac{X_i - \overline{X}}{s_x}\right).$$

Other forms of standard scores have also been used. The Army, with its AGCT scores, has used standard scores having a mean of 100 and a standard deviation of 20; the Air Force, in order to make use of IBM cards derived the so-called stanine or standard-nine scores having standard score with a mean of 5 and a standard deviation of 2. Similarly, the College Entrance Examination Board makes use of a system in which the mean is 500 and the standard deviation is 100.

A standard score, z', having any desired arbitrary mean, M', and arbitrary deviation, $S.D'.$, may be obtained from raw scores by applying the following formula:

$$(4) \qquad z' = M' + (S.D.')\left(\frac{X_i - \overline{X}}{s_x}\right).$$

Standard scores are much more useful than other types of derived scores for those who wish to carry out further analyses with such measures. Because they represent a linear transformation of the raw scores (that is, because differences in them are proportional to differences in raw scores), standard scores may be used without the kind of distortion that appears when calculations are performed on percentile ranks. Finally, when standard scores are used, the zero point and what is meant by an equal unit of measure (the standard deviation) is specifically defined, thus preventing any misunderstanding.

The major disadvantage of standard scores is that their meaning is not readily apparent to many lay persons to whom scores are interpreted. Fortunately, if the scores form the normal frequency distribution, there is a specific relationship between percentile ranks and standard scores. For example, in a normal distribution, the mean plus and minus one standard deviation includes 68 percent of the cases. Thus, a person situated one standard deviation unit above the mean (with a standard score of $+ 1.00$) would have a percentile rank of $50 + 34$ or 84. Similarly, a person one standard deviation unit below the mean (that is, with a standard score of $- 1$) would have a percentile rank of $50 - 34$ or 16. Figure 6 illustrates the relationship among percentile ranks and various forms of standard scores when the score distribution follows a normal curve.

Expectancy Tables

Finally, when the necessary information is available, there is a much better way of presenting norms. This is in terms of expectancy tables, which provide the user with an interpretation of a raw score directly in terms of likely future behavior.

To see the advantage of this method over the others, the reader might ask himself what it means, in terms of behavior in other situations, to say that a person has done as well or better than 60 percent of the standardization group. Does it mean he will succeed, or fail, or what? If this is the only information which is available, there is no evidence on the basis of which to make a predictive statement except, of course, subjective impression and familiarity with what has happened to individuals with similar percentile ranks in the past.

Basically, the purpose of an expectancy table is to provide empirically obtained probabilities indicating that persons achieving a given test score will behave in a certain way in some second situation. For example, suppose one is interested in using scores on a test of mechanical ability to make decisions concerning whether or not a given individual should seek to become a mechanic. It would be necessary to have both test scores and some kind of a measure of success as a mechanic for each member of the standardization group. Suppose, for purposes of illustration, such information were available on a standardization group of 25 individuals (see Table 5).

The first step is to divide each of the two variables, the test score and the rating of success as a mechanic, into reasonable and meaningful class intervals. To keep computational procedures

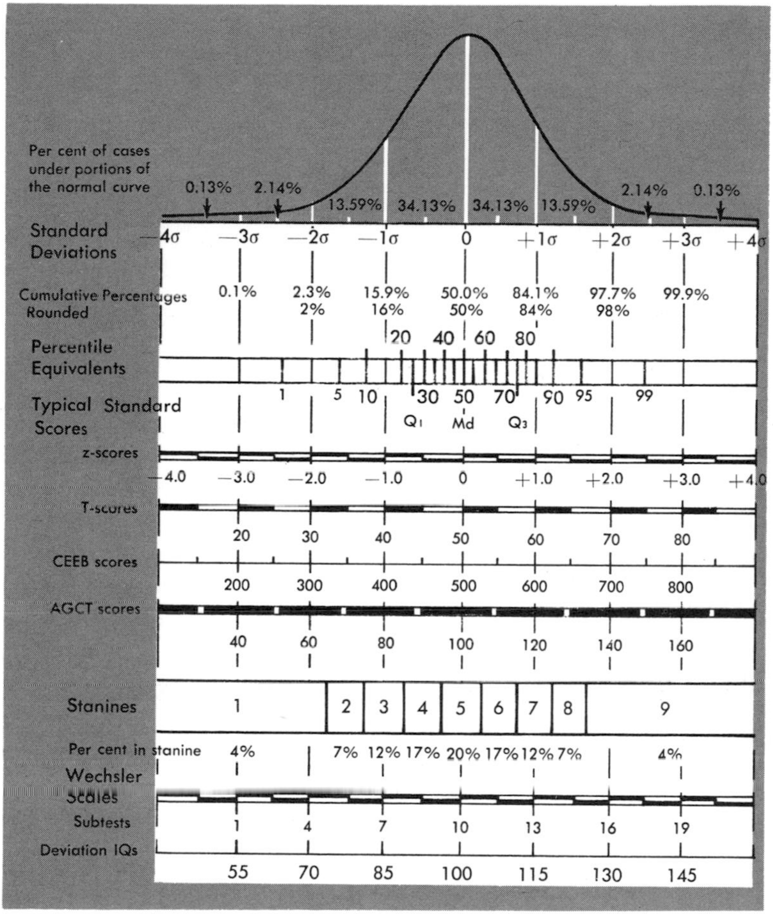

FIGURE 6: Methods of Expressing Test Scores

SOURCE: Methods of expressing test scores, *Test Service Bulletin*, 1955, 48, The Psychological Corporation, New York.

TABLE 5: Test Scores and Ratings of Success for Twenty-five Mechanics

Person	Test Score	Mechanic Rating	Person	Test Score	Mechanic Rating
1	42	3	14	54	5
2	32	5	15	8	1
3	59	8	16	25	4
4	17	4	17	5	0
5	32	2	18	53	7
6	0	1	19	37	5
7	50	4	20	16	2
8	24	7	21	43	7
9	30	3	22	15	4
10	20	0	23	26	3
11	50	8	24	30	6
12	15	2	25	57	7
13	35	8			

simple, let it be assumed that three categories on each characteristic would provide sufficient accuracy. That is, degree of success as a mechanic will be recorded in the expectancy table only as below average, average, and above average; and the test scores will similarly be grouped into high, medium, and low categories. Since the highest rating is 8 and the lowest is 0, class intervals of 0 to 2, 3 to 5, and 6 to 8 would seem convenient. Likewise, since the test scores vary from 0 to 59, class intervals on this variable of 0 to 19, 20 to 39, and 40 to 59 could be used. With these categories, the headings of an expectancy table as illustrated in Table 6 can be set up.

TABLE 6: Expectancy Table for Success as a Mechanic

Test Score	Degree of Success			
	Below Av. 0–2	Av. 3–5	Above Av. 6–8	Total
High 40–59	0 .00	/// 3 .38	7++/ 5 .62	8
Medium 20–39	// 2 .20	7++/ 5 .50	/// 3 .30	10
Low 0–19	7++/ 5 .71	// 2 .29	0 .00	7

The next step is to determine how many persons in the standardization group fall into each of the nine categories. The simplest way to do this is to go down the list and make tallies. Then, the rows are summed to determine the total number of persons who achieved high, medium, and low test scores. Finally, each cell frequency is divided by the total number in its respective row. The result is an estimate of the proportion of people falling into a given score category on a test who achieve various degrees of success as a mechanic.

Obviously, the small number of cases used in this example would yield estimates of success which are too unstable for actual use. Ideally, there should be at least twenty persons in each cell of the expectancy table and certainly no fewer than five. An example of *expectancy norms* which have been used to interpret extreme test scores in a state university is given in Table 7.

TABLE 7: Expectancy Table for Prediction of Grade Point Average at a State University

Estimated Chance in 100 That a Person With a Given
Predictive Index Will Get a Given First-Quarter Grade-Point Average
(Based upon total of 1350 cases, Fall 1956)

	First Quarter Grade-Point Average								
Predictive Index **	2.00 or Better	0.00 to 0.49	0.50 to 0.99	1.00 to 1.49	1.50 to 1.99	2.00 to 2.49	2.50 to 2.99	3.00 to 3.49	3.50 to 4.00
150-up	100	*	*	*	*	*	*	33	67
135-149	100	*	*	*	*	10	29	33	27
120-134	89	*	*	*	8	21	31	27	11
105-119	74	*	*	7	16	34	25	13	*
90-104	63	*	5	10	21	37	20	5	*
75-89	36	2	9	22	31	27	8	*	*
60-74	21	6	23	27	22	17	2	*	*
45-99	16	11	25	25	24	12	*	*	*
0-44	3	30	22	27	19	*	*	*	*

*Less than 5 cases in this cell
** Predictive Index = CAT-T $+ 59 \left(\dfrac{\text{Hi-school class size — Rank in Hi-school class}}{\text{Hi-school class size}} \right)$

The major advantage of the expectancy approach to interpreting scores is that it provides, directly, the kind of evidence which is needed in order to use the test scores meaningfully. Unlike standard scores, expectancy tables can be readily interpreted even by a person unsophisticated in measurement. Further, an expectancy table makes obvious the probabilistic nature of test scores and does not leave the scores in numbers which are likely to be used inappropriately in future calculations.

The major disadvantage of using expectancy tables in order to avoid interpretive errors is that they require considerable additional information which may not be available. Furthermore, expectancy tables are not generalizable to new situations; that is, a separate expectancy table must be constructed for every different location and for every different use of the test score which is anticipated.

OBJECTIVITY

The objectivity of a test, it will be recalled, refers to the extent to which the instrument is free from personal error—the personal bias of the one who is doing the scoring. Just as a speedometer in an automobile could be designed (for example, by putting a mirror behind the indicator needle) so as to reduce the inaccuracies which result because each passenger reads the dial from his own position, so a measure of behavioral characteristic can be constructed so as to reduce the amount of personal error. Thus, for example, a test composed of questions asked in multiple-choice form is almost always more objective than one composed of free response items.

An index measuring the degree of objectivity of any test could easily be developed by using something like Kendall's coefficient of concordance to indicate the degree of consistency which is obtained when several different persons score the same test. However, a specific measure of this characteristic of a test is seldom used in practice,[4] simply because a lack of objectivity is directly reflected as a lack of test reliability. Thus, any test which has an adequate

---

[4] On occasion, an interrater reliability (usually the correlation between the two sets of scores obtained when the responses from a single set of subjects are scored by two different individuals) is reported. In the terminology used here, this would be called an *index of objectivity.*

reliability as indicated by the measures discussed in the next chapter may be assumed to possess sufficient objectivity for use. On the other hand, a separate index of objectivity as described above may prove valuable to a test constructor by suggesting a specific cause of unreliability in an instrument under development.

3

Evaluation of Tests – Reliability

IN CHAPTER 2, RELIABILITY was described as an indication of the extent to which a test contained variable errors—that is, errors which differed from person to person during any one testing and which varied from time to time for a given person measured twice by the same instrument. This chapter will develop this concept more fully, present several experimental procedures by which such an index is actually obtained, and finally discuss a number of factors and conditions which effect test reliability.

VARIABLE ERRORS AND TRUE SCORES

To help clarify the concept of variable error, consider again the analogy of measuring the length of a table. Earlier it was noted that because of many and varied chance inaccuracies, two separate measurements of the same table might produce slightly different results. The only difference between this situation and the measurement of behavioral characteristics is that, in the latter case, the size of these variable errors is much greater.

If it can be assumed that the length of the table does not change from time to time, then any differences in reported (that is, observed) table length can be regarded as error. But, which of the two measurements is correct? Is there any justification for accepting one as a true length and rejecting the other as an erroneous observation? If both measurements were made with equal care there obviously is no way of determining whether one observation or the other or both are somewhat in error.

Since it is not possible with any one measurement to know the true length of the table independently of the error of measurement[1], it seems reasonable to consider that every observation is composed of two components: (1) the true length of the table, and (2) an error which has occurred on this specific measurement occasion. For example, if the length of the table is reported to be $61\frac{1}{2}$ inches long, it could be that the true length was $61\frac{1}{4}$ and that the measurement was $\frac{1}{4}$ inch too much. Perhaps, on the second measurement, the length was reported as $60\frac{3}{4}$ inches. If the true length is $61\frac{1}{4}$ inches, then the error component is $-\frac{1}{2}$ inch. Similarly, it could happen that Johnny knows the answer to forty-three items but guesses the correct answer to four items he does not know, or he might have marked the wrong place on the answer sheet for one of the items even though he knew the correct response. In both instances, his true score on the test is 43, but in the first instance there is a positive error of 4, yielding an observed score of 47, and in the second case the error is -1, thus giving a score of 42. The person who administered the test to Johnny does not, of course, know what the true score is; all he knows is that on one occasion, Johnny received a score of 47, and that when the test was given a second time, Johnny got a score of only 42. The problem is to find a way of estimating how much of Johnny's reported score is attributable to error and how much can be said to represent his true knowledge. While this cannot be

---

[1] If a sufficiently large number of measurements of a single object are taken and the errors are truly chance inaccuracies, it might be assumed that errors which lead to overestimates exactly balance the errors which lead to underestimates, and therefore the average of all the reported measures will be the true length. This concept is used to derive the *standard error of measurement* discussed on page 76.

done by making two measurements on just one person, if many people are measured twice with the same test, it is possible to derive an index which will serve as an indication of the amount of variable error in that test.

DEFINITION OF RELIABILITY

Consider now that there are many tables to be measured. Assume, for the moment that they are all exactly the same length —that is, assume that the true component of the observed measurement is the same for each object. Under these conditions, any variation in reported table length would be attributable to error. If the observed measures were very close together we would assume that there was very little error in the measurement, while if these reported values differed by a great deal, it could be assumed that the error of measurement was large. Thus, when the true lengths of the tables are identical, the variance of the observed table lengths would provide a good index of the amount of error.

But, what if all the tables are not of the same length? (This, of course, is a much more realistic analogy since it can seldom be assumed that a group of persons to whom a test has been given all have precisely the same amount of ability, or of knowledge, or of whatever trait is being measured.) In this circumstance, the total variation in observed table lengths is partly due to true differences in table size and partly due to errors which vary from one measuring to the next. Thus, the total variation in the reported table lengths can no longer be used as an index of error. However, just as was the case when considering a single score, it is possible to conceive of the total variance as involving an error component and a true component. Then, it seems reasonable to ask what proportion of the observed or measured differences in table length is attributable to true or actual differences in length. If this proportion is large, then the measurements reflect true differences; on the other hand, if the proportion is small, a large part of what has been observed is error. This proportion of the amount of variation in true scores to the total variation has been given the name *reliability*. Thus, in terms of tests, reliability is

defined as the ratio of the true score variance to the variance in
the scores as observed.

The concepts just described can be very easily expressed algebraically. To begin with, each person's observed score can be
represented as:

(5) $x_i = t_i + e_i,$

where:

x_i = the score actually obtained by person i

t_i = the true score for person i

e_i = the amount of error which occurred for person i at the time
the measurement was made.

Thus, in the previous example, Johnny's first actual score, x_i, was
17; his true score t_i, was 43, and the error at the time of the first
measurement, e_i, was +4. The second time he was measured, x_i
was 42; t_i, (assuming Johnny did not change) was still 43; and the
error (on this second occasion), e_i, was − 1.

From a theorem of statistics, if two scores are normally and
independently distributed, the sum of the scores will have a normal distribution such that the variance of the combination is the
sum of the variances of the two components. Thus,

(6) $\sigma_x^2 = \sigma_t^2 + \sigma_e^2,$

where:

σ_x^2 − the variance of the observed scores

σ_t^2 = the variance of the true scores

σ_e^2 = the variance of the errors.

Reliability, defined as the ratio of true score variance to
observed score variance can now be expressed as:

(7) $\text{reliability} = \dfrac{\sigma_t^2}{\sigma_x^2}$

(8) $= \dfrac{\sigma_x^2 - \sigma_e^2}{\sigma_x^2}.$

From this latter expression, it can be seen that if the measurement
involves nothing but error (recall, for example, the situation where

all tables were of the same length and thus any variation in observed length was entirely attributable to error) then $\sigma_x^2 = \sigma_e^2$
and the reliability is zero. On the other hand, when there is no
variable error at all, $\sigma_e^2 = 0$ and the ratio defined as reliability
becomes

$$\frac{\sigma_x^2}{\sigma_x^2} = 1 .$$

Thus, reliability, defined as the ratio of true score variance
to observed score variance, is an index of the amount of variable
error in a test. The reliability varies on a scale from zero to one,
having the former value when the measurement involves nothing
but error and reaching the latter value only when there is no
variable error at all in the measurement.

PROCEDURES FOR ESTIMATING RELIABILITY

As has been seen, it is not possible to ever know, directly, an
individual's true score independent of the amount of error which
occurs on any particular measurement. Thus, it is never possible
to calculate exactly the values σ_t^2 or σ_e^2. Consequently, the *true*
reliability of a test can never be computed. Rather, various experimental procedures have had to be devised for obtaining information from which the ratio σ_t^2/σ_x^2 may be estimated. At the present
time, there are four classical ways of estimating reliability. Each
of these procedures is basically different in that it defines what is
meant by error in a slightly different way.

To help point out these differences it will be convenient to
recall that reliability can be expressed in terms of observed scores
and error:

$$\text{reliability} = \frac{\sigma_x^2 - \sigma_e^2}{\sigma_x^2} .$$

As each of the basic procedures is described, the formulas expressing the estimated reliability will be written in a form analogous
to the above. Thus, exactly what is defined as error in each procedure will be readily seen.

Test-Retest Reliability

One obvious way of defining what is meant by variable error is in terms of random fluctuations in performance from one testing session to another. That is, error can be defined as anything which leads a person to get a different score on one testing than he obtained on another testing. The kind of reliability which is obtained in thinking about errors in this way is commonly called test-retest reliability. Since, however, any fluctuation in score from one time to another is called error by this procedure, such an index is sometimes referred to as the coefficient of stability.

The logic for deriving an index from this definition is as follows: First, assume that the test has been given to a group of individuals. Then, represent the scores obtained on this test by a long oblong which is designated x.

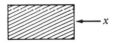

Now suppose the same test were given to the same people at some later time, denoting the scores on this testing by the symbol x'.

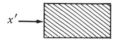

Then, assuming the persons measured did not change with respect to the characteristic measured, the extent to which the scores are identical on both testings represents a true component, and the extent to which the results are different indicates the size of the error component. Graphically, this can be represented by the overlap of the two boxes.

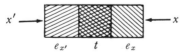

Where the extent of the overlap represents the true score component, those portions which do not overlap can represent the error components.

Now, from elementary statistics, it may be recalled that a measure of the overlapping of two variables is the correlation between them. Thus, it would seem reasonable that the correlation between the two sets of scores, one obtained on the first testing and the other obtained on the second testing, might be related to reliability as defined. To show that this is, indeed, true, simple algebraic representation will be used.

As above, the observed score x_i obtained by person i on the first testing can be expressed as $x_i = t_i + e_i$. Similarly, let the observed score obtained by the same individual on the second testing be x_i'. Since error, in this instance, is defined as any fluctuation in score which has occurred between the two testings the second score can be represented by two components: t_i, which is identical to the t_i in the first equation and e_i, which, being different, must be represented with a prime. Thus, $x_i' = t_i + e_i'$.

Assuming these scores to be deviation scores, the correlation between the two can be expressed as:

$$(9) \qquad r_{xx'} = \frac{\Sigma xx'}{N s_x s_{x'}} \; ;$$

but

$$(10) \qquad \Sigma xx' = \Sigma(t_i + e_i)(t_i + e_i')$$
$$= \Sigma t_i^2 + \Sigma e_i t_i + \Sigma t_i e_i' + \Sigma e_i e_i'.$$

Since e_i and e_i' represent random fluctuations (by definition) it can be shown that:

$$\sum_i e_i t_i, \qquad \sum_i e_i' t_i, \qquad \text{and} \qquad \sum_i e_i e_i'$$

all equal zero. (The covariance of two random variables and the covariance between a random variable and any other variable is zero.)

Furthermore, since there is no reason to expect the overall amount of error to change from one situation to the other situation (that is, if the administration is carefully carried out) and since, therefore, the amount of true score remains the same, it can be said that:

$$(11) \qquad s_x = s_{x'}.$$

Inserting these values in the original expression for the correlation
it can be seen that:

(12) $$r_{xx'} = \frac{\Sigma t_i^2}{N s_x^2} \; ;$$

but

(13) $$\frac{\Sigma t_i^2}{N} = s_t^2 \, ,$$

and therefore

(14) $$r_{xx'} = \frac{s_t^2}{s_x^2} .$$

Thus, the correlation between scores on the first testing and the
scores on the second testing provides an estimate of reliability
defined as a ratio of the true variance to the observed variance.

Although, at first this might seem to be a completely adequate
solution to the problem of estimating test reliability, there is one
important difficulty with the procedure. Were the values obtained
measures of the length of a desk or the weight of a coin it would
be completely reasonable to assume that the properties being
examined did not change and that any difference in observed
length or weight was error. Not so, however, with human characteristics. Many traits of personality, interest, and attitude are
conceived of as not being static but rather continually in a state of
flux. It may, therefore, be inappropriate to consider any and all
changes in score from one measurement in time to a second such
measure as being error. Even with measures of achievement,
ability, and aptitude, there are problems. For if a considerable
time lapses between testings, because of some different experiences
in the meantime, some subjects learn and others forget. Thus,
many of the changes in score are not actually error, and, to this
extent, reliability is underestimated. On the other hand, if re-
testing is administered immediately or after only a short period,
the subjects, remembering their earlier responses tend to answer
the questions in the same way. The resulting effect is to produce a
spurious increase in the estimated reliability. The test-retest procedure, then, may either overestimate or underestimate the true

reliability of the test, and in many instances it is difficult to determine which has occurred.

Parallel Test Reliability

One way of overcoming the problem of the recall of specific items (and thus a spurious overestimate of the reliability) is to administer, not the same test twice, but two tests composed of different items, but designed to measure exactly the same trait in the same way. Such tests are called parallel tests, or parallel forms of the same tests, and the estimate of the reliability obtained by computing the correlation between scores obtained by the same individuals on two such tests is known as parallel test reliability.

With this procedure there is, of course, the problem of determining when the test constructor has developed two tests which are, in fact, parallel. Strictly speaking, two tests are parallel, if and only if, they sample the same content universe in the same way and result in scores (when both are administered to the same group of persons) such that the means, variances, and interitem covariances are equal. While statistical tests have been developed (see Wilks, 1946 and Gulliksen, 1950) to test whether the scores and items meet the latter condition, the checking, with respect to content must be on a judgmental basis. If the test constructor has been careful in defining and classifying his content universe, and stratified sampling procedures are used in selecting items for the two parallel forms, it is possible to have considerable confidence that the two tests are actually parallel with respect to content. Then, and then only, if the statistical criteria are also met can it be said that the two tests are in fact parallel.

The logic by which it can be shown that the computed correlation between scores obtained on two forms of a test provides an estimate reliability defined as the ratio of true score variance to observed score variance is exactly the same as that presented for test-retest reliability. Therefore, the procedure will not be repeated here. One need only let the "primed" symbols represent the scores and their components on the parallel test rather than the second testing.

What is called error, however, is different in the parallel form procedure from the test-retest procedure. It is obvious that anything which causes a person to receive a score on one of the parallel forms which is different from that he obtained on the other is termed error. Since it is impossible to administer two tests to the same individuals simultaneously, all the time to time fluctuations of the test-retest procedure are called error. But this is not all. Different scores on the two tests might also be obtained because the tests were not exactly equivalent. For example, since different items are used, one form may be slightly more difficult for one person and at the same time slightly easier for a second, or the items may not get at precisely the same trait. Thus, *both* time to time and form to form (sample to sample) fluctuation in performance are called error. For this reason, the parallel form procedure yields what has been termed a measure of *equivalence and stability*.

Split-Half Reliability

Although parallel form reliability eliminates the effects of remembering responses from one test to another, it does not overcome the difficulty of calling real fluctuation in the trait under consideration error. To do this it would be necessary to administer both tests to the same people simultaneously. An approach which approximates this is to first administer a test and then, after the answers have been obtained, to divide the items into two equivalent parts, each scored separately. The correlation between the scores on one part of the test and those obtained on the other part may then represent a measure of form to form fluctuation only. Such an index is often called a *coefficient of equivalence*.

As was true with parallel test reliability, there remains the problem of getting the two parts to be approximately equal. One could, of course, be very rigorous. It is possible to perform an item analysis on the results, pair items according to difficulty, content, discrimination,[2] and so forth, and to assign one item of each pair to each half. However, a much less laborious way, and one which in practice seems to work out very well, is to simply place all the

[2] See Chapter 7.

even numbered items in one half and all the odd numbered items in the other.

Once again, the logic by which it can be shown that the correlation between the scores obtained on the two parts of the test is, in fact, an estimate of the reliability of a test, is identical with the procedure outlined for test-retest reliability. Only, this time, the observed scores x and x' represent the scores on the two halves of the test.

There is, however, one additional problem to be faced when using the split-half reliability that does not occur with the other procedures so far discussed. It so happens that test reliability is a function of the test length as measured by the number of items that comprise a test. The reason for this will be discussed in a later section. For the present, it is sufficient to note that as the length of a test increases, so does its reliability. Thus, since the split-half procedure is based upon a correlation between scores obtained on only half the test, a correction is needed to determine the reliability of the entire test.

For this purpose, the so-called Spearman-Brown prophecy formula is used. In completely general terms it is expressed as:

$$(15) \qquad r_{xx'} = \frac{mr'_{xx'}}{1 + (m - 1)r'_{xx'}},$$

where:

$r'_{xx'}$ = the reliability obtained from the original calculation

m = the multiple of the original test length by which the test has been lengthened or shortened

$r_{xx'}$ = the reliability of a test m times as long as the original.

In the case of the split-half reliability, $m = 2$ since the whole test is twice as long as the half test on which the original reliability was computed. Thus, when used to correct the correlation found between scores on two halves of a test in determining split-half reliability, the Spearman-Brown formula becomes:

$$(16) \qquad r_{xx'} = \frac{2r'_{xx'}}{1 + r'_{xx'}}.$$

When using this formula it is assumed that the items added to make the test longer measure the same trait, and further that the variances of the two half scores are equal (that is, for example, that $\sigma^2_{odd} = \sigma^2_{even}$). If the division of the items into two parts is done carefully, both assumptions can readily be met. However, on occasion when the odd-even approach is used, the variances may not turn out to be equal. A second and more recent formula which does not require this second assumption (though the first should still hold) has been developed by Guttman (1945). Thus the formula:

$$(17) \qquad r_{xx'} = 2\left(1 - \frac{\sigma_{x_a}^2 + \sigma_{x_b}^2}{\sigma_x^2}\right),$$

where:

$\sigma_{x_a}^2$ = Variance of the scores obtained on half a of the test

$\sigma_{x_b}^2$ = Variance of the scores obtained on half b of the test

σ_x^2 = Variance of the scores obtained on the entire test

may be used with the split-half procedure for estimating reliability.

To compare this formula with the original definition of reliability as

$$\frac{\sigma^2_{observed} - \sigma^2_{error}}{\sigma^2_{observed}},$$

the Guttman expression for reliability can be rewritten as:

$$(18) \qquad r_{xx'} = \frac{\sigma_x^2 - (2\sigma_{x_a}^2 + 2\sigma_{x_b}^2 - \sigma_x^2)}{\sigma_x^2}.$$

Thus, the error variance is

$$(19) \qquad 2\sigma_{x_a}^2 + 2\sigma_{x_b}^2 - \sigma_x^2$$

$$= \frac{4\sigma_{x_a}^2 + 4\sigma_{x_b}^2}{2} - \sigma_x^2.$$

The term $4\sigma_{x_a}^2$ represents an estimate of the total test variance from the variance of only those items grouped to form half a[1].

[1] From previous statistics it will be recalled that if $x_a \overset{d}{=} N(\bar{x}_a, \sigma_{x_a}^2)$ then $Kx_a \overset{d}{=} N(K\bar{x}_a, K^2\sigma_{x_a}^2)$ and thus $2x_a \overset{d}{=} N(2\bar{x}_a, 4\sigma_{x_a}^2)$.

Similarly the term $4\sigma_{x_b}{}^2$ represents an estimate of the total test variance from the variance of these items grouped to form half b. Thus the expression

(20)
$$\frac{4\sigma_{x_a}{}^2 + 4\sigma_{x_b}{}^2}{2}$$

is seen to be the average of the two estimates of the total variance from each of the halves of the test. According to the Guttman procedure, then, error variance is the difference between the total score variance as estimated from the two halves of the test and that computed from the scores on the total test.

Kuder-Richardson Reliability

A fourth classical way of thinking about variable error is in terms of inconsistency of performance on the items within the test. Ideally, when test items are arranged in order of increasing difficulty, each person who takes the test should reach a point prior to which he has correctly answered all items in the test and beyond which he will be able to answer none. If such a perfect division as this occurred for each person who took the test (the break coming at different points for different individuals) the test would be perfectly reliable according to the conceptions of Kuder and Richardson (1937). To the extent that there is an area of overlapping where examinees get some of the more difficult items correct and the easier items wrong, error occurs and the test is unreliable.

While this view of variable error seems perfectly reasonable if the test is a relatively pure measure of a single trait (that is, if it is a unifactor test) such as arithmetic, vocabulary, or spelling, such a definition is not acceptable where the test items lack complete homogeneity—that is, measure different things. For, if a test measures both quickness in arithmetical computations and vocabulary, a person may miss some easy arithmetic items and get more difficult vocabulary items correct (or vice versa), not because of happenstance, but because he has achieved more in one area than another.

Because of this characteristic, the Kuder-Richardson reliabilities have sometimes been referred to as a measure of an entirely
different characteristic of a test—homogeneity.

Certainly, if a test is a complex one—that is, if it measures
more than one trait (not necessarily a difficult one!)—it is difficult
to say to what extent the inconsistencies in performance result
from error and to what extent they reflect intraindividual differences in the traits involved, and Kuder-Richardson reliability
should not be used. However, when the test is obviously unifactor,
this approach is perfectly acceptable.

The mathematical derivation of the Kuder-Richardson reliability formula is rather complex and will not be presented here.
However, an examination of the formula for the index, frequently
called K-R 20, in the light of our basic definition of reliability will
be of value in showing how this concept of error is incorporated
into the estimation of reliability.

According to this formula,

$$(21) \qquad r_{xx'} = \left(\frac{n}{n-1} \right) \left(\frac{\sigma_x^2 - \sum\limits_{j=1}^{n} p_j q_j}{\sigma_x^2} \right),$$

where:

n = the number of items in the test

σ_x^2 = the variance of the observed test scores

p_j = the proportion of persons who got item j correct

$q_j = 1 - p_j$.

The term n/n-1 is the common correction for bias when an
estimate of the variance of a set of values is obtained by taking the
square of the standard deviation in small samples.

The only thing in the formula which may be unfamiliar is
the item variance, $p_j q_j$. This is the expression of the variance of
scores on a single item where a score of 1 is assigned to a person
who gets the item correct and a score of 0 is given to a person who
gets it wrong.

Suppose, for example, ten persons took a test composed of just one item—item j. The scores on the test would be represented as follows:

Scores for item j

$i =$	1	2	3	4	5	6	7	8	9	10
$x =$	0	0	1	1	0	1	1	0	1	1

Here,

$$\Sigma x_i = 6 \quad \text{and} \quad \Sigma x_i^2 = 6.$$

Now,

(22)
$$s_x^2 = \frac{\Sigma(x - \bar{x})^2}{N} = \frac{\Sigma x^2}{N} - \left(\frac{\Sigma x}{N}\right)^2.$$

But, since, when all values are 0 and 1

(23)
$$\Sigma x^2 = \Sigma x$$

and

(24)
$$\frac{\Sigma x}{N} = p_j,$$

it is seen that

(25)
$$s_x^2 = \frac{\Sigma x}{N} - \left(\frac{\Sigma x}{N}\right)^2$$
$$= \frac{\Sigma x}{N}\left(1 - \frac{\Sigma x}{N}\right)$$
$$= p_j(1 - p_j)$$
$$= p_j q_j,$$

and, for this particular example

$$s_x^2 = \left(\frac{6}{10}\right)\left(\frac{4}{10}\right) = .24.$$

Thus, it is apparent that error variance, for Kuder-Richardson reliability, is measured by the sum of the item variances over all items of the test.

Hoyt Reliability

Hoyt (1941) has presented a procedure for estimating reliability which defines a variable error in a slightly different way from other approaches presented so far. As it turns out, however, the results are identical with Kuder-Richardson reliability. Nonetheless, it is instructive in terms of understanding the concept of reliability, to examine his conceptual approach.

The final basic way of defining what is meant by variable error involves a slightly different breakdown of observed score variance from what has been previously presented.

According to Hoyt's formulation, variation in the performance of an individual from item to item is not considered to be error at all. Rather, it is a real (non-error) difference, an *intra*-individual difference, and one which should not be involved in the estimation of reliability. That is, total variation observed is conceived to be made up of three components: true *inter*individual differences; *intra*individual differences (measured by item variance), and error *inter*individual differences. In our previous notation, this concept can be expressed as

$$(26) \qquad \sigma_x^2 = \sigma_t^2 + \sigma_i^2 + \sigma_e^2,$$

where:

σ_i^2 = item variance

and the other terms are defined as before.

Transposing, the *intra*individual difference term we get

$$(27) \qquad \sigma_x^2 - \sigma_i^2 = \sigma_t^2 + \sigma_e^2$$

as the appropriate observed variance to be used. According to Hoyt, then, a better definition of reliability is

$$(28) \qquad r_{xx'} = \frac{\sigma_t^2}{\sigma_x^2 - \sigma_i^2} = \frac{(\sigma_x^2 - \sigma_i^2) - \sigma_e^2}{\sigma_x^2 - \sigma_i^2}.$$

Using an analysis of variance procedure, then, this reliability can be estimated by

$$(29) \qquad r_{xx'} = \frac{MS_{\text{individuals}} - MS_{\text{residuals}}}{MS_{\text{individuals}}},$$

where:

$MS_{\text{individuals}}$ = mean square of deviations from the individual's means

$MS_{\text{residuals}}$ = mean square of the deviations left over after individual and item variation has been removed.

FACTORS INFLUENCING ESTIMATED RELIABILITY

Procedure for Estimating Reliability

Since each of the approaches to estimating reliability defines error in a slightly different way, it is not difficult to imagine that when all procedures are applied to the same test, each one produces slightly different results. It is thus essential for a person who is evaluating a test with respect to reliability to know exactly what procedure was used and also to be aware of which procedures yield higher and which lower estimates of reliability.

First, it should be apparent that the parallel form estimate of reliability, when computed for a given test on a given group of subjects, will result in a lower coefficient than will the test-retest procedure. This is so not only because parallel test reliability includes form to form as well as time to time fluctuations in its definition of error, but also because it eliminates the spurious increase in consistency of score which results from the fact that people remember from one time to the next how they responded to the question previously. Because it is a more conservative estimate, parallel test reliability is the preferred measure. It is often considered a lower bound—that is, the true reliability is likely to be no lower than this estimate.

Split-half reliability, on the other hand, is usually felt to represent the upper bound. In other words, the true reliability is likely to be no higher than this estimate. While there is no reason to expect form to form fluctuation in general to be smaller than time to time fluctuations, it so happens that any single trial method of estimating reliability (that is, reliability estimates requiring only one administration of the test, for example, split-half, Kuder-Richardson, or Hoyt) will result in a serious overestimate if applied to tests having a large speed component. Exactly why this is so will be discussed in a later section. For the present, one simply needs to remember that almost every test depends to some degree, upon how fast the examinee works, and to that extent the split-half index will be an overestimate of the reliability. Thus, some instruments may appear highly acceptable with respect to reliability when in fact this is an illusion due to severe time limits on the test and the use of a split-half procedure to assess the reliability.

As has already been pointed out, the Kuder-Richardson procedure is not appropriate as a measure of reliability except with tests which are pure measures of some trait. To the extent that a test is complex (that is, measures more than one characteristic)— and, as will be seen later, the best predictors today are complex measures—the K-R procedure will underestimate the true reliability. On the other hand, since the Kuder-Richardson is a single trial estimate, it will overestimate the true reliability. Thus, no general statement can be made as to whether any given coefficient will be too large or too small.

Similarly, it is difficult to generalize about the Hoyt reliability coefficient. However, because of its sophisticated rationale and the fact that it can be used with weighted options (while the K-R cannot) as well as be conveniently computed by means of analysis of variance, this form of reliability is often preferred by persons working in test theory.

Test Length

A second major factor which has an influence upon test reliability is the length of the test. In the discussion of the split half reliability, the Spearman-Brown prophecy formula was presented as a quantitative expression of this effect. It remains to indicate why such a relationship is reasonable.

Perhaps the easiest explanation will result from considering any set of items which are organized into a test as but a sample of all possible items which represent a given content universe. If the entire universe could be used, the test would be one of infinite length, and a person's score on it would be his true score. Because only a sample is taken in a practical situation, the score observed is only an estimate of the true score. From principles of sampling design it is known that the larger the sample (and therefore the longer the test), the more precise the estimate and the smaller the error is likely to be on any particular testing. Thus, as a larger and larger sample is taken, the longer and more reliable the test becomes.

At this point it is interesting to note that Lord (1953), approaching the entire problem of reliability from a sampling point of view, arrived at formulas equivalent to those of Kuder and Richardson.

Group Heterogeneity

A third important influence upon the reliability, as estimated, is the range of abilities in the analysis group. This problem arises because, by definition, reliability, as the ratio of true score variance to observed score variance, is a relative measure. Suppose that the actual amount of error in the test remains the same, but the observed variation in score changes considerably (as might well happen if a scholastic ability test were administered first to a group of high school students and then to a population of college graduates). From the formula

$$(30) \qquad r_{xx'} = 1 - \frac{\sigma_e^2}{\sigma_x^2}$$

it is apparent that the decrease in observed variance resulting from the restriction in range of ability, would sharply increase the second term of the expression and reduce the reliability by a considerable amount.

To circumvent this problem, many test publishers are now reporting separate reliability coefficients for different subgroups of the entire analysis sample. Thus, a different reliability might be given for a high school student, for college students, and for the general adult population.

A second way of overcoming this difficulty, which has become popular in recent years, is to report an index which, while a function of reliability, is independent of the variability of the group on which it is computed. This index is called the *standard error of measurement,* and represents an estimate of the standard deviation of the errors obtained in repeated sampling.

Suppose it were possible to put in one group all persons having exactly the same degree of ability—i.e., having identical true scores. The scores actually observed on a test administered to them would not be the same because of errors which varied from person to person. That is, $\sigma_x^2 \neq 0$. If, then, a frequency distribution of the observed scores were made and the error components

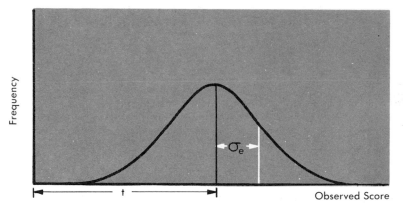

FIGURE 7: **Frequency Distribution of Observed Scores Obtained by Persons with a Given True Score**

were, as seems reasonable, normally and independently distributed with a mean of zero, the mean of this distribution would be t and its variance σ_e^2 (i.e., its variance would be the error variance for persons of this level). Similarly, the frequency distribution of observed scores obtained from groups of other ability levels would have a mean equal to their true score and a variance which would be the error variance for persons of that ability level. Now, if it occurred that the error variance was the same regardless of the ability level, the standard deviation of any one of these distributions would be the standard error of measurement. However, error variance does differ from one ability level to the next, and thus, the standard error of measurement must be thought of as a kind of an average or overall estimate of the standard deviation of these distributions.

Since, like reliability, the standard error of measurement is defined in terms which can never be obtained in practice, it is necessary to estimate it from indices obtained in an analysis group. Since the standard error of measurement is a function of reliability, the usual procedure is to first estimate the test reliability by one of the procedures already described and to use it to estimate the standard error of measurement. Thus, from the definition of reliability,

$$(31) \qquad \rho_{xx'} = \frac{\sigma_x^2 - \sigma_e^2}{\sigma_x^2},$$

it is possible to obtain:

$$\rho_{xx'}\sigma_x^2 = \sigma_x^2 - \sigma_e^2$$

$$\sigma_e^2 = \sigma_x^2 - \rho_{xx'}\sigma_x^2$$

$$(32) \qquad \sigma_e = \sigma_x \sqrt{1 - \rho_{xx'}},$$

and the standard error measurement is thus estimated by taking

$$(33) \qquad s_e = s_x \sqrt{1 - r_{xx'}},$$

where s_x is the computed standard deviation of the observed scores and $r_{xx'}$ is the estimated reliability.

Although the standard error of estimate gives an index of variable error which is not effected by the homogeneity of the group on which the reliability is determined, it is a measure in terms of test score units. Thus, while the index will not spuriously fluctuate with the homogeneity of the analysis group, it is not possible to make direct comparisons from one test to another. It seems, then, that the choice between reliability and standard error of measurement may be six of one and half a dozen of another. The main point is that before any evaluation of the amount of variable errors in a test can be made, it is necessary to know exactly what group was used for the analysis.

Speededness

A fourth influence on the reliability of a test as estimated is the extent to which a test is a measure of speed as contrasted with power. It was mentioned in an earlier section that any single trial estimate of reliability such as the split-half, the Kuder-Richardson, or Hoyt procedures will result in an overestimate of the reliability of tests which have a large speed component.

A test is referred to as a pure speed test if it is such that everyone who reaches an item gets it correct. Thus, any differences among scores will depend entirely upon the rate at which the examinees work. An example of this kind of instrument is the Minnesota Vocational Test for Clerical Workers which contains items similar to those seen in Figure 3 (Chapter 1). Since the task is simply to check those pairs of names or numbers which are different, it is obvious that a person who had unlimited time would be able to attain a perfect score. With a time limit, every item reached is usually answered correctly, and thus the score will depend almost entirely upon how many items are reached.

Contrasted with this, a pure power test is one in which unlimited time is available. Under these circumstances, everyone is able to try all items and the score will depend entirely upon the number of items the examinee was able to answer correctly. For practical reasons, almost all tests have a time limit. A common practice is to set a time limit such that between 75 percent and 90 percent of the examinees on whom the test is tried are able to finish. Thus, almost every published test has at least a small component of speed.

The spurious effect of speededness on test reliability is most readily seen in the case where the odd-even form of split-half reliability is used with a pure speed test. Here the maximum difference between any person's score on the even items and his score on the odd items is one. For, if an examinee gets every item he tries correct, he must have the same number of odd and even items right if the last item worked is an even numbered one, and one more odd than even item correct if the last one attempted was odd numbered.

Also, since, in a pure speed test, no errors are made on the items reached there are no inconsistencies in performance from item to item. Thus, methods of estimating reliability like Kuder-Richardson, which define error in terms of such item score fluctuations, would also be increased spuriously.

It is necessary, therefore, to use a test-retest or parallel form approach to reliability with highly speeded tests. One of the best and simplest procedures is to break the items into two parts or sections *before* the test is administered. Then, each half can be separately timed and scored. The reliability for the total test can then be properly estimated with Guttman's formula or by computing the correlation between the scores obtained in the two parts and using the Spearman-Brown prophecy formula, to correct to a result for a test twice as long.

It might be noted that even with such a procedure, speeded tests will generally be found to have higher reliability than power tests. This is not a mathematical artifact, however, but seems to reflect the fact that in actual behavior a greater consistency exists in rate of work than it does in quality of performance.

Before leaving this topic, it would seem appropriate to try to answer the question of how one tells when a test is so highly speeded that single-trial estimates of reliability should be avoided.

There are several ways of measuring the degree of speededness. Perhaps the most simple is to take the ratio:

$$(31) \qquad\qquad\qquad \frac{s_r^2}{s_c^2},$$

where:

s_r^2 = variance of scores obtained by counting the number of items reached regardless of whether they are right or wrong;

s_c^2 = variance of scores obtained by counting the number of items correct.

If all items are reached, as in a pure power test, s_r^2 will be 0. If the test is pure speed (all items reached are correct) then $s_r^2 = s_c^2$ and the ratio takes on a value of 1.00. But, what size this ratio has to be to be critical as far as estimating reliability is concerned has not been determined. Certainly, if it is over .50, the test can be considered highly speeded; below that it is hard to tell.

In actual practice, however, such an index is seldom computed. Rather, parallel test or retest procedures are used whenever, looking at the test content and time limits, the author feels the test is speeded. The main thing is for the consumer of tests to be on guard against estimates of reliability which have used single trial procedures with speeded tests in order to make the instrument look respectable. When this is done, the purchaser can only know that the reliability is certainly no higher than that reported, and most likely is considerably lower.

Construction and Administration of the Test

A final set of factors or conditions which can effect the reliability of a test are those having to do with the way in which items are written and the way the test is administered.

Knowing what is meant by variable error and bearing in mind that by and large reliability relates to consistency of score (from time to time, form to form, or item to item), it will not be difficult for the student himself to list many things which might be done to improve the usefulness of a test in this respect. Thus, no attempt will be made here to present a complete list. Rather, the factors mentioned should serve as examples.

First, there are many things within the test itself. For example, the arrangement of items can sometimes make a difference. If there is a wide range of difficulty among the items, it is usually best to place the easier items near the beginning of the test. This prevents the examinee from wasting time on items beyond his ability and thus not reaching items he might be able to do. Interdependent or nearly identical items will reduce the reliability. If the ability to answer one item depends on whether or not an examinee has correctly responded to a previous question, or if two items are essentially the same question asked in two different ways, the test is, in effect, shortened. Such things as "catch" questions or emotionally loaded items will also reduce reliability. This occurs because on one occasion the examinee may "see through" the gimmick or overcome his emotional response, while on a second situation, by chance, the circumstances may prevent him from doing this.

Another important influence is the form of the item. To the extent that the correct response can be obtained by chance, the test will be less reliable. Thus, a true-false item form is not as desirable as a five-answer multiple-choice item. The problem of guessing is often a serious one and will be discussed in greater detail in a subsequent chapter. One final important influence within the test itself is the appropriateness of the difficulty level of the test. A test which is too easy or too difficult for the group contains many items which do not discriminate and thus serve no purpose. This, in effect, shortens the test. In addition, an overly hard test leads to considerable guessing.

There are also some factors which lower the reliability which are attributable to the person taking the test. Lack of familiarity with the type of question is one which in the early days of objective testing was quite prevalent. For this reason, many early tests contained several practice problems. It has been shown that the first time a person takes a new type of test, such things as multiple-choice items and separate answer sheets may be bothersome. However, after one experience with such tests, sufficient familiarity is acquired so that future performances are not likely to be affected. Since, nowadays, almost every school child has taken a variety of such tests, practice sessions and overly elaborate directions (except in tests for very young children) are seldom used.

Another characteristic of the person taking the test which may influence reliability is his general attitude. This may be manifest as a set to respond positively or negatively, a tendency to guess, a motivation to fake the results, and so forth. To the extent that such feelings as these vary from time to time, the test results may be inconsistent. In any case, it is usually assumed that this factor can be sufficiently controlled by establishing rapport in the test situation and by using adequate standard directions in the test administration.

It might be noticed that no mention has been made of the examinee's physical well-being. Contrary to expectation, it has been found that persons who "do not feel well," "have headaches," "are sick to their stomach," etc., do no more poorly on a test under these conditions than they do when they think they are at their best physically. It is the personal subjective feeling of how well one performs that is lowered, not the test score. Obviously, when an examinee is so violently ill that he actually cannot see, or must interrupt the test, the above generalization does not hold. In most instances when an examinee claims he received a low score because he did not "feel well" when he took the test, it might be a good idea for public relations purposes to give it to him again. But, it is not likely that the score will change beyond normally expected fluctuations.

The final set of factors in this group are those resulting from the person giving the test. Failure to establish rapport, to communicate the importance of responding honestly and to the best of one's ability, and so forth, permits the personal attitudes just described to multiply in their effect. Also, it is obvious that insufficient or varying instructions, a misread stopwatch, a kindly attitude of "oh, let's let him have a few extra minutes to finish," or a special hint in answering a question, can reduce the reliability of a test. This is why it is so extremely important that persons administering the test read the directions verbatim and follow the other instructions for test administration explicitly.

MINIMUM DESIRABLE RELIABILITY OF A TEST

One final word about reliability concerns the question as to how reliable a test should be before it is useful. This, of course, is an extremely difficult question to answer. It has already been mentioned that the reported reliability may vary considerably depending upon the procedure used to estimate it and the homogeneity of the analysis group. Of course, reliability varies, too, with the degree of speediness, the test length, the item construction, and the directions for test administration. But these latter are traits which in part comprise the quality of the measuring instrument itself and therefore must not be partialled out or ignored when evaluating it. There are, however, some additional considerations when one is attempting to determine the adequacy of a test with respect to its freedom from variable errors.

One of these is the purpose for which the test is to be used. Many years ago T. L. Kelley (1927) devised a classical guide to be used with achievement tests. Assuming that a test must make discriminations of a difference as small as .26 times (i.e., approximately one-fourth of) the standard deviation of a grade-group with a chance of 5 to 1 of being correct, the following represents minimum reliabilities for different purposes:

1. To evaluate level of *group* accomplishment, .50
2. To evaluate differences in level of group accomplishment in two or more performances, .90
3. To evaluate level of individual accomplishment, .94
4. To evaluate differences in level of individual accomplishment on two or more performances, .98

Although these requirements are quite stringent and seldom adhered to today, they amply illustrate that the needed degree of reliability varies considerably with the purpose for which the test is to be used.

Similar to this is a statement often heard in test circles that the maximum possible validity (in this case, the correlation between a test and some independent measure of performance) is the square root of the reliability. Actually this relationship is derived from Spearman's famous correction for attenuation, which is usually given as follows:

$$(32) \qquad r_{XY} = \frac{r_{xy}}{\sqrt{r_{xx'}} \, \sqrt{r_{yy'}}},$$

where

r_{XY} = relationship between two traits measured with perfect reliability

r_{xy} = relationship between two traits as measured

$r_{xx'}$ = reliability of the measure of one trait

r_{yy} = reliability of the measure of the second trait.

Considering the test measure to be represented by the symbol x and the independent measure or criterion by y, and multiplying both sides of the expression by the denominator of the right hand term,

$$(33) \qquad r_{xy} = r_{XY} \sqrt{r_{xx'}} \, \sqrt{r_{yy'}},$$

the maximum validity may then be conceived as occurring when the true relationship between the test and the independent or criterion measures is perfect (that is, when $r_{XY} = 1.00$).

Thus, the maximum observed correlation between test and criterion is

$$(34) \qquad r_{xy} = \sqrt{r_{xx'}} \, \sqrt{r_{yy'}}.$$

If it is further assumed that the criterion is measured without error (that is, that $r_{yy'} = 1.00$), then

(35) $$r_{xy} = \sqrt{r_{xx'}} \, ,$$

and it can be stated that the maximum test criterion correlation is the square-root of the reliability of the test.

In addition to the purpose for which a test is to be used, it is necessary to consider the content of the test when evaluating the adequacy of its reliability. In discussing test-retest reliability it was hinted that measures of certain trait areas would tend to be less reliable than those of others. As it turns out, generally speaking, aptitude and ability tests will have slightly lower reliabilities than those of achievement tests, and measures of typical perform-ance have reliabilities much lower than tests of maximum per-formance. For example, by simply recording reported reliabilities for well known tests in each of several areas, the author obtained the medians and ranges shown in Table 8.

TABLE 8: Range and Median Values of Reliabilities Reported for Various Types of Measures

Type of Test	Number of Reliabilities	Value of Reported Reliabilities		
		Low	Median	High
Achievement Batteries	32	.66	.92	.98
Scholastic Ability	63	.56	.90	.97
Aptitude Batteries	22	.26	.88	.96
Objective Personality	35	.46	.85	.97
Interest Inventories	13	.12	.84	.93
Attitude Scales	18	.17	.79	.90

Closely related to the above, the final consideration before deciding whether a particular reliability is adequate is the gen-eral run of coefficients reported for other measures of the same trait. In some instances a reliability which is far from perfect may be the best yet, or much better than impressionistic judgment or than simply ignoring the trait because no measuring device is available.

In summary, then, a reliability coefficient must be interpreted in terms of the procedure used and the homogeneity of the analysis group and is to be evaluated in the light of the purpose for which the test is to be used, the content area measured, and the success with which other similar instruments have met in eliminating variable errors.

4

Evaluation of Tests – Content Validity

BASIC KINDS OF VALIDITY

IT WILL BE RECALLED that the problem of validity arises because psychological measurement is indirect. Under such circumstances it is never possible to be completely certain that a test measures the precise characteristic for which it was designed. Thus, it is always necessary to gather some sort of evidence which provides confidence that a test score really represents what it appears to represent.

As in the case with reliability and variable errors, the determination of the extent to which a test is affected by constant errors (errors which are the same for every person who takes the test and a given person each time he is measured) involves a variety of experimental procedures. These many different approaches may be conceived as representing three basic kinds of validity, each primarily concerned with a different aspect of the total testing situation as represented in Figure 8. This total testing situation for each individual can be thought of as involving three major components: the test-taking behavior, the mental traits

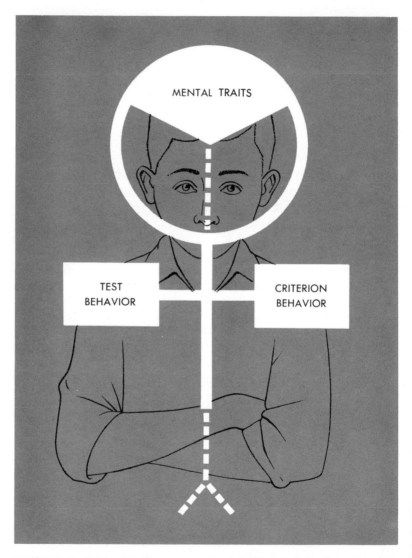

FIGURE 8: Schematic Representation of the Total Testing Situation
for an Individual

which supposedly determine behavior, and behavior in some external (non-test-taking) or criterion situation.

One way of gathering evidence which will support the idea that a test measures certain characteristics is to make a careful examination of the test-taking situation and the test behavior in and of itself. When this is the primary emphasis of the study, the concern is for what is known as *content validity*. Contrasted with this, the evidence used to indicate that a test measures what it is designed to measure might be entirely restricted to the relationship between the test behavior and the criterion behavior. This kind of evidence is called *empirical validity*. Finally, when the evidence gathered implies or depends upon the existence of some mental trait (seen earlier as a hypothetical construct), it is referred to as *construct validity*.

Each of these three basic types of validity—content, empirical, and construct—includes several kinds of evidence and has special value under certain conditions. Thus, each type will be discussed at some length in the remaining sections of this chapter.

CONTENT VALIDITY

Face Validity

The most common variety of content validity (or of any type of validity, for that matter) is face validity. Face validity refers *not* to what a test actually measures, but to what it appears, on the basis of a subjective evaluation, to measure. Of all the concepts of validity, face validity is the least justifiable. Obviously, reading over the items of a test to see if the items look satisfactory and if the content appears to be appropriate is not a very scientific form of evidence. Yet, time and time again, casual examination of the items by a prospective test user rather than inspection of data reported in a test manual has determined whether or not a particular test was used.

Even though face validity is never to be regarded as a substitute for more objective kinds of evidence, it does have a place in testing. First of all, in the original writing of items, face validity is about all there is upon which to rely. It is difficult to believe that anyone would create test items which did not appear (either ostensibly or because of some empirically observed or hypothetical relationship) as if they would work. But, once items have been written, face validity in test construction is not at all important. As will be seen in the next chapter, there are objective ways of determining whether an item is doing a good or a poor job for the specific purpose for which the test was conceived.

A second way in which face validity has some importance is in gaining rapport and maintaining good public relations. Particularly when tests are used in industry, in military situations, or in connection with civil service examinations, it is of some importance that the items and the test as a whole appear to be plausible and relevant to the stated purpose. If they are not, those taking the test are likely to exhibit negativism and a public which is uninformed as to the better and objective criteria for evaluating the worth of a test may be severely critical of both the specific agency involved and the use of tests in general. Fortunately, it is almost always possible to develop tests which combine face validity with other types of validity. If a choice is unavoidable, however, the test which has been found valid by some procedure other than face validity is the one to be preferred.

Logical or Sampling Validity

The second variety of content validity has been variously termed logical validity, validity by definition, content validity proper, and sampling validity. Actually, it is the last term which comes closest to describing what is meant. Here, the primary concern is whether a specifically defined universe of behavior is adequately sampled by the test in question.

Although logical validity, like face validity, depends upon the judgment of an expert in the field, it involves far more than merely looking at the items to see if they appear to do the job. First, it requires a careful definition in behavioral terms of the trait or content area to be measured. Second, it involves a breakdown of the total area defined into categories which represent all major aspects of the area. Finally, it involves a judgment as to whether there is a sufficient number of items in each of the categories which do in fact discriminate between those persons who have the particular characteristic or possess the knowledge and those who do not.

A good example of the kind of breakdown required for logical validity is reproduced in Figure 9. In this exhibit, the subject

Table 1:	Table of Specifications for *Latitude and Longitude**			
	General Type of Behavior			
Subject Matter Content	Recall of Information	Understanding of Concepts and Relationships	Application in Practical Situations	Total
Globe as a useful model of the earth	8	6	0	14
Movements of the earth	5	6	5	16
Lines of the globe	15	20	15	50
Finding locations	0	8	12	20
TOTAL	28	40	32	100

* A short instructional program prepared by Learning Incorporated and published by Coronet Instructional Films.

FIGURE 9: Sample Description of a Content Universe which can be used for Judging the Content Validity of a Test

matter content covered by a short instructional program is summarized in a table of specification which indicates the percent of emphasis given to various subject matter and behavioral categories.

Although this particular table of specification was used in planning a test for evaluating the program, a person who wishes to make use of any test might follow a similar procedure in judging its logical validity. Preferably, the consumer should define and break down the content area to fit his particular need. Then, he should carefully examine the test and classify the items into his own categories to see to what extent the test measures both the type of behavioral changes and the subject content area in which he is interested.

Before turning to the final variety of content validity, it should be pointed out that logical validity properly finds its greatest use in measures of achievement. While in a few vocationally oriented courses an external criterion concerning how much an examinee has profited from a particular learning experience can be found, most school situations offer no such possibility. What, for example, might a teacher of ancient history use for validation of a final examination other than a careful analysis of its content to determine whether it covers the objectives of the course and the material presented in reading, lecture, and classroom discussion?

Factorial Validity

Probably the most sophisticated form of content validity is that which makes use of the technique called *factor analysis* to determine to what extent a given test measures various content areas. Because a factor analysis involves gathering empirical data on test performance for a variety of measures, some writers classify factorial validity as a type of empirical validity. Since most such studies include only test behaviors and their primary purpose is to analyze test content, however, it logically fits into the scheme presented here as content validity. In those few studies which include both other test behaviors and some external or criterion measure, the factor analysis would seem to provide one way of gathering evidence for construct validity. The term empirical validity, as earlier determined, is restricted to those studies concerned only with the relationship between a test and a criterion measure.

To understand fully the meaning of factorial validity it is necessary to know some of the basic tenets of factor analysis. Thus, without going into the computational details, the major purposes, the fundamental concepts, and some of the logical implications of factor analysis for testing will be discussed.

Basically, factor analysis is a technique for examining a table of all the intercorrelations among a set or battery of measures which has been administered to a single group of examinees, in order to:

1. Ascertain the minimum number of traits or factors which will account for all the observed relationships among the tests.
2. Determine the extent to which each such factor is measured by each of the tests included in the battery.
3. Develop equations by which it is possible to determine each person's score on the factors when given his score on each of the tests in the battery.

A complete explanation of the procedures by which these purposes are achieved is beyond the scope of this book. However, a rough idea of the logic involved and an acquaintance with some of the terminology, particularly with respect to the second purpose, is useful at this point.

The starting place for a factor analysis is the observed relationship among many test performances as shown in a table or matrix of intercorrelations such as Table 9. Each cell in this correlation matrix represents an observed relationship between scores on the tests represented by its respective row and column. For example, the correlation .51 was found between scores on test one and test two; the correlation .07 between scores on tests eight and fourteen, and so forth.

Logically, the analysis itself provides a means by which first one "new" trait or factor is postulated and then another, each in turn accounting for as much as possible of the "common performance" observed among the tests that remains after the effects of the preceding variable have been removed. The result is a so-called *factor matrix* or *table of factor loadings* such as that shown in Table 10.

These factor loadings provide an index of the extent to which the given test measures each of the traits or content areas involved, and thus of the factorial validity of each test listed.

TABLE 9: Correlation Matrix Representing the Observed Relationships Among Eighteen Tests

Correlation Matrix R, Sub-Study A

	1	2	6	8	10	11	13	14	15	21	23	26	30	31	32	33	34
1.																	
2.	511																
6.	302	179															
8.	330	033	490														
10.	347	328	466	440													
11.	522	416	305	218	408												
13.	407	383	205	225	365	521											
14.	456	333	271	072	289	442	619										
15.	541	494	377	319	459	655	496	418									
21.	398	198	090	163	170	260	141	196	198								
23.	260	046	—036	010	092	206	—035	082	078	821							
26.	360	232	287	080	178	208	237	236	470	—130	—191						
30.	398	195	062	037	144	179	148	129	138	804	701	—150					
31.	300	234	187	114	082	169	121	167	247	107	011	476	055				
32.	386	198	145	160	020	358	204	224	353	249	206	455	177	638			
33.	314	306	229	048	250	346	290	212	390	163	136	478	100	374	402		
34.	417	358	172	101	135	372	210	187	341	090	036	525	—002	505	568	517	
35.	497	377	323	166	400	662	256	354	497	242	233	426	061	336	346	389	479

Decimal points have been omitted.

SOURCE: Ingvar Werdlin, *The Mathematical Ability: Experimental and Factorial Studies.* Lund, Sweden: C. W. K. Gleerup, 1958, Table VI:10, p. 154.

**TABLE 10: Factor Matrix Representing the Loadings of
Eighteen Tests on Five Factors**

Rotated Factor Matrix V
Sub-Study A

Test	Factor					
	R	D	V	S	N	Res.
1. Number Series I	06	41	17	23	27	—12
2. Number Series II	14	37	00	09	07	—29
6. Same-Opposite	11	01	62	08	—04	—03
8. "Wrong Word"	—04	02	68	01	07	10
10. Completion	25	10	49	—14	03	—08
11. Arithmetic II	44	27	06	—01	09	20
13. Syllogisms I	—03	62	09	—02	—05	16
14. Reasoning	01	56	—01	03	04	09
15. Arithmetic III	30	33	22	09	00	06
21. Addition I	01	13	05	05	89	03
23. Multiplication	20	—11	—08	00	87	10
26. Solid Figures	22	01	06	54	—27	—13
30. Addition III	—11	23	03	01	85	—12
31. Figures	—09	01	14	76	00	03
32. Lozenges	02	09	—02	67	16	27
33. Form Boards I	29	01	01	42	03	—08
34. Form Boards II	26	—01	—04	60	—04	—07
35. Plane Geometry	57	—02	05	19	08	04

Decimal points have been omitted.

SOURCE: Ingvar Werdlin, *The Mathematical Ability: Experimental and Factorial Studies*. Lund, Sweden: C. W. K. Gleerup, Table VI:14, p. 156.

In the last chapter, it was seen that the total observed score variance in a test given to a group of individuals could be broken down conceptually into a true and an error component. This notion was expressed mathematically as:

$$(36) \qquad \sigma_x^2 = \sigma_t^2 + \sigma_e^2,$$

where:

$\sigma_x^2 =$ the variance of the observed scores

$\sigma_t^2 =$ the variance of the true scores

$\sigma_e^2 =$ the variance of the errors which occurred on this particular measurement occasion.

The logic of factor analysis conceives of the true score component of this equation as being further broken down into subcomponents each representing a different underlying trait. Thus, the mathematical expression now becomes:

$$(37) \qquad \sigma_x^2 = \sigma_i^2 + \sigma_{ii}^2 + \sigma_{iii}^2 + \ldots + \sigma_s^2 + \sigma_e^2,$$

where i, ii, iii, and so forth, represent the different factors which contribute to performance on this particular test.

Dividing both sides of this equation by the observed score variance,

$$(38) \qquad 1 = \frac{\sigma_i^2}{\sigma_x^2} + \frac{\sigma_{ii}^2}{\sigma_x^2} + \frac{\sigma_{iii}^2}{\sigma_x^2} + \ldots + \frac{\sigma_s^2}{\sigma_x^2} + \frac{\sigma_e^2}{\sigma_x^2}.$$

Then, each ratio

$$\frac{\sigma_i^2}{\sigma_x^2}, \frac{\sigma_{ii}^2}{\sigma_x^2}, \frac{\sigma_{iii}^2}{\sigma_x^2}, \qquad \text{and so forth}$$

indicates that proportion of the total variance in performance on a test which is attributable to each factor—in a completely analogous fashion to the familiar ratio σ_t^2 / σ_x^2 which, as was noted in the last chapter, is called reliability, and which represents the proportion of the variance in observed scores which is attributable to true differences among individuals. The factor loadings of Table 10 are simply the square roots of the above proportions.

It is not difficult to see how factor analysis fits in with the idea of content validity. Suppose, for example, it was desired to ascertain the validity of a paper and pencil test of mechanical ability. One approach would be to ask about the extent to which the test content depends upon (or, perhaps more accurately, is related to) such things as spatial perception, a knowledge of barnyard physics, tool familiarity, manual dexterity, and other traits which seem logically related to mechanical ability, rather than upon such things as reading achievement, general scholastic ability, and so forth, which, should not be too highly related to mechanical ability, but which must come into play to a certain extent whenever a paper and pencil test is used.

Instead of merely making a subjective judgment after looking over the instrument, it is possible to administer this test along with two or three separate measures of each of the more or less pure traits mentioned above. Then, a factor analysis is likely to yield a separate factor for each of the major different types of tests included in the battery, and the factor loadings of the test for mechanical ability will provide an indication of the extent to which that test measures scholastic ability, reading, tool familiarity, barnyard physics, spatial perception, and so forth. These factor loadings, of course, represent the factorial validities of the test. While it is obvious that, with this procedure, no factor can come out of the analysis which does not go in with the tests selected for inclusion, such a procedure will quickly reveal important content lacks and point out the extent to which scores are likely to be dependent upon some obviously irrelevant characteristics.

The technique of factor analysis has also been used to suggest hypotheses about the nature and organization of the basic mental traits found in man. This, of course, involves gigantic studies (or a series of studies) in which a great variety of tests measuring all conceivable traits are administered to the same group of typical individuals. The hope has been that instead of the hundreds of aptitude, ability, and personality tests now required to get at human traits, only a relatively small number will someday be needed for a rather complete description of man's behavioral characteristics.

A significant problem with this application of factor analysis, however, is that there are an infinite number of factor matrices which can result from a single set of observed intercorrelations. That is, there are many, many different sets of postulated factors which could produce the one observed correlation matrix. Thus, the reader who pursues the study of factor analysis further, will find discussions about such things as rotation, orthogonal versus nonorthogonal factors, and simple structure. All of these refer to attempts to arrive at some agreement as to which of the possible solutions to accept. As a result, modern psychologists no longer look upon factor analysis as providing *the* basic underlying organization of mental traits. Rather, it is viewed as suggesting a taxonomy of traits which may or may not be useful in further theoretical and applied work.

Before leaving this topic of factorial validity, therefore, it will be worthwhile to take the time to view the various theories of mental organization which have grown out of factor analysis and to note the implications which each has for the construction and use of tests.

About the same time that Binet, in France, was formulating his concept of a single complex trait called general intelligence, Spearman, in England, developed the beginnings of factor analysis.

On the basis of the results he obtained with this new method, Spearman formulated his famous two-factor theory of mental organization. Basically, this conception holds that all mental activity is made up of one common element, or trait (described at one time by Spearman as mental energy), or general factor plus a large number of independent, specific elements. Thus any activity involves two components: the general factor and a factor unique to the particular activity in question.

Spearman's theory can be represented graphically[1] as:

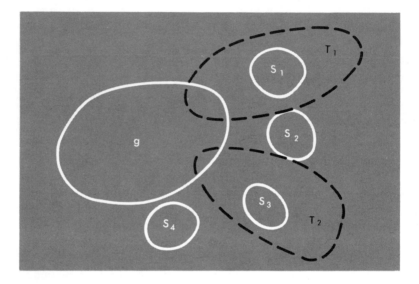

where:

g = general factor
S_i = any specific factor
T_i = any test activity.

Each test, Spearman felt, contained some g and the S unique to the activity of answering the particular items in the test. Thus, the observed correlation between any two tests resulted because they both, to a certain extent, were measures of g.

[1] All of the graphic representations of the three older theories of the structure of the intellect have been adapted from *Psychometric Methods* by J. P. Guilford. Copyright 1954. Used by permission.

The implication of Spearman's theory for testing is quite clear. Since the specific traits are too numerous to be of practical value, test construction should concentrate on the development of tests highly saturated with *g*. Although the exact nature of *g* was never precisely stated, tests dealing with abstract relationships (for example, verbal, numerical, or graphic analogies) seem to come closest to representing what was meant.

As more and more data were gathered, it became apparent that some modification of this theory was necessary. In many instances, tests involving quite similar activities showed correlations greater than would be anticipated on the basis of overlap with *g* alone. Thus, a new, intermediate class of factors, group factors, was postulated. These group factors can be shown diagrammatically by permitting the specific factors to overlap slightly, thus:

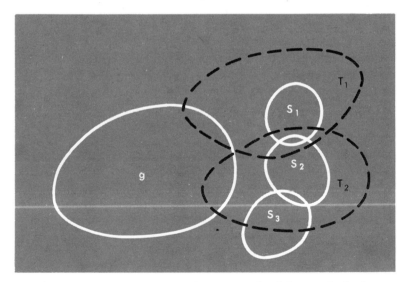

Such group factors, however, have remained in a relatively unimportant position in Spearman's theory, and its proponents today—and this includes most psychologists outside the United States—still feel that *g* is the most important influence in intellectual behavior. For example, an examination of new tests currently being developed in the Scandinavian countries, in Australia,

in France, and in England, would reveal all sorts of new and ingenious ways of getting at the ability to see abstract relationships.

A second major theory of trait organization is called *the
sampling theory* and was most concisely formulated by G. Thompson, also an Englishman. According to this theory, mental makeup
consists of a vast number of relatively minute ability elements
which have been variously identified with genes, neural elements,
stimulus-response bonds, specific experiences, and so forth. The
behavior of any person in a given activity—such as taking a test
—is a reflection of the particular sample or pool of such elements
called forth. Correlation among various measures results from an
overlapping of the different elements. Diagrammatically this can
be represented as

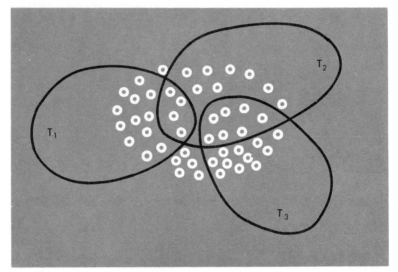

The major implication of this sampling theory for testing
is quite different from Spearman's theory. Rather than develop
pure measures of a single trait which is important in all activities,
a special test needs to be developed for each different activity and
ideally should duplicate as closely as possible the situation which
it is designed to predict. Thus, in business and industry, particularly in this country, many work sample tests are used.

Experience has shown that such tailor-made tests do, in fact,
produce the highest predictive correlation for a specific situation.

However, a test of this sort which is useful for one job in a particular factory, may not be at all useful in another situation—even one which appears to be quite similar. Thus, such tests are of limited usefulness in a guidance situation where the counsellee needs to be provided with information about his likely success in each of several families of related but not identical occupations. Also, tests designed for maximum prediction in one specific situation are not likely to be of great value in studying human behavior. Usually the composition of such tests is too complex to be useful in research studies designed to discover lawful relationships between human characteristics and behavior.

Although no special group seems to strongly advocate this particular conception of the organization of traits, it is interesting to note that it fits in best with today's widely accepted association theories of learning.

The last major theory of trait organization which has definite implication for test construction and use is the *multi-factor theory* largely developed by L. L. Thurstone and most widely accepted by contemporary American psychologists. This theory proposes a relatively small number of broad group factors, each of which enters with different weights into performance of specific tasks. Schematically, the mental organization suggested by the group factor theory is:

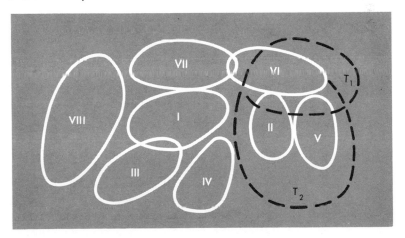

In this conception, the intercorrelation of tests results from an overlap of these common factors. Ideally, then, each test should be a pure measure of one of the group factors. Once all of the group factors have been identified and tests developed which accurately measure each one independently of other traits, it should be possible to predict any given criterion. This would be done by administering all of the group factor tests and assigning weights appropriate to the particular situation at hand. Such an approach should ultimately lead to a tremendous economy of testing, since a measure of the extent to which a person possesses these "pure" traits would be useful in any job situation. As it turns out, however, complex (that is, multifactor) tests, tailor-made for a particular job or task, still produce the highest predictive correlations. Thus, tests developed following this theory are not as useful in employee selection as they are in guidance situations where a considerable gain in generalizability of the results often offsets a relatively small loss in accuracy of prediction.

FIGURE 10: Sample Items from Primary Mental Abilities, Verbal Meaning Test

Reprinted by permission of Science Research Associates, Inc. from *Primary Mental Abilities*, Form AH by L. L. Thurstone and Thelma Gwinn Thurstone. Copyright 1947 by Thelma Gwinn Thurstone.

Thurstone and other early workers following group factor theory felt that the number of traits ultimately needed for complete prediction in all tasks would be relatively small. For example, Thurstone's early test of primary mental ability included only the following seven basic traits:

1. *Verbal Comprehension.* This is the principle factor found in such tests as reading, verbal analogies, disarranged sentences, vocabulary. Typical items from such tests are given in Figure 10.

2. *Word Fluency.* This trait is found in such tests as anagrams, rhyming, naming words in a given category, listing synonyms, etc. Examples of items from tests of this sort are given in Figure 11.

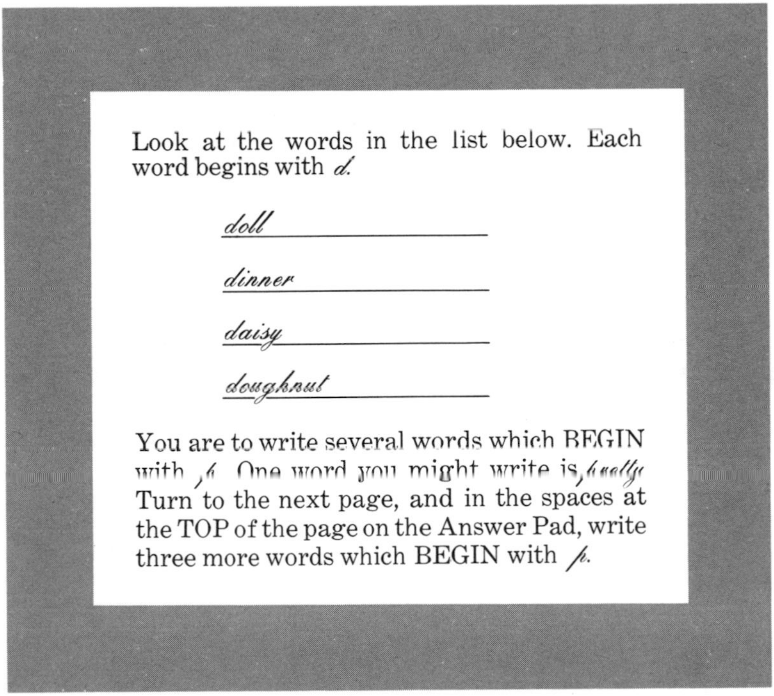

Look at the words in the list below. Each word begins with *d.*

doll _____

dinner _____

daisy _____

doughnut _____

You are to write several words which BEGIN with *d.* One word you might write is *deadly.* Turn to the next page, and in the spaces at the TOP of the page on the Answer Pad, write three more words which BEGIN with *d.*

FIGURE 11: Sample Items from Primary Mental Abilities, Word Fluency Test

3. *Number*. This is a factor which is closely associated with speed and accuracy in simple arithmetical computations, and illustrated by sample items in Figure 12.

Now check the sums of the problems below. If the answer is Right, put an × in R . If the answer is Wrong, put an × in W . If you wish to change an answer, draw a circle around this box like ⊗ . Then mark the new answer in the usual way. _____

A	B	C
17	35	63
84	28	17
29	61	89
140	124	169

FIGURE 12: Sample Items from Primary Mental Abilities, Number Test

Reprinted by permission of Science Research Associates, Inc. from *Primary Mental Abilities*, Form AH by L. L. Thurstone and Thelma Gwinn Thurstone. Copyright 1947 by Thelma Gwinn Thurstone.

4. *Spatial Relations*. This trait represents an ability to visualize spatial relations in two or three dimensions. Most modern tests, such as the Revised Minnesota Paper Form Board Test (see Figure 13) are paper and pencil instruments and limited to two dimensions.

5. *Associative Memory*. This factor is identified chiefly with tests of rote memory and for paired associates. Sample items from one such test are presented in Figure 14.

6. *Perceptual Speed*. This trait represents an ability to quickly and accurately grasp visual details or to rapidly recognize similarities or differences. The Minnesota Vocational Test for Clerical Workers described in Chapter 1 as a pure speed test is typical of the measure of this trait.

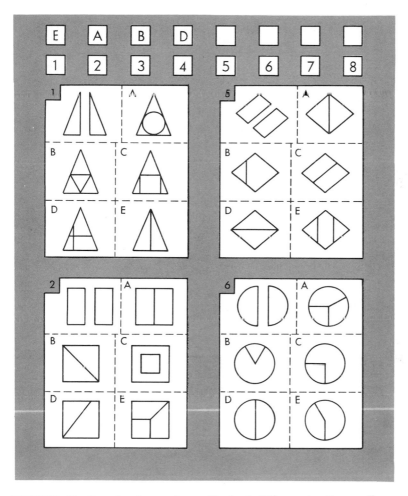

FIGURE 13: Sample Items from Revised Minnesota Paper Form Board Test

**READ THE FOLLOWING DIRECTIONS VERY CARE-
FULLY WHILE THE EXAMINER READS THEM ALOUD**

Look at the problems on the right side of this page. You will notice that there are eight of them, numbered from 1 to 8. Notice that the problems go DOWN the page.

First look at Problem 1. There are two parts in the upper left-hand corner. Now look at the five figures labelled A, B, C, D, E. You are to decide which figure shows how these parts can fit together. Let us first look at Figure A. You will notice that Figure A does **not** look like the parts in the upper left-hand would look when fitted together. Neither do Figures B, C, or D. Figure E **does** look like the parts in the upper left-hand corner would look when fitted together, so E is PRINTED in the square above 1 at the top of the page.

Now look at Problem 2. Decide which figure is the correct answer. As you will notice, Figure A is the correct answer, so A is printed in the square above 2 at the top of the page.

The answer to Problem 3 is B, so B is printed in the square above 3 at the top of the page.

In Problem 4, D is the correct answer, so D is printed in the square above 4 at the top of the page.

Now do Problems 5, 6, 7, and 8.

PRINT the letter of the correct answer in the square above the number of the example at the top of the page.

FIGURE 13: Continued

This is a test of your ability to remember numbers that you have associated with things. The memory page presents 20 picture-number pairs like this:

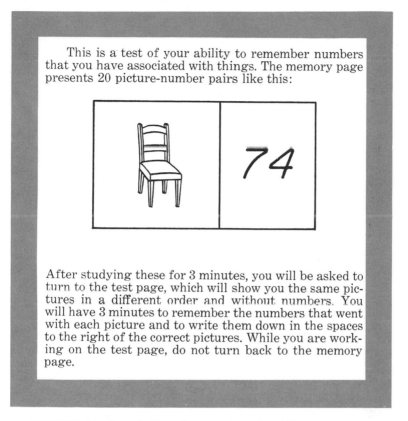

After studying these for 3 minutes, you will be asked to turn to the test page, which will show you the same pictures in a different order and without numbers. You will have 3 minutes to remember the numbers that went with each picture and to write them down in the spaces to the right of the correct pictures. While you are working on the test page, do not turn back to the memory page.

FIGURE 14: Sample Item from an Associated Memory Test

SOURCE: John French, ed., *Kit of Reference Tests for Cognitive Factors*, Test Ma-1 *Picture-Number*. Copyright, Educational Testing Service, Princeton, N. J.

7. *General Reasoning.* Of all the factors presented, general reason is probably least clearly defined. Originally Thurstone postulated two reasoning factors—one of inductive reasoning and one of deductive reasoning. Later data, however, failed to provide evidence for such a distinction, and thus many modern tests, such as Thurstone's, illustrated in Figure 15, attempt to get at but a single general reasoning factor.

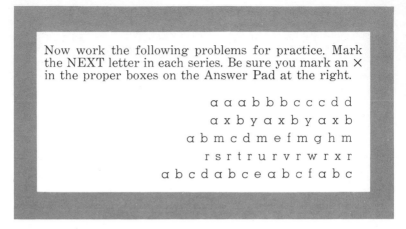

Now work the following problems for practice. Mark the NEXT letter in each series. Be sure you mark an X in the proper boxes on the Answer Pad at the right.

a a a b b b c c c d d

a x b y a x b y a x b

a b m c d m e f m g h m

r s r t r u r v r w r x r

a b c d a b c e a b c f a b c

FIGURE 15: Sample Items from Primary Mental Abilities, Reasoning Test

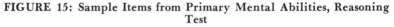

Reprinted by permission of Science Research Associates, Inc. from *Primary Mental Abilities*, Form AH by L. L. Thurstone and Thelma Gwinn Thurstone. Copyright 1947 by Thelma Gwinn Thurstone.

As work in factor analysis has continued, however, more and more factors have been found. French (1951) and (1953) made a thorough review of the literature in factor analysis, summarizing the results in two publications. One listed some fifty-nine factors which had been identified in the area of aptitude and achievement, and the other described sixty-two different factors found in attitude and personality measurement. At the same time, Guilford has argued that if psychologists are to ever understand the nature of intellect, more attention should be given to the superior human adult. Thus, rather than working with school children as Thurstone had done, Guilford has carried out studies with Air Force Cadets, and high level Naval personnel. As a result, over forty different *intellective* factors have now been satisfactorily identified.

Further, in 1956, Guilford presented a first attempt at a systematization of the many factors observed. As seen in Figure 16, Guilford represents the organization of intellectual traits in three dimensions. Along one dimension are represented the things which the "mind" can do—the operations; along the second are the different contents with which the operations can be performed;

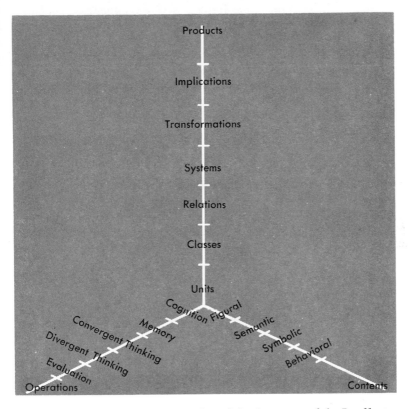

FIGURE 16: Guilford's Conception of the Structure of the Intellect

SOURCE: *Review of Educational Research* (Washington, D.C.: National Education Association, 1959)

and along the third axis are listed the different products which can result when the various operations are performed with one or more of the contents.

Basically, Guilford sees four major operations:

1. *Cognition*—becoming aware of the existence of something.
2. *Memory*—simply remembering what was once known.
3. *Productive Thinking*—the operations of organizing, by reasoning, or other processes, the contents in such a way as to result in useful solutions to problems.

4. *Evaluation*—the operation of making judgments and decisions.

Productive Thinking is further broken down into convergent
and divergent problem solving. The convergent problem-solving
operation occurs when the task has but a single solution, as is the
case with many problems in mathematics, science, and engineer-
ing. On the other hand, divergent problem solving occurs in a
situation in which many many solutions are possible, as is the
case in many musical, artistic, and political applications. Although somewhat similar to the older breakdown of deductive
and inductive reasoning, Guilford's conception is much more
inclusive. Reasoning is but one way of solving problems, and
divergent problem solving includes what has heretofore been only
loosely described as creativity.

It is also worth noting that the term *productive* rules out
reverie, fantasy, and other forms of thinking which are *not* primarily intellective.

The contents with which these different operations can be
performed are listed as:

1. *Semantic*—contents having to do with language.
2. *Symbolic*—contents having to do with numerical ideas and
   concepts.
3. *Figural*—contents related to visual, auditory, etc. configura-
   tions, patterns, and shapes.
4. *Behavioral*—contents related to the way in which persons
   and animals behave.

Previously, a person who could perform all the operations
well with semantic contents was said to have verbal ability; a
person who effectively performed the various operations with
symbolic contents was said to have mathematical ability; persons
with facility with figural contents were said to have artistic ability;
and those who could recognize, remember, think productively
about, and make evaluations effectively with behavioral contents
were said to have a high degree of social ability.

Finally, Guilford divides the products into *elements,* or bits
of information; *classes* or groupings of elements; *relations* or

similarities, differences, and contingencies among the classes; *theories* or systems of relationships; *transformations* or concepts of how things change; and *implications* or projections of the theories to events which have not yet been observed or thought about.

While admittedly a rough, first attempt, this classification scheme, somewhat analogous to the periodic table in chemistry, has provided for meaningful classification of the forty-odd factors already developed and has further suggested areas in which new factors might be found. Subsequent work has verified the existence of some of these additional traits, illustrating the tremendous value of such taxonomic work in the area of testing, as well as the usefulness of the factorial approach to content validity.

5

Evaluation of Tests –
Empirical Validity

EXPRESSING EMPIRICAL VALIDITY

IN THE LAST CHAPTER it was noted that empirical validity provides the evidence that a test score can be interpreted in a particular way by showing that a relationship exists between the test performance on the one hand, and on the other, behavior in some second (criterion) activity. This relationship between test and criterion performance can be expressed in several ways.

Because it represents a measure of association between two continuous variables, the Pearson product-moment correlation coefficient is the most common index of empirical validity. Thus, a measure of scholastic ability is validated by correlating test scores with subsequent grade-point average; a test of mechanical ability is assessed for validity by means of the correlation between scores on the measure and ratings of performance on the job; and so forth. If either the criterion or the test or both variables are not measurable on a ratio scale (see Chapter 1) then some other form of correlation such as rank order, biserial, tetrachoric, or the correlation ratio may be used.

Sometimes direct measurement of the criterion behavior is expensive, unreliable, or nearly impossible to obtain. Under these

circumstances other ways of describing the relationship between
the two behaviors must be found. One possibility is that of noting the mean difference in performance among readily recognized
groups. Thus, for example, evidence of the empirical validity of a
measure of art aptitude might be expressed in terms of the differences in mean scores obtained by people in general, by art students, and by professional artists. If the test is empirically valid,
scores should increase considerably from the first group to the last.
Similarly, a test of scholastic ability might be empirically validated by showing that the average of the scores obtained on the
test increases as it is administered to persons at successively higher
levels of education.

Another somewhat different approach is to express the relationship between test and criterion performance in terms of the
percentage of individuals who would be correctly classified by
the test according to their known group membership. Thus, an
interest measure which was designed as an aid in occupational
guidance might be empirically validated by showing that a high
proportion of persons presently on the job could be correctly
classified according to their occupation from the test scores alone.

To effectively present evidence of empirical validity to the
statistically untrained consumer of tests, the data summarized by
the indexes just described can be presented in graphic or tabular
form. Thus, the expectancy table of Chapter 2 might be used to
show the relationship between test and criterion scores as well as
to provide a means for direct interpretation of the scores; and differences in scores among several groups might be presented as
shown in Figure 17.

INTERPRETING VALIDITY COEFFICIENTS

When empirical validity is expressed, as it usually is, in terms
of the correlation between test scores and performance on some
criterion, the further question arises as to how high the validity
coefficient should be for the test to be useful. In general, this question can be answered in two ways: first, it is possible to determine
the amount of error which would be made if the test were used
to predict an individual criterion score; second, it is possible to

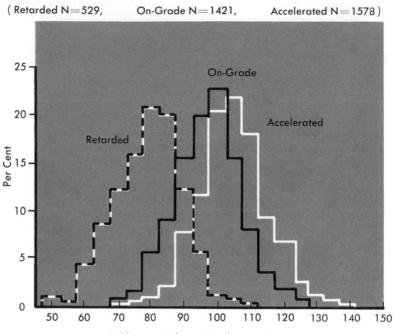

(Retarded N=529,   On-Grade N=1421,   Accelerated N=1578)

Kuhlmann-Anderson Intelligence Quotients

FIGURE 17: Evidence of Validity Shown by a Difference in Performance Among Groups

Source: F. Kuhlmann and R. Anderson, *Master Manual, Kuhlmann-Anderson Tests*, 6th ed. (Princeton, N. J.: Personnel Press, Inc., 1952).

compare the number and kind of selection errors made when using a test for screening purposes with those errors made without the use of the test. Each of these answers to the question will be discussed in turn.

Predicting an Individual Criterion Score[1]

[1] It should be recognized that for most practical situations, it is not actually necessary to predict exact criterion scores, but only to assign the individual to broad categories like *pass-fail, satisfied-unsatisfied, likely to profit from treatment-not likely to profit from treatment,* and so forth. Nonetheless, the logic of predicting an individual score represents an important theoretical notion and does provide a way for interpreting validity coefficients in the absence of information about the base and validity rates described in the next section.

Consider the problem of attempting to predict the likely success of a boy who is about to enter college. Since grade-point average at the end of the first year is the index used to determine whether the boy will be allowed to return to school the next year, assume that it is the criterion score which is to be predicted.

Without any information at all about this boy, except that he hopes to enter a particular college, it is still possible to make a prediction about what his grade point will be. Logically, the best guess as to his grade point would be that typically received by entering freshmen. That is, if the average grade point earned by freshmen at this particular institution was 1.76, then, in the absence of other relevant information, the best guess as to this new entering freshman's performance would be 1.76. Suppose, however, some information were available as to this entering student's performance on an entrance test known to be related to grade point. No longer is the best estimate as to his future grade point the average of that achieved by all freshmen. Rather, from the basic logic of prediction as described in Chapter 1, the best guess is now the grade point typically achieved by those students who received the same score on the entrance test as did this new applicant.

Just how such a prediction would be made can be seen from the schematic scatterplot between entrance test scores and grade points as shown in Figure 18.
The curve to the left of the Y axis can be thought of as representing the frequency distribution of grade points achieved by all freshmen and the curve to the left of the vertical line at point X can be thought of as representing the frequency distribution of the grade points achieved by those freshmen who received a score of X_o on the entrance test. The line $Y = a + bX$ represents the regression line for predicting Y from X and, as usual, the thickness of the ellipse which circumscribes the scatterpoints representing the individual students can be used to judge the degree of relationship between the two variables. In this figure, then, $\overline{Y}$ represents the best estimate of grade point when no test information is available and the value $\overline{Y}_{x_o}$ represents the best estimate of grade point for an applicant who received a score of X_o on the entrance test.

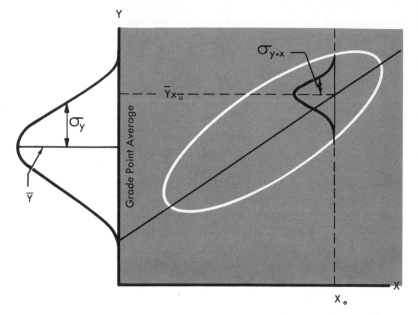

Scores on Entrance Exam

FIGURE 18: Errors of Predicting an Individual Performance with and without Test Information

Next, it is necessary to consider how accurate the estimate of grade point would be, first without, and then with, the test score information. If every entering freshman received exactly the same grade point, then there would be no error whatsoever in the estimate of grade point. At the other extreme, if the grade points of freshmen varied all the way from 0.00 to 4.00 (where 4.00 represented a straight *A* average) the estimate of 1.76 (the average of the grade points achieved by all freshmen) could be as much as 1.76 above and 2.24 below the actual achievement of the new applicant. Within these extremes, it is easy to see that the larger the spread of freshmen grade-point averages, the worse the estimate of 1.76 might be and the smaller the spread, the less likely the value 1.76 will deviate from the grade point actually achieved by a significant amount. Thus, it is reasonable that the variance of the grade points achieved by all freshmen can be used as an index of how far off the estimate is likely to be when *no* test information is available. Similarly, it is reasonable that the variance of the grade points achieved by freshmen who received an entrance score of X_o can be used as an index of how far off the estimate is likely to be when predicting the grade point of an applicant who gets a score of X_o on the entrance test. Thus, the amount of error anticipated when estimating a grade point without any test information is represented in Figure 18 by the value σ_y^2 and the amount of error anticipated when estimating a grade point with the test information is represented by the value $\sigma_{y \cdot x}^2$.

As might readily be expected, there is a direct mathematical relationship among the values r_{xy} (the correlation between the test and the criterion measure) and the values σ_y^2 and $\sigma_{y \cdot x}^2$ as defined above. This relationship can be expressed as:

$$(37) \qquad r_{xy}^2 = \frac{\sigma_y^2 - \sigma_{y \cdot x}^2}{\sigma_y^2}.$$

Three different indexes, each making use of this relationship, have been used to provide more direct information as to the usefulness of the test for predicting a criterion score than is given by the validity coefficient itself. These indexes are the standard error of estimate, the coefficient of alienation, and the relative reduction of error variance.

The Standard Error of Estimate. This index can be thought of as a kind of average of the standard deviations of grade points calculated separately for those freshmen who received each of the different possible scores on the entrance test. That is, the value $\sigma_{y \cdot x}^2$ really represents a kind of average of the values $\sigma_{y \cdot x_1}^2$, $\sigma_{y \cdot x_2}^2$, $\sigma_{y \cdot x_3}^2$, and so forth, where x_1, x_2, x_3, and so forth, represent the various possible scores on the entrance test.

The standard error of estimate can be computed by means of a formula obtained by solving the equation given above for $\sigma_{y \cdot x}$. Thus,

$$(38) \qquad \sigma_{y \cdot x} = \sigma_y \sqrt{1 - r_{xy}^2}.$$

This standard error of estimate can then be used to set confidence limits about an estimated criterion score in exactly the same way that the standard error of measurement was used in determining the confidence limits of a true score. Suppose that an applicant to

college achieved a score of 119 on an entrance test known to have
a correlation of .60 with grade-point average at that institution.
If the average of the grade points achieved by past freshmen who
got a score of 119 was 2.9 and the standard deviation of the grade
points achieved by all freshmen was .5, then the 95 percent confidence limits would be determined by taking: $2.9 \pm 1.96\sigma_{y \cdot x}$. The
value $\sigma_{y \cdot x}$ would be calculated as follows:

$$\sigma_{y \cdot x} = \sigma_y \sqrt{1 - r_{xy}^2}$$
$$= .5 \sqrt{1 - (.60)^2}$$
$$= .4.$$

The confidence limits become $2.9 \pm 1.96(.4)$ and thus it would be
anticipated, with 95 percent confidence, that the grade point
achieved by the applicant, were he to be admitted, would be
somewhere between 2.1 and 3.7.

The Coefficient of Alienation.   While the standard error of
estimate provides an excellent practical measure of the amount
of error when estimating a criterion score, it is always expressed
in the same units as is the criterion measure. When the criterion
is measured with large numbers, the standard error of estimate
will be large and when the criterion is measured in terms of small
numbers, the standard error of estimate will also be small in
absolute magnitude. Thus, the actual size of the standard error
is always a function of the size of the standard deviation of the
criterion distribution.

This bothersome problem of having an index of error which
is affected by the units of the criterion measure can be overcome
by the use of a relative index. One such index is the coefficient of
alienation which can be expressed as the ratio of the standard
error of estimate to the standard deviation of the criterion scores.
That is,

$$(39) \qquad \text{Coefficient of Alienation} = \frac{\sigma_{y \cdot x}}{\sigma_y} = \sqrt{1 - r_{xy}^2}.$$

When the standard error of estimate is small in relation to the
standard deviation of the criterion distribution, the efficiency of
predicting an individual score is high and the coefficient of aliena-

tion is low. As the standard error of estimate approaches the criterion standard deviation, the efficiency of prediction becomes less and less and the coefficient of alienation is an inverse measure of the effectiveness with which a prediction can be made from a test.

The Relative Reduction in Error. A much simpler and more direct relative measure of the efficiency of predicting a criterion score can be obtained by simply squaring the correlation between the test and the criterion measure. It has already been noted that:

$$(40) \qquad r_{xy}^2 = \frac{\sigma_y^2 - \sigma_{y \cdot x}^2}{\sigma_y^2}.$$

Since $\sigma_{y \cdot x}^2$ represents the amount of error with the use of the test and σ_y^2 represents the amount of error when estimating the criterion score without the use of the test, the difference $\sigma_y^2 - \sigma_{y \cdot x}^2$ represents the reduction in error which results from using the test. Dividing this difference by the original amount of error, then, gives the relative reduction in error achieved through the use of the test.

Thus, if the correlation between a test and a criterion were .30 the relative reduction in error would be only .09; while, if the correlation between a test and criterion were as high as .70 we would be .49 or nearly 50 percent more accurate in estimating the criterion scores with the test than without it.

Using Tests to Improve Decisions

Those readers who are aware that, with the present state of knowledge, the obtained correlations in predicting success in college centers around .60 may be quite shocked to realize that the reduction in error over pure chance (that is, over guessing the mean grade-point average of all freshmen for every new student) when predicting a specific grade-point average by the use of a test is only slightly more than one-third. Fortunately, except for individual counselling purposes, it is seldom necessary to predict an individual's exact criterion score. In most situations, tests are used for screening or selection purposes and the determination of the extent to which a test is useful in these circumstances takes a different form from that just described.

The General Schema. A typical screening situation has been represented graphically in Figure 19. In this figure, the ellipse represents the scatterplot indicative of the degree of relationship between the test scores and the criterion scores. At some

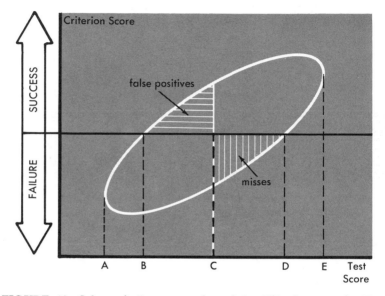

FIGURE 19: Schematic Representation of the Effectiveness of a Test in a Selection Situation

point along the *Y* axis is a place at which, administratively or otherwise, quality of performance is considered to be entirely unsatisfactory. Thus, all measures of performance exceeding this value lead to the decision, *successful,* and all persons performing less well would be termed *failures* (that is, they would be dismissed from school, fail to receive a degree, be fired from a job, and so forth). Any one of the possible cutting scores on the test, such as those represented by points *A, B, C, D,* and *E,* is a score to be selected as representing the test performance which must be achieved by a person in order to be accepted (that is, admitted to school, hired for a job, given a license, and so forth).

With the cutting score on the test somewhere near the middle of the score range, say at point *C*, the ellipse, containing all individuals, will be divided into four sections. In the lower left quadrant will be persons who would not be acceptable if the cutting score were used and who would have failed had they been given the chance. In the upper right quadrant are points representing persons who would have been selected for the task and who would have succeeded. Thus, the decision based on the arbitrary cutting score to accept or reject would have been correct for every person falling in these quadrants. Not so individuals whose test and criterion scores place them in the upper left or lower right quadrants. In both of these latter instances, an error would have been made had the cutting score *C*, as pictured, been selected. Persons falling in the upper left portion of the ellipse are those who would not have been accepted by their test performance, but who would have succeeded had they been given an opportunity; those in the lower right are persons who would have been accepted, but who would have failed at the task. The former are designated *false positives* and the latter *misses*.[2]

To evaluate the effectiveness of a test in a screening situation, two conditions other than the size of the correlation (which is represented in the figure by the narrowness of the ellipse) between test and criterion scores must be known. The first of these is the cutting score itself. The second is the *base rate,* that is, the proportion of persons who succeed prior to the use of the test. The base rate represents the proportion of correct decisions which are made when selecting individuals without the use of the particular test under evaluation. For, in effect, when individuals are all given an opportunity to try out, a prediction is made for each person that he will succeed. To evaluate the effectiveness of a test in a particular situation, then, the proportion of correct decisions made when the test is used (the validity rate) must be determined and compared with this base rate.

---

[2] This terminology may seem backward to those interested in employee selection who might ordinarily think of persons hired who later failed as false positives and persons not hired who could have done the job as misses. The notations, however, derive from medicine where a false positive test implies that disease was indicated when it did not exist; and the person who has the disease but is not detected is called a miss.

Determining Base Rates.   Unfortunately, test publishers or authors of validity studies reported in the literature do not often provide data in such a way that a potential user can evaluate its probable effectiveness by noting the number and kinds of errors made when tried in other similar situations. Rather, the usefulness of the test for a selection situation is described only in a summary statement giving such information as the percentage of persons in each group who failed the test or the proportion of successes selected with the test as compared with the proportion of successful persons selected without the test. With only this latter information, incorrect conclusions may be drawn about the usefulness of the test or scale in question. The only alternative open to the potential user is to obtain his own estimate of the base rate in the situation in which the instrument will be used and to calculate for himself the actual validity rate of the scale.

For example, in one study reviewed by Meehl and Rosen (1955) an attempt had been made to devise a scale which would be useful in military induction stations for detecting men who would not complete basic training because of psychiatric disability or AWOL recidivism. What the original investigators did was to apply a number of scales to two groups of men—415 who had made a good adjustment and 89 who had had to be discharged on psychiatric grounds. Noting that the best scale diagnosed as failures 55 percent of the poorly adjusted group and only 19 percent of the well-adjusted group, the authors advocated the use of the scale throughout the service.

As pointed out by Meehl and Rosen, the base rate (the proportion of successes without the use of the scale) was completely ignored by the original authors when reporting the success of their instrument. Thus, the conclusion that the scale would be highly useful throughout the service could be quite unjustified. To correctly determine the efficiency of the scale, it is necessary to prepare an expectancy table which properly includes the base rate.

For purposes of illustration, Meehl and Rosen assumed that the base rate at the particular induction station at which the study was executed had been estimated to be 95 percent (that is, it was estimated that 5 percent of the inductees failed to finish their basic training because of psychiatric disability or AWOL recidivism).

With this estimate and the information provided by the original
authors, all the necessary information for making a sound judgment can be obtained. The results of the calculations are presented
in Table 11 which has been reproduced from the Meehl and Rosen
article.

**TABLE 11: Number of Inductees in the Poor Adjustment and Good
Adjustment Groups Detected by a Screening Inventory**

(55% valid positives; 19% false positives)

Predicted Adjustment	Actual Adjustment				Total Predicted
	Poor		Good		
	No.	%	No.	%	
Poor	275	55	1,805	19	2,080
Good	225	45	7,695	81	7,920
Total Actual	500	100	9,500	100	10,000

SOURCE: P. Meehl and A. Rosen, Antecedent probability and the efficiency of psychometric signs,
patterns, or cutting scores. *Psychol. Bull. 1955, 52,* 194–216, Table 1, p. 195.

To construct Table 11, the percentages of 55 and 19, as presented by the original authors, can first be inserted into the appropriate cells. From these, the 45 percent and the 81 percent can be
obtained by subtraction from 100. Next, an arbitrary grand total
of 10,000 has been selected for purpose of illustration and placed
in the lower right hand cell of the table. Then, using the error
rate of 5 percent, the total actual adjustment numbers of 500 and
9,500 can be determined. Multiplying these total numbers by the
appropriate percentages, frequencies of 275, 225, 1,805 and 7,695
are found. Finally, adding the numbers for each row, the total
predicted figures of 2,080 and 7,920 are obtained.

Thus, if predictions are made according to the authors' recommendations for the entire 10,000 inductees, 275 + 7,695 or a
total of 7,970 correct decisions would be made. That is, using the
inventory, the prediction is right 79.7 percent of the time. This
validity rate would be quite impressive were it not for the fact
that an even better percentage of correct decisions could have
been achieved without ever having seen either the scale or the
inductees. Simply by predicting that every one of the 10,000 re-
cruits would be successful, a correct decision would be made 95
percent of the time; for, only 5 percent of the entire group will

not make it through basic training for reasons of psychiatric disability or AWOL recidivism.

This latter assessment, of course, assumes that misses and false positives are equally serious errors and that the scale is used in a particular way. Thus, in using the base rates for prediction, the number of false positives is reduced to few, but the proportion of misses is more than doubled. Also, Cureton (1957), in a later discussion of the problem of assessing the usefulness of a test in a prediction situation, has demonstrated that every valid, continuous predictor can (at least when an optimal cutting score[3] is used) provide better predictions than those given by the base rate alone. Thus, in the situation just described, the scale was evidently not used in such a way as to minimize the error of prediction.

Locating Cutting Scores.   Referring again to Figure 19, it is obvious that the proportion of incorrect decisions which are made (the error rate) will change as the cutting score on the test is moved from an extremely low score to the highest possible score. Starting at the left of the figure, point *A* represents a cutting score just below the lowest score obtained on the test. This situation is that which would exist if the test were not used. The entire area inside the ellipse below the criterion point taken as the boundary between success and failure is the proportion of errors made without the test. In this instance all errors are misses—that is, persons who were given the opportunity but who failed.

As the cutting score is increased to point *B*, the number of misses is decreased, the proportion of errors now being that area inside the ellipse in the lower right quadrant of the figure. If the cutting score is further raised, the total number of errors—the area inside the ellipse in the upper left and lower right quadrants —will continue to be reduced. To the right of point *B*, however, the type of error will change.[4] Although fewer misses will occur, the selection procedure now overlooks some persons (false positives) who would succeed had they been given an opportunity. Near point *C* the overall error will be at a minimum, but the

---

[3] According to Cureton, the optimal cutting score to predict a dichotomous criterion from a continuous predictor is the point of intersection of the smoothed predictor frequency distributions of the two criterion categories.

[4] The considerations required to set an appropriate cutting score when there are two types of error are discussed in a later paragraph.

incorrect decision will involve both a number of misses and false positives. If the cutting score is raised beyond the region of point C, the total number of errors again begins to increase. This time, however, the incorrect decisions are primarily those of not selecting people who could succeed and only to a small extent those of choosing individuals who later fail. At point D no person would be selected who later failed and all the error would involve overlooking persons who could have succeeded had they been given a chance. Raising the cutting score beyond this point (as lowering it below point B) would serve no useful purpose since the number of false positives would increase without a corresponding drop in the number of misses. The extreme, point E, represents the completely trivial solution of setting a cutting score just above the highest score made, thus rejecting everyone.

In summary, then, the evaluation of a test in a selection situation consists of the following steps:

1. Administer the test to all individuals who would be selected under the procedures as they would be followed *without* the test.

2. Allow *all* persons so tested to work on the task until an adequate measure of their criterion performance has been obtained.

3. Determine, for alternative cutting scores, the number of misses, the number of false positives, and the total proportion of errors made when so using the test. By subtraction, obtain the total proportion of correct decisions.

4. Compare the proportion of correct decisions made with the test with those without the test. (That is, compare the validity rate with the base rate.)

As an example, of this procedure, consider the results obtained when a preliminary form of a selection test was administered to 151 candidates admitted to the school of veterinary medicine at a midwestern state university. The data necessary for setting cutting scores to minimize errors of decision in this selection situation are presented in Table 12. At the end of the DVM program these students were classified as successful or nonsuccessful according to whether or not they graduated, and a

TABLE 12: Data Necessary for Setting Cutting Scores to Minimize Errors in Making Selection Decisions

Score	Not Successful Tally	Not Successful Cum. f.	Successful Tally	Successful Cum. f.	Total Errors
24			/	/	
29	/	78			
30	/	77			
32	//	76			
34	/	74			
35	//	73			
36	//	71			false positives
37	//	69			
38	/	67	misses		
39	//	66	/	②	← 66
40	卌	64	//	4	← 63
41	////	59	/	5	← 60
42	卌 //	55	//	7	← 55
43	///	48	////	11	← 56
44	////	45	///	14	← 55
45	//	41	///	17	← 56
46		39	卌 ///	25	← 64
47	///	39	////	29	← 65
48	卌 //	36	卌	34	
49	////	29	//	36	
50	卌 /	25	卌	41	
51	////	19	卌	46	
52	//	15	卌 /	56	
53	/	13	///	55	
54	//	12	卌 /	61	
55	卌 /	10	////	65	
56	/	4	////	69	
57	//	3	//	71	
58		1	/	72	
59		1	/	73	
60	/	1			

separate frequency distribution was made for each group. Next, a cumulative frequency was obtained for each different test score, starting at the *low* end of the distribution for the successful group but at the *high* end of the distribution for the unsuccessful group. For any given score the number of persons who received that score or lower and were graduated is indicated in the cumulative frequency column for the successful group, and the number of persons who received a higher score but failed is indicated in the cumulative frequency column for the unsuccessful group in the row corresponding to the next higher score. For example, looking at a test score of 39, we can see that only two successful persons got this or a lower score, while sixty-four persons got a score higher than 39 and yet failed. Thus, if 39 were taken as the lowest passing score for admission purposes, there would be a total of sixty-six errors: two false positives and sixty-four misses. Similarly it can be seen that had 41 been taken as the lowest qualifying score, fifty-nine misses and four false positives or a total of sixty-three errors would have occurred.

Continuing this process with successively higher scores, it can be seen that the minimum number of total errors is fifty-five, obtained using either a score of 43 or a score of 45 as the lowest qualifying mark. Although, with 55 errors in 151 cases the validity rate of $\dfrac{151 - 55}{151}$ (100) or 64 percent may not seem high, this is an improvement over the base rate of 52 percent (78 correct decisions in 151 cases) which has been achieved by a selection system previously in use which did not involve the test performance.

While two different cutting scores resulted in the same minimum number of errors, the kind of errors which occurred in each case would have been different. Thus, a choice between the two alternatives would depend upon whether a miss or a false positive were considered to be the most serious type of error. As a matter of fact, it often is not desirable to minimize the overall error as was done in the illustration just presented. In an ordinary college selection situation, for example, it is usually felt that a false positive (keeping a person out who might succeed) is a far more serious error than admitting someone who later fails (a miss). On the other hand, say in the selection of airplane pilots, when the supply of candidates is plentiful and/or the cost of training highly expensive (and perhaps even dangerous to potential failures), a false positive may be a far less serious kind of error than a miss. In such situations as these, some sort of weighted error can be minimized. In the former situation, for example, each miss could be counted as three errors while each false positive as one, and the cutting score which led to the minimum error under these conditions determined.

Using Taylor-Russell Tables.   In industrial situations, the value of a test as a screening device is often assessed by means of a series of tables developed by Taylor and Russell (1939). Information such as that given in Table 13 is provided for each of eleven different base rates, and indicates, for a given correlation between test and criterion and for a given selection ratio (that is, proportion of applicants who will be accepted), the proportion of persons among those selected who will be satisfactory. It should be noted, however, that such an index provides an evaluation of the usefulness of a test only in terms of the misses, and completely ignores the number of false positives. Thus, a Taylor-Russell evaluation would have given preference to the use of the military screening inventory previously discussed over base rate predictions even though the number of false positives is thereby increased from 0 to 1,805 in 10,000 cases, while the number of misses is reduced only from 500 to 225 in 10,000.

TABLE 13: Sample Taylor-Russell Table for Assessing the Usefulness of a Test in a Selection Situation

Proportion of Employees Considered Satisfactory = .40

Selection Ratio

r	.05	.10	.20	.30	.40	.50	.60	.70	.80	.90	.95
.00	.40	.40	.40	.40	.40	.40	.40	.40	.40	.40	.40
.05	.44	.43	.43	.42	.42	.42	.41	.41	.41	.40	.40
.10	.48	.47	.46	.45	.44	.43	.42	.42	.41	.41	.40
.15	.52	.50	.48	.47	.46	.45	.44	.43	.42	.41	.41
.20	.57	.54	.51	.49	.48	.46	.45	.44	.43	.41	.41
.25	.61	.58	.54	.51	.49	.48	.46	.45	.43	.42	.41
.30	.65	.61	.57	.54	.51	.49	.47	.46	.44	.42	.41
.35	.69	.65	.60	.56	.53	.51	.49	.47	.45	.42	.41
.40	.73	.69	.63	.59	.56	.53	.50	.48	.45	.43	.41
.45	.77	.72	.66	.61	.58	.54	.51	.49	.46	.43	.42
.50	.81	.76	.69	.64	.60	.56	.53	.49	.46	.43	.42
.55	.85	.79	.72	.67	.62	.58	.54	.50	.47	.44	.42
.60	.89	.83	.75	.69	.64	.60	.55	.51	.48	.44	.42
.65	.92	.87	.79	.72	.67	.62	.57	.52	.48	.44	.42
.70	.95	.90	.82	.76	.69	.64	.58	.53	.49	.44	.42
.75	.97	.93	.86	.79	.72	.66	.60	.54	.49	.44	.42
.80	.99	.96	.89	.82	.75	.68	.61	.55	.49	.44	.42
.85	1.00	.98	.93	.86	.79	.71	.63	.56	.50	.44	.42
.90	1.00	1.00	.97	.91	.82	.74	.65	.57	.50	.44	.42
.95	1.00	1.00	.99	.96	.87	.77	.66	.57	.50	.44	.42
1.00	1.00	1.00	1.00	1.00	1.00	.80	.67	.57	.50	.44	.42

SOURCE: H. Taylor and J. Russell, The Relationship of validity coefficients to the practical effectiveness of tests in selection: discussion and tables. *J appl. Psychol.*, 1939, 23, 565–578, p. 575.

Nonetheless, the Taylor-Russell tables present a striking example of how very valuable a test can be for screening purposes, even though the validity coefficient is quite small. For example, with a test-criterion correlation as low as .30, the proportion of satisfactory workers can be increased by as much as 25 percent under fairly stringent selection ratios and with base rates (proportions of employees considered satisfactory without any selection) between .40 and .50.

SPECIAL PROBLEMS IN EVALUATING TESTS BY MEANS OF VALIDITY COEFFICIENTS

It would be ideal if it were possible, when evaluating tests by means of empirical validity coefficients, to simply choose that test which had the highest reported validity coefficient. Although it is generally true that the higher the validity coefficient, the more useful the test for predicting an individual criterion score or for screening purposes, two specific situations arise in which the validity coefficient is not truly representative of the effectiveness of the test. In one case, the value of the test may be underestimated; in the other, it will be exaggerated. The user of tests, therefore, needs to be aware of what these circumstances are and the way in which they operate to spuriously affect the validity coefficient.

Concurrent Validity

In almost all of the previous discussion of empirical validity coefficients it has been assumed that the test data was gathered first, and then, at some later time, by means of a follow-up study, the criterion data was gathered. This approach to gathering empirical validity results in information often referred to as *predictive* validity.

On the other hand, it is sometimes expensive, inconvenient, ethically undesirable, or otherwise nearly impossible, from a practical point of view, to obtain data in this way. Rather, it is necessary to obtain criterion data at the same time or even prior to securing the test information. For example, it may not be possible to administer a test to hundreds of children and then to wait five or ten years to follow them up to see how many have become successful mechanics. It is obviously much less costly to simply search out mechanics who are presently on the job and administer to them the test at the same time ratings or other criterion information are gathered from their employers. In contrast to the predictive validity described earlier, empirical validity data gathered in this latter way would provide information referred to as *concurrent* validity.

Although such a time-wise distinction may seem pedantic and even superficial at first, it turns out to be of considerable importance when attempting to assess the usefulness of a test in a particular practical situation. This is because test results, if they are to be useful (as contrasted with just interesting) must, in the final analysis, be predictive. Thus, immediately, the student will suspect that predictive validity is a much more valuable type of evidence than concurrent validity. Beyond this, however, there is a very serious limitation of concurrent validity: a restriction in range (on both test and criterion scores) as a result of preselection.

The usual procedure in obtaining concurrent validity is to administer a battery of tests to a group of employees already on the job or to students while they are in school. At the same time, supervisor ratings, productivity indices, grade-point averages, or other criterion data are gathered. Then, the correlation between test results and criterion scores is computed and reported as the validity evidence. The restriction in range occurs because such a study omits one very, very important group. It does not include persons who, either through failure or as a result of their own self-selection, have already left the situation. It is obvious that the effect of this preselection will be to reduce the computed relationship between the two variables. The danger, however, is that such an effect is greatest on those very characteristics which are the most important and useful as far as prediction of success is concerned. Thus, a crucial variable may be overlooked or discarded.

To take an extreme example, it is conceivable that the most important single factor in determining success or failure as a musician is whether a person is tone deaf. If this were the case and a battery of tests were administered to professional musicians, little relationship would be found between a measure of tone deafness and ratings of performance, salaries, or other criteria. Thus, simply because no person on the job as a musician is tone deaf, it might be erroneously concluded from the empirical study alone that a measure of this trait is of little importance. Yet, for guidance work and for early identification of the musically talented, it would be, perhaps, the most important characteristic of all.

Cross-Validation

Failure to consider the effects of the restriction in range when it is necessary to gather empirical data by the process of concurrent validation results in underestimating the usefulness of a test. On the other hand, neglecting to gather new information as to the effectiveness of the test *after* the prediction or selection system has been worked out—that is, failure to cross-validate—can lead to exaggerated claims as to the effectiveness of the prediction or selection.

Whenever a test is used either to predict a specific criterion score or for screening purposes, the resulting prediction equation or cutting score is determined in such a way that error is minimized for the specific data at hand. In doing this, many of the chance fluctuations occurring in the particular observations obtained are used to advantage. This tends to spuriously increase the estimated accuracy of prediction over that which can actually be accomplished when the findings are applied to new observations. Therefore, to properly evaluate the usefulness of a test, the prediction equation or cutting score must be derived from one sample of information and validated on a second sample of subjects from the same universe. If this has been done, the test is said to be cross-validated for that universe.

A person who attempts to apply the test, even to a second sample of the same universe, without cross-validation should anticipate a reduction in the test-criterion correlation found in practice as compared with that calculated in the original analysis. In general, when a single test is used, the smaller the size of the original sample, the greater the shrinkage of the validity coefficient in cross-validation. If more than one measure is used in the prediction or selection system, the amount of shrinkage will also be a function of the number of variables tried out: the larger the number of original predictors used and the smaller the proportion of variables retained, the greater the reduction in actual validity from that found with the original sample.

In many instances, a potential user of a test examines validity coefficients reported in the literature in the hope of determining whether the test would be useful in his own situation. Judgments of this sort require inferences beyond the original universe and thus the actual validity in the new situation can be expected to be smaller than the reported coefficient, even if the latter was cross-validated on a second sample in the original situation.

To accurately assess the usefulness of the test in a new situation, it is necessary to carry out other forms of cross-validation studies. If the additional information is obtained by checking the effectiveness of the test on a differently defined population, but using the same criterion as in the original study, the process is called *validity generalization*. If the test validity is checked against a new criterion as well as with a different population, *validity extension* has been carried out. Other designs for cross-validation studies which may be useful in special circumstances have also been worked out and described by Mosier (1951).

Cross-validation is especially important in the selection of items for a test and in discovering so-called *psychometric signs* (score characteristics, empirically derived, which distinguish between two or more groups). For example, suppose an attempt were being made to develop a system for distinguishing between clinically diagnosed groups of psychopathic deviates and schizoids. Further, suppose that scores are available for each patient on ten personality variables. If it were felt that the relevant information was to be found in score differences rather than the scores themselves, there could be different indexes which might be tried. Suppose that upon testing the significance of differences between mean index values for the two groups, three of the forty-five possible indexes were found to be significant at the 5 percent level. Could it be said, from this evidence alone, that the three significant indexes were psychometric signs which could be used for distinguishing between the two clinical groups studied?

The answer is no. By the very meaning of the 5 percent level of significance one should expect to find differences this large or larger five times in 100 even though the null hypothesis (that is, no difference) was true. Roughly, (45)(.05) or between two and three significant differences might be expected even though the null hypothesis held in every case.

While no one with any statistical sophistication at all would fail to determine the significance of any observed correlation (or multiple correlation), too many researchers have failed to compare the observation of psychometric signs with a chance distribution. The best answer to the question of how to tell if the "significant" psychometric signs represent real differences or expected chance occurrences is to cross-validate by taking a new sample and seeing if the same psychometric signs appear. If they do, the researcher can have a fair degree of confidence that his finding will hold up in subsequent studies.

The person who is selecting items for a test or developing a system for distinguishing between two or more groups on the basis of psychometric signs must be careful, however, not to confuse successive refinements of the instrument with cross-validation. Having identified a number of test items or signs which significantly distinguish between the criterion groups obtained in one sampling of the two universes, the worker may wish to try them out on a second sample. If he then further refines the instrument by retaining only those items which turned out to be significant on both trials, the final measure cannot be considered to have been cross-validated, for, at no time has the predictor been tried out exactly as it will be used on a new sample. Proper cross-validation begins only after all refinements of the procedure have been completed, and requires that the selection or prediction system be applied to a new situation *unchanged* from the previous trial.

In summary, then, cross-validation serves to provide more accurate information about the usefulness of a test in a particular situation than can be obtained from a validity coefficient calculated on the original group of subjects used to develop the prediction or screening system. Cross-validation is accomplished by trying out a previously developed and refined test (or series of psychometric signs) on a completely new group as close as possible to that for which the test will ultimately be used. To the extent that the original sample used for the test development was small (or different), to the extent that a large number of predictors was tried and only a small proportion ultimately retained, there is likely to be considerable shrinkage in the cross-validation validity coefficient from that obtained with the original analysis group.

6

Evaluation of Tests —
Construct Validity

THE NATURE OF CONSTRUCT VALIDITY

CONSTRUCT VALIDITY IS THE most recent addition to the conceptual ideas concerning kinds of evidence which are required before a test user can feel justified in interpreting test scores in certain ways. The idea first appeared in two reports of an APA committee in Psychological Tests (1952, 1954). More recently, Cronbach and Meehl (1955) have elaborated and clarified the concept. Most of the ideas and even some of the examples discussed in this section have been taken from this latter article.

In an earlier chapter it was pointed out that human characteristics such as mechanical ability, musical talent, clerical aptitude, intelligence, and in fact, all mental (including, attitude, interest, and personality) traits which one might attempt to measure with tests, scales, and inventories are hypothetical constructs, each carrying with it a number of associated meanings relating how a person who possessed the specified traits would behave in certain situations. Thus, as can easily be imagined, the process of establishing the construct validity of a test is no simple one. Every validation study becomes an evaluation not just of the test alone, but also of the theory and concept of the trait as well.

As Cronbach and Meehl describe it, the logical process of construct validation requires: First, setting forth the proposition that this test measures trait A; next, inserting this proposition into present theory about trait A; third, working through the theory to predict behavior characteristics which should be related to test scores and those which should show *no* relation to test scores if the test truly measures trait A as presently conceived; and finally, securing data which will empirically or experimentally confirm or reject the hypothesis.

If the anticipated relationships are found, all is well. For the moment, the test is considered valid, and the hypothetical trait with its associated meanings is a useful construct. On the other hand, as Cronbach and Meehl (p. 295) point out, if the predictions (positive or negative) do not hold up, there are three possibilities:

1. The test does not measure the construct variable
2. The theoretical network which generated the hypothesis is incorrect
3. The experimental design failed to test the hypothesis properly.*

Thus, a decision must be made as to which of these three conditions has occurred. As can be imagined, a great many of the claims and counter claims about tests and their interpretation stem from disagreement as to which of the three possibilities is the culprit. The practical test user or the theory builder is likely to say, "That was a nice try, but your test just didn't work out." The test constructor, on the other hand, will reply, "If you had used the appropriate statistical technique, or controlled on such and such, you would have obtained the expected results"; or, if he can find nothing wrong with the experimental design, will say, "So much the worse for your theory."

Sometimes, it is relatively easy to tell what has happened. A well-trained researcher, with adequate knowledge of the subject matter involved, through an examination of the procedure followed, would be able to determine whether the design of the

---

* L. Cronbach and P. Meehl. Construct validity in psychological tests. *Psych. Bull.* 1955, 52.

study itself was adequate. In some cases, a theory, through much other evidence, is already so well confirmed that a particular validity study is relevant only to the usefulness of the test. Once in a while, when a test has already successfully predicted a great many and a wide variety of criterion behaviors, it may be that in a specific situation where predictions fail to hold up, it is appropriate to reject a part of the theory or some of the associated meanings of the postulated trait.

Perhaps the best way to clarify the nature of construct validation is to point out several features of the process which need special emphasis. First, it should be noted, that a specific criterion used in the early stages of the development of a test may be later rejected as less valid than the test itself. According to Cronbach and Meehl (1955, p. 286):

We start with a vague concept which we associate with certain observations. We then discover empirically that these observations covary with some other observation which possesses greater reliability or is more intimately correlated with relevant experimental changes than is the original measure, or both.*

These authors then cite as examples the measurement of temperature and scholastic ability with the Binet scale. (1955, p. 206.)

For example, the notion of temperature arises because some objects feel hotter to the touch than others. The expansion of a mercury column does not have face validity as an index of hotness. But it turns out that (a) there is a statistical relation between expansion and sensed temperature; (b) observers employ the mercury method with good interobserver agreement; (c) the regularity of observed relations is increased by using the thermometer (for example, melting points of samples of the same material vary little on the thermometer; we obtain nearly linear relations between mercury measures and pressure of a gas). Finally, (d) a theoretical structure involving unobservable microevents—the kinetic theory—is worked out which explains the relation of mercury expansion to heat. This whole process of conceptual enrichment begins with what in retrospect we see as an extremely fallible "criterion"—the human temperature sense. That original criterion has now been relegated to a peripheral position. We have lifted ourselves by our bootstraps, but in a legitimate and fruitful way.

Similarly, the Binet scale was first valued because children's scores tended to agree with judgments by schoolteachers. If it had not shown

* L. Cronbach and P. Meehl. Construct validity in psychological tests. *Psych. Bull.* 1955, 52.

this agreement, it would have been discarded along with reaction time and the other measures of ability previously tried. Teacher judgments once constituted the criterion against which the individual intelligence test was validated. But if today a child's IQ is 135 and three of his teachers complain about how stupid he is, we do not conclude that the test has failed. Quite to the contrary, if no error in test procedure can be argued, we treat the test score as a valid statement about an important quality, and define our task as that of finding out what other variables—personality, study skills, and so forth—modify achievement or distort teacher judgment.*

Second, a consumer of tests needs to know not only the test itself, but also the theory behind the test *and* the evidence which supports the theory. That is, it is absolutely essential that a test user know what interpretations of a test are theoretically possible, and which of these have been empirically verified.

As Cronbach and Meehl have pointed out (1955, p. 291), unless essentially the same theory is accepted by all test users, no general scientific validation is possible. A person who does not accept the test author's theory, must validate the test for himself in his own situation following his own conception of the trait involved.

Third, scientists can properly evaluate a claim supporting the usefulness of a test and the associated theory of the trait it measures only if the evidence is made public. It is worth noting that failure to meet this latter qualification—that is, refusal to make evidence available to others—has resulted in severe criticism of a number of test authors and publishers by the American Psychological Association's committee on ethics as well as suspicion on the part of many psychologists that the tests involved have not really been validated. Excuses that no really adequate criterion for validation purposes exists are not acceptable, and rationalizations about a trait which fail to result in observable consequents cannot be considered construct validation.

Fourth, it should be perfectly clear that each positive study results in greater and greater confidence that a test is a valid measure of a certain construct. On the other hand, in spite of hundreds of prior successes, one well-established negative finding can completely destroy any belief in the absolute reality of the

---

* L. Cronbach and P. Meehl. Construct validity in psychological tests. *Psych. Bull.* 1955, 52.

trait as measured. Such a pronouncement may seem harsh and actually contrary to what happens in practice—for, very few workers would, as a result of one contrary finding, stop using the test in those situations where positive results had been repeatedly obtained. This apparent conflict can readily be resolved by conceiving of any mental trait (and for that matter, any other hypothetical construct which appears anywhere in science) not as representing or failing to represent underlying Truth (with a capital T) but as being a relatively useful or useless conception in certain practical and/or theoretical situations. While one solid, negative finding does destroy the logical necessity of the trait as representing the truth—it only sets a boundary on the usefulness of the construct and its measure.

Finally, it should be apparent that it is quite naive to ask whether a test is valid. As Cronbach and Meehl (1955, p. 297) point out, a test is never really "validated" at all. Rather, a principle for making certain kinds of inferences about persons who obtain given test scores is verified or refuted. Thus, if a test yields many types of inferences, some may be valid and others not. The question should not be "Is the test valid?", but "Is the test valid for such and such?"

EVIDENCES WHICH SUPPORT CONSTRUCT VALIDATION

From the preceding, it might well be anticipated that no single, numerical estimate of the degree of construct validity will be found. Rather, a wide variety of approaches and evidences may be used to support claims about what a test measures (and consequently the ways in which it can be used). Cronbach and Meehl (1955) list five types of evidence which might be appropriate. In reviewing these, the reader will note that procedures previously suggested in assessing content and empirical validity reappear. Although some writers have expressed a fear that so-called construct validity allows test authors and publishers to neglect crucial validity studies, what it actually does is to increase the types of evidence which are required for adequate validation. No longer will a single study in one specific situation involving one particular criterion measure be acceptable as complete evidence that a test measures what its authors claim.

Group Differences

The first general type of evidence which might lend support to a claim of construct validity is Group Differences. Many traits are postulated in such a way that persons in different groups are conceived to possess different amounts of the characteristics involved. Thus, men as a group, would be expected to perform differently from women as a group in any valid test of mechanical ability or of clerical ability; persons of different age groups (at least through the early years) would be expected to perform differently on any valid test of intellectual development; persons who have had specific training should do better on any valid measure of achievement in the area than persons not having such training; and overachievers should be different from under-achievers (as distinguished in some manner independent of the test under consideration) with respect to a valid measure of scholastic information. To be sure, some overlap would be anticipated, and in many circumstances a positive finding would not add greatly to the degree of confidence in the test; but a finding of no difference at all would certainly lead to real doubt about the validity of the test in question.

Changes in Performance

Somewhat similar to this kind of evidence would be changes in performance over occasions. Roughly speaking, this kind of data differs from the former in the same way that a longitudinal study differs from a cross-sectional one. Rather than making comparisons among groups of different individuals, the same persons are studied upon two or more occasions.

Whether or not any observed changes in score add to or detract from the confidence in the test will depend upon the conception of the trait it measures. If such traits as musical talent or scholastic aptitude are postulated as constant with age, observed changes in score over a period of time would be discouraging.

Similarly, a measure of elation which resulted in an identical score for the same person on all occasions would not be very satisfying.

More convincing than general stability or fluctuation in score over time, as the case may be, is evidence that the introduction of specific variables result in predictable changes (or lack of change) in score. Thus, performance on an aptitude measure should remain the same in spite of the introduction of a training program, while performance on an achievement test in the same situation should increase. Similarly, an increase in scores on a measure of frustration administered immediately following an experimentally induced humiliation over what was found prior to the experiment might be anticipated and a scale measuring authoritarianism should produce the same result whether the questions are stated positively or negatively.

Correlations

Another type of evidence which can shed light on construct validity is correlational. Certainly, two measures of the same trait (whether the one is considered a criterion or simply another measure of the same characteristic) ought to correlate highly. On the other hand, to the extent that a measure correlates with an obviously irrelevant variable, it may be thought of as lacking validity. Thus, student evaluations of classroom teaching which correlate very highly with the grades received would generally not be considered as satisfactory a measure of teaching competence as a scale of opinions which resulted in a somewhat lower relationship between these two characteristics.

While a single correlation between a test and a criterion is generally not considered sufficient evidence in and of itself to establish construct validity, an appropriately designed factor analytic study may. If a trait is conceived such that its function is somewhere in between two others and is completely unrelated to a third, the measure of it might be included in a battery of tests designed to establish these other factors. Then, a factor analysis would indicate whether the measure in question had the predicted interrelationships. It should be noted that such a pro-

cedure need not imply that the factors found are the true underlying dimensions of the "mind." Rather, they are best thought
of as reference points set up specifically for an experimental test
of certain predictions about the measure under examination. Such
a form of reference is more appropriately viewed as being useful
or useless for describing and summarizing certain observed phenomena and for predicting new relationships. (See, for example,
Eysenck, 1950.)

More recently, Campbell and Fiske (1959) have suggested
a way of systematically studying correlational evidence for purposes of inferring construct validity which does not involve a
factor analysis. First of all, they point out that a test is always a
trait-method unit. That is, a trait cannot be measured independently of some method. Thus, some of the observed score
variance on any test is attributable to the particular method
used rather than to just the trait involved. While this method
variance is of no particular problem in a purely empirical situation where the object is to predict some practical criterion, it can
be misleading when attempting to determine whether a test
measures some specific trait. Conceivably, two separate tests might
correlate highly simply because the same method of measurement
was used and not because the same trait was involved.

Second, Campbell and Fiske emphasize the importance of
the idea mentioned by Cronbach and Meehl that any measure
is clearly described only by means of a joint method of similarities
and differences. It is necessary to tell both what a test measures
and what it does not. Evidence of the construct validity of a test
must, therefore, make use of both a convergent principle which
suggests that two measures of the same trait should correlate
highly with one another even though they represent different
methods, and a discriminant principle which suggests that two
measures should not correlate highly with one another if they
measure different traits even though a similar method is used.

As a result of these considerations, Campbell and Fiske advocate a validation process which requires the computation of intercorrelations among tests which represent at least two traits each
measured by at least two different methods. To illustrate the
technique, these authors prepared the fictitious multitrait-multi-

TABLE 14: A Synthetic Multitrait-Multimethod Matrix

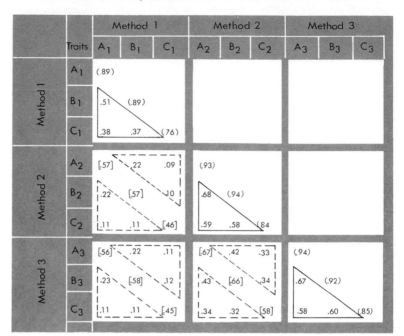

( )=reliability coefficients in three reliability diagnosis

[ ]=validity coefficients in three validity diagonals

◹ =heterotrait—monomethod triangle

⌐◹ =heterotrait—heteromethod triangle

SOURCE: D. Campbell and D. Fiske. Convergent and discriminant validation by the multitrait-multimethod matrix. Psych. Bull. 1959, 56, 81–105.

method matrix presented as Table 14. The major components of this table are the following:

1. Three *reliability diagonals,* each containing three reliability coefficients in parentheses representing the degree of relationship between the same trait measured in the same way on different occasions;

2. Three *validity diagonals,* each containing three "validity coefficients" in brackets representing the degree of relation-

ship between the same trait measured by different methods;

3. Three *heterotrait-monomethod triangles* each containing three correlation coefficients representing the degree of relationship between measures of different traits using the same method; and

4. Six *heterotrait-heteromethod triangles* each containing three correlations representing the degree of relationship between measures of different traits using different methods.

According to Campbell and Fiske, evidence of convergent validity occurs when the entries in the validity diagonal are significantly different from zero and high enough to encourage further investigation. Discriminant validity is suggested when (1) values in the validity diagonal are higher than the values in the heterotrait-heteromethod triangle adjacent to it; (2) the validity diagonal values are higher than those found in heterotrait-mono method triangles (so that the trait variance is larger than the method variance); and (3) the same *pattern* (regardless of the size of the coefficients) is found in all heterotrait (both monomethod and heteromethod) triangles.

The use of the multitrait-multimethod matrix as suggested by Campbell and Fiske does not provide a system which will automatically determine whether a test has or does not have construct validity. Indeed, the very concept of construct validity prohibits this possibility. However, such an arrangement of validity information does facilitate the meaningful interpretation of crucial information and, perhaps even more important, provides a means for suggesting steps which might be taken to further improve the measurement of a particular trait.

Internal Consistency

A fourth type of evidence useful in determining the construct validity of a test is that which comes from studies of its internal consistency. Again, whether high or low internal consistency is encouraging in so far as the usefulness of the measure is concerned, will depend upon whether the concept of the trait requires a pure or a complex measure. As in the case of factor analysis, the study should involve more than just applying a specific mathematical technique to a set of data which has been gathered in a conventient way. In both cases, a careful, logical analysis of the trait and its relationship to other variables and to special characteristics of the measuring device, should lead to specific predictions as to what to expect in terms of observables if the trait concept is appropriately formulated and if the test devised to measure it is adequately designed.

Study of the Test-Taking Process

A final kind of evidence which provides information by which a test may be evaluated as a measure of a construct is that which comes from a study of the process which the subject undergoes when taking the test. Informally, one of the best ways to judge what accounts for variability in the scores is to take the test oneself, listing the activities required to answer the items.

To be completely acceptable as validity evidence, however, a more formal procedure should be followed. Thus, the listing of the activity types might be done by a group of judges or by observers watching subjects perform and then used for the construction of special measures for the purpose of gathering correlational evidence. Sometimes a simple count of the frequency with which various distractors are marked on an examination, or an analysis of scratch paper, or an interview with persons who have taken the test may be very revealing. Lucas (1953), for example, by such a procedure showed that the Navy Relative Movement Test actually involved two different abilities: spatial visualization and mathematical reasoning. In addition, an analysis of the scoring procedures (see Helmstadter, 1957) may reveal such things as the influence of response sets.

Actually, there are no set procedures which can be spelled out and recommended for the analysis of the "mental" processes required to take a test. It can only be pointed out that, with ingenuity, rigorous studies of the test taking process can be made which will produce excellent evidence about the construct validity of a test. Once again, this illustrates the point made at the beginning of this section that no single index or even study will, in and of itself, be adequate evidence of construct validity. Rather, a diverse attack, much as is expected for the verification of any psychological theory, will be required before any measure and its corresponding trait, the construct, will be accepted.

SPECIAL PROBLEMS IN INTERPRETING TEST RESULTS

Since, as has been pointed out earlier, it is the principle for making inferences from scores and not the test itself which is validated, all the special problems faced when interpreting test results are directly related to construct validity. Thus, in this final section, three areas of special concern—the criterion problem, guessing and faking, and response sets—will be discussed.

The Criterion

The so-called criterion problem refers to the fact that in many cases it is extremely difficult to obtain adequate evidence for the validity of a test simply because no criterion appears to be completely satisfactory. The concept of construct validity and the resulting idea that many varieties of evidence may legitimately support test validity has alleviated the situation somewhat. Nevertheless, on many occasions, even in a practical prediction situation where empirical validity is of prime importance, a satisfactory criterion will be far from simple to obtain. Yet, one must be found if the test is to have any usefulness at all. Thus, it is worthwhile to discuss the general nature of criteria.

Generally speaking, as a measure of success, a criterion might include either or both a standard of performance set up independently of the person evaluated, or an indication of the satisfaction which the individual derives from the activity. No matter which of these aspects constitutes the major proportion of the criterion, difficulties arise. For an adequate measure of satisfaction it is necessary to consider life from the viewpoint of the subject involved. To what extent does he value money, prestige, living in a particular geographical area? What are some of the pressures exerted on him by his family, his community, etc? And, if an attempt is made to avoid some of this indirection by simply asking the person about the extent to which he is satisfied, additional difficulties are encountered. For example, inferences based on verbal reports are usually less satisfactory than observation or measurement of other overt behaviors—what a person *says* and what he *does* are often two different things. In any case, there will also be a problem resulting from natural selection. All those persons remaining on the job, are, to a certain extent, satisfied. Persons who were sufficiently unhappy to overcome the pressures (or just plain inertia) to stay will have left the job or occupation. Such individuals are practically impossible to trace down for inclusion in the analysis sample. If the selection has been severe, the resulting restriction in range may make it impossible to develop an adequate measure.

If the concern is primarily that of establishing performance standards, the difficulty is one of accounting for all sorts of specific situational factors which may operate entirely independently of the individual to raise or lower his apparent level of performance. For example, if an attempt is made to use something like the dollar volume on individual sales in a given period, there is the problem of equating different sales territories. A person selling a minimum in one area may be doing better than another who sells twice as much in a region richer in prospects.

Whatever criterion is developed, there are several qualities by which its value may be judged. The one absolutely essential characteristic is that the criterion be *relevant* to the purpose for which the test is used. Such a statement may at first seem trite and of no consequence. Yet time and again attempts have been made to validate tests against criteria which are of little ultimate importance. For example, at the start of World War II tests designed to predict success in gunnery were validated against grades in a training situation. The ultimate goal, of course, was success in hitting the prescribed target in combat. As it turned out, grades in training courses were largely dependent upon the student's ability to memorize nomenclature and related only slightly to the ultimate criterion. Once this became apparent, the content of the gunnery school course was changed—but, of course, all the selection tests then had to be reevaluated. Thus, it can, and all too often does, happen that an immediately available criterion is not always relevant. This is particularly true when success in a training or educational program is involved.

In addition to relevancy, the criterion should be free of variable errors. If the criterion is a continuous measure, this means it must have reliability; and if it is a discrete variable, it means the same people should always fall into the same category upon repeated classification. Relative freedom from variable errors is, of course, a necessary but not a sufficient quality of a good criterion. That is, a certain degree of reliability is necessary in order that it contain some relevant variance—but a high degree of reliability does not guarantee that the criterion has relevance.

Similarly, it is important that the criterion be relatively free from so-called *constant errors*. Lack of relevancy of the criterion represents one form of constant error. Another, not so apparent, arises when a population is divided into subgroups, and scores obtained by the two or more groups on the test to be analyzed are contrasted in order to obtain evidence of validity. If the procedure used to select subjects for the study produces biased samples, the difference between mean scores obtained by the two groups may be either over or underestimated, depending upon the direction of the bias. Thus, to take an extreme example, suppose an attempt were being made to validate a scale designed to measure social maturity by comparing scores made by freshmen, sophomores, juniors, and seniors in high school. If the sampling included students from schools located in very high and very low socioeconomic areas, the natural attrition (i.e., student drop-out) might result in a biased sampling of groups which could effect the results. Thus, if social maturity were a trait related in a positive direction to socioeconomic level, and the dropout rate in high school were higher (as it seems to be) for students from lower socioeconomic backgrounds than for those at the upper end of the scale, differences between freshmen and seniors might not be as large as they would be had an unbiased sample of persons from the age groups involved been obtained.

Before turning to other areas, a word of caution should be given about a remark all too often made by certain test authors or publishers to the effect that "no suitable criterion was possible to obtain." Usually such a statement is intended to excuse the test author from the responsibility of providing any validity data at all. The test publisher just assumes that the test will work and leaves the burden of gathering the evidence upon the user. Most of the time, a criterion *can* be found if careful consideration is given to the reasons why the test is to be used. If, after spelling out exactly what it is that the test is expected to do, no criterion becomes apparent, then the user has no business in using the test for this particular purpose (unless, of course, there is considerable other evidence that the test is a measure of a particular construct and that the theory which suggests that the trait measured is related to the desired, but unmeasurable criterion is well established on an empirical and/or experimental basis).

The person who uses a test without such evidence is only misleading himself when he interprets the scores without evidence that the interpretation is legitimate. Worse than this, such a person is hiding his ignorance behind something which has the appearance of being rigorous. To most professionals in the area of testing the use of tests under such circumstances is completely unethical, both because the client (that is, either the person whose score is being interpreted or the person for whom the test is interpreted) is being swindled and because such a use can lead to distrust of test results even when the interpretation is well supported by good, solid evidence.

Faking

The second major problem in interpretation of test results is that of faking. Faking is the term used any time an examinee deliberately attempts to alter the results in some specific way. Whether the measure is one of maximum performance or of typical behavior, such malingering is possible.

If the measure is one of aptitude, ability, or achievement—that is, one of maximum performance—there is usually little opportunity to increase the score. This can be done, of course, by guessing or through some sort of cheating during the test taking—copying, marking more than one answer on a machine-graded exam, using "crib" notes, and so forth—or through special coaching on specific items in the test (which may momentarily raise the score without a concomitant, long-term increase in knowledge or performance). With formulas which correct for guessing, with adequate safeguards to keep the tests secure, with sufficient supervision during the examination period, and with simple checks when scoring the papers, these types of faking can be practically eliminated.

On the other hand, deliberate attempts to *reduce* scores on measures of maximum performance are much more difficult to prevent and practically impossible to detect. This kind of malingering seems to occur because an individual feels that if he receives a high score too much will be expected of him. He may be afraid, for example, that he will be placed in a higher section in some college course and therefore be graded more stiffly or that in a military situation he will be sent for special training in some area in which he thinks he is not interested. About the only means of prevention in such cases is by emphasizing, in the test directions, the advantages of obtaining the best score possible. In most selection situations, the user of the results can console himself by the fact that a person who malingers in this way is probably not very well motivated in the desired direction anyway, and a prediction of his likely success in a training program or future activity in the area of the test might even be improved as a result of his having deliberately obtained a low score. For general counselling, however, the results can be quite misleading. Fortunately, though, in a counselling situation, there is greater opportunity for convincing the examinee that it is to his own benefit to do his best and to find out whether the subject did attempt to fake the test results.

As might be expected, the problem of faking is infinitely more important when it comes to the measurement of typical performance. Faking is much easier to do with interest, attitude, and personality measures, and much more difficult to prevent. As a result, it occurs far more frequently, and it has been in this area of measurement that the most attention has been devoted to the problem. Thus, it is in this context that some of the current solutions to the problem will be described.

Theoretically, one should be able to prevent faking by convincing the examinee that it is to his own advantage to obtain the truest picture possible of his interests, attitudes, and personality. However, in many situations this is just not possible. Sometimes, the subjects lack sufficient foresight to see the advantages, sometimes their motivation to fake—for example, in the case of job applicants who want to make a good impression—is so strong that they cannot be so convinced, and sometimes people act on the basis of family and other social pressures of which they themselves are not entirely aware.

Thus, a number of devices have been developed to help discourage faking. Perhaps the simplest is to include in the directions instructions to "work rapidly." While very few measures of typical behavior have time limits, if the subject can be cajoled into making quick, spontaneous judgments, he will not have time to think of all the implications of his responses and is less likely to be influenced by some of the subtle pressures of which he is not fully aware.

A second approach to this problem has been an attempt to disguise the purpose of the test. Usually, this amounts to giving the test or scale an ambiguous or misleading name—such as calling a measure of cynicism a measure of criticalness. Unfortunately, however, this usually does not fool anyone except the most naive, who probably would not be able to do a good job of faking anyway.

Another way of discouraging faking is to use item forms such that the weighting or implication of the responses is not clear to the casual observer—which the subject certainly is if he is working through the instrument as rapidly as possible. Perhaps the best example of this approach is the development of a forced-choice scale in which either of the responses is equally popular, but one has been shown empirically to be indicative of one of the traits under consideration, and the other either not indicative or a measure of some second trait. A typical item from a scale of this sort is shown in Figure 25 (Chapter 8). While the original studies using such a scale held forth tremendous promise, later investigation indicated that the results were not quite as outstanding as had at first been supposed and suggest that the important thing which brought about what improvement did occur may have been the care in construction of the scale rather than the particular format in which it was presented.

A different technique, which has become more and more popular recently, has been the development of what are called *faking, lie,* or *validity* keys. In this instance, a study is made of responses given under conditions in which it is very unlikely that faking has occurred; and these responses are compared with those given when faking has occurred (usually upon the explicit instructions from the experimenter). Knowing how responses change when an individual is attempting to fake, a test constructor can develop a key which yields a score indicating the extent to which a person has responded as do malingerers. Thus, the results obtained with a person who scores high on the "validity" key are held in doubt. A recent example of the use of this principle can be seen in data presented in the manual of the Kuder Preference Record, form *D*. These are reproduced in Figure 20.

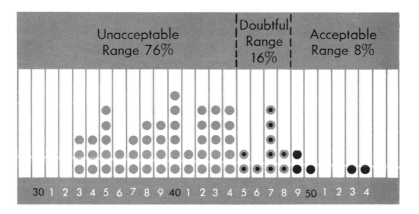

FIGURE 20: Distribution of *V* Scores of Sixty-two College Students Attempting to Conceal the Fact that They Were Faking

Reprinted by permission of Science Research Associates, Inc. from Kuder Preference Record, Manual for Occupational, Form D. Copyright © 1956, 1959. G. Frederic Kuder.

While this technique was originally developed in the area of personality measurement to identify those who tried to show themselves in a good light, it can be used in aptitude measurement to identify those who are purposely trying to appear dull. A key which compares malingerers with truly retarded persons could be readily developed. Perhaps, more simply, a study could be made of individual responses in relation to the item difficulty. Item difficulty is often hard to judge and if an individual is found to have correctly answered difficult items while missing many easier items, he may be suspected of faking.

Before leaving this topic, it should be noted that faking is not a problem in a strictly empirically oriented test—at least for the particular situations in which the test was developed and evaluated. Here, the test user is not so much interested in what the examinee does as what he *says* he does. Thus, if an item asks "Do you have headaches often?" the interest is not to place persons in order on a scale in terms of the number of headaches they do have but rather in order on a scale with respect to whether they *feel* the number of headaches they have is large or small.

Similarly, if a test has been developed to select salesmen on the basis of their interests and if the key has been derived by administering the tests to job applicants and noting the differences in responses made by those who later were successful and those who later failed, then one need not worry about attempts to fake *when the test is administered in similar selection situations.* In a sense, the *lie* key is already built in.

However, as is true with all empirically constructed tests, the extent to which they can be generalized to other situations is limited. Thus, if the test were given in a counselling or other nonselection situation where faking was not likely to occur, the results might turn out to be rather peculiar. At least, the user should be aware that without additional evidence he has no right to attempt to interpret the scores in the same way in the two situations.

Response Set

Some years ago, Cronbach (1946) called attention to the fact that a score received on a test was sometimes a function of the way in which the items happened to be presented rather than (or, at least, as well as) the trait being measured. Thus, for example, if interest is measured by having the respondent simply check each of those items presented on a list which represent things that he likes to do, the tendency to like a great many or a few things will have a marked effect on the result. Had the individual been asked to check exactly half of the items, indicating those he liked best, quite different results probably would have been obtained. This important source of "methods" variance in test scores has been labeled response set.

Specifically defined by Cronbach as "any tendency causing a person to give different responses to test items than he would when the same content is presented in different form," response sets have been increasingly recognized as important influences on scores obtained on tests of all types. Thus, Metfessel and Sax (1958) found that one-third of the fifteen well-known standardized measures of aptitude and achievement which they reviewed were keyed in such a way that persons with a set to select a particular alternative (for example, the first, or the last, or true, or false choices) could be spuriously helped or hindered in obtaining high scores; Barnes (1956) concludes ". . . that response sets . . . play a larger part in personality testing than has been suspected"; and Loevinger (1959) has cautioned that "Proliferation of tests of high sounding psychological constructs in disregard of response bias is a conspicuous waste of research." Best known among the rather wide variety of response sets already identified are those which represent a tendency to guess, a tendency to acquiesce (that is, to respond "yes" regardless of the content of the statement), a tendency to be critical (that is, to deny or disagree with any assertion), a tendency to check or list many adjectives, a tendency to take an extreme position, and a tendency to always describe oneself as socially desirable.

Response sets like those just listed are known to occur primarily when tests or inventories have but two or three alternatives for each item. Further, this effect is most likely to be greatest when a decision among the alternatives presented is extremely difficult for the subject to make. Obviously, for example, if a person knows the answer on an aptitude or achievement test, or if he has a strong preference with respect to the content of the item on an interest or personality inventory, his tendency to guess or select more "likes" than "dislikes" will not appear.

When response sets do occur, they may represent either an undesirable influence which needs to be eliminated or they may reflect a real and important dimension of human differences which is potentially useful for making predictions about behavior. As Broen and Wirt (1958) point out in a discussion of the results of their factor analysis of eleven different response sets, such effects should be eliminated

. . . only in those cases where there is no correlation between the response set itself and the criterion for which prediction is being attempted. If there is a correlation between a response set and a criterion, then either the suppression of that set or the neglect to use tests in which that response set can operate may lead to lower validities.

To be able to capitalize upon the effect of response set when it is useful and to eliminate it when it is undesirable, some procedure is necessary for obtaining the separate set and content components of a test score. Both Helmstadter (1957) and Webster (1958) have presented ways of accomplishing this. While the detailed discussion of the various procedures available is beyond the scope of this book, it would seem worthwhile to examine at least one logical basis for separating the two components and to note one of the simpler formulas by which separate set and content components of a test score can be obtained.

Consider an inventory designed to measure attitude toward socialism. Suppose the scale listed a series of principles and practices representing both socialistic and nonsocialistic approaches and the respondent was asked to indicate agreement or disagreement with each. Under these circumstances, the responses made would be a function of both one's attitude toward socialism (content) and one's tendency to agree with whatever is said (set). The relationship between the keyed responses and the examinee's responses can be seen in the score matrix presented in Table 15. In this matrix N_s is the number of items representing socialistic principles and practices and N_{ns} is the number of nonsocialistic statements. A_s represents the number of socialistic statements with which the respondent agrees, and D_s the number with which he disagrees. Similarly, A_{ns} and D_{ns} represent the number of nonsocialistic statements with which the respondent agrees and disagrees respectively.

TABLE 15: Response Matrix for a Scale Designed to Measure Attitude Toward Socialism

Type of Statement	Response Made		Number of Statements
	A = agree	D = disagree	
s = socialistic	A_s	D_s	N_s
ns = non-socialistic	A_{ns}	D_{ns}	N_{ns}

Thus, the ratio A_s/N_s represents the tendency to agree with socialistic statements; the ratio D_{ns}/N_{ns} represents the tendency to disagree with nonsocialistic statements. A most reasonable and simple content score can then be taken as the sum of these two ratios. That is,

$$(41) \qquad C = A_s/N_s + D_{ns}/N_{ns}.$$

In this specific example, as in most instances, it seems quite reasonable to feel that a person's attitude should not be related to his tendency to agree to whatever is said. Thus, a desirable set score would be the mathematically simplest measure which was both independent of C and a logically sensible index of the tendency to mark everything agree. Since the ratio D_{ns}/N_{ns} represents a tendency to disagree, it certainly seems reasonable that the difference between a respondent's tendency to agree (the ratio A_s/N_s) and his tendency to disagree would provide a useful index. Thus, the simplest set score which meets the requirements is

$$(42) \qquad S = A_s/N_s - D_{ns}/N_{ns}.$$

The value S does represent a score which is independent of C and which has the further advantage of being positive when the tendency to agree is greater than the tendency to disagree, negative if the tendency to disagree is greatest, and zero when the two tendencies balance each other exactly.

It should be emphasized that the user of the above formulas, or any other system for obtaining separate set and content components of a test, must not assume that the resulting scores will automatically be reliable and valid. Additional studies will be needed to ascertain whether the set, as identified, is consistent from testing to testing, and whether the corrected content score or the new set score, or both, are valid measures of human characteristics. As a matter of fact, in the final analysis, all three of the problems discussed in this section—the criterion problem, faking, and response sets—are most adequately handled through careful construct validity studies. Such studies must not merely relate test scores to a readily available criterion measure (which everybody admits is inadequate) but rather must consider the form in which the items are written, the various circumstances under which they are administered, the alternative ways of deriving scores from the responses, and the specific kinds of inferences which it is hoped can be made from such results.

7

Test Development

THUS FAR, THE BASIC logical principles of testing have been presented in a way which describes the use and evaluation of the test as a whole. It takes little imagination to realize, however, that if a test or scale is composed of a series of individual items, then the characteristics of the items will ultimately determine the characteristics and quality of the test. This chapter, therefore, will examine the "stuff" of which tests are made. Its purpose is not that of providing skills in item writing as a manual on test construction might do, but rather to present the logical, if not actual, steps through which a test constructor must go if he is to develop a satisfactory device for quantifying observations of human characteristics. In the process of reviewing these steps it is anticipated that the reader will find specific applications of some of the principles of testing already encountered and may find some additional generalizations which are part of the body of knowledge in testing as it is known today.

PREPARATION OF MATERIALS

Planning the Test

The first step in the construction of a test or measuring device is one of the most important yet most often neglected. It requires careful delimitation and breakdown of the area or trait involved. If the measure is one of achievement, the process is the straightforward development of a table of specifications as was described in the discussion of content validity. If the measure is to be one of aptitude, interest, attitude, personality, or the like, the task is more difficult but just as important. Obviously, no single instrument can measure all human characteristics. While a factor analysis can describe the extent to which tests already in existence overlap, sound judgment on the part of the test constructor is the only means of pinpointing those specific characteristics which a particular measuring device must tap.

In general, there are no specific rules or techniques which can tell a person exactly what to measure in a particular situation. The use of plain common sense and a carefully thought out answer to the question "Why do I want to measure this characteristic?" will start the worker in the right direction. Trial and error, and perhaps some not-so-common sense, must be depended upon beyond this point.

In some situations the so-called *critical incidents* technique, introduced by Flanagan (1949) may be of help. In attempting to devise specific ability tests which would predict success on the job, Flanagan hit upon the idea of making a careful study of those particular on-the-job incidents which led to the dismissal or advancement of an employee. Using an interview and/or anecdotal technique (in which an employer writes a verbal description of such an incident immediately after it happens), with many different employers each providing data on a large number of employees, information can be obtained which will provide a wealth of ideas as to what areas must be included in an instrument if it is to have predictive value. When using such an approach, however, the test constructor must watch for two things which can lead him astray. Sometimes, information obtained in this way will be concerned with relatively rare occurrences. A happening or circumstance which arises only once in a lifetime for one of the employees is not something very useful for inclusion in a general measuring device to be used with thousands of workers across the country who may seek to enter a particular trade. Second, many of the stated reasons for failure or unusual success may be only the superficial happenings—the stimulus which set off an action truly motivated by an accumulation of subtle events not fully apparent to either the employer or employee. The so-called critical incident may have been merely the straw that broke the camel's back. Thus, while the critical incidents approach may serve as a stimulator of ideas, suggesting the type of things which need to be considered, the test constructor, applying his experience and judgmental skill, ultimately decides exactly what will or will not be included in the measure.

Writing the Items

Once the areas of knowledge and/or particular traits which need to be included have been carefully laid out, the next step is to list the behaviors which the examinee should (or should be able to) exhibit if he possesses the knowledge or characteristics under consideration. This should lead directly to the first writing of the items. If possible, the items should stimulate the examinee in such a way that if he usually does or can go through the desired behavior, he will respond in one way, while if he typically behaves in a different way or is unable to carry through the desired sequence, he will respond another way. Sometimes, however, it is impossible to get at the knowledge or characteristic desired in such a direct manner. Then, the item writer must look for necessary and unique consequents of possessing the particular characteristic (be it knowledge of some subject matter, a skill, an attitude, or a personality trait) being measured. That is, when the desired behavior cannot be measured directly, the test constructor must ask: "If a person possesses this characteristic, what ought he be able to do that he could not do if he did not possess this characteristic?" Such an indirect approach may lead to a test or scale which appears to get at many, many details while omitting the main point, but which may be an extremely valuable instrument, particularly for a selection situation where the major objective is to eliminate those who might fail at some future activity. Because no one item, nor even set of items, can be considered sufficient conditions for success, tests constructed in this way—as most are—will enable the user to predict negatively (that is, predict failure) much better than positively.

While the listing of the specific behaviors, direct or indirect, which are to be measured will suggest the item content, the test constructor is faced with the additional task of developing the particular format in which the content will be presented. Manuals or texts which are primarily concerned with item-writing skills, present a number of rules of thumb which the test constructor can follow. Generally, such suggestions have evolved from experience in item writing which has led experts to believe that certain formats or phraseology produce better results than others. Some of the rules for writing items have been logically derived from those principles of testing concerning objectivity, reliability, and validity described in previous chapters. Very few of the specific suggestions for item writing and format have come from experimental studies designed to provide specific evidence as to the best way in which to present the material. Thus, the reader should bear in mind that the suggestions mentioned in the ensuing paragraphs are means to an end. The ultimate evaluation of the items must depend upon whether or not the items possess certain desirable characteristics as shown by an item analysis of the results of an experimental trial of the test.

The essay examination, as a measuring instrument, has been criticized earlier, both in connection with test objectivity and the discussion of content validity. If an essay test is to be worth the extra time, effort, and expense required to administer, read, and grade it, it should result in a reliable measure of an important characteristic which cannot be obtained through a more objective item format. No one has yet been able to demonstrate that essay exams meet this requirement. A vast amount of evidence has led most experts in the field of measurement to agree with Stalnaker (1950) who states:

. . . none of the . . . broad, higher-order abilities for which the essay test has long been considered especially suited has yet even been established as subject to dependable measurement, let alone measurable by essay questions.*

and again,

. . . many teachers expect it (the essay question) to measure attainment of objectives that probably cannot be measured adequately in the typical test situation and possibly cannot be measured at all.*

* J. Stalnaker, "The Essay Type of Examination," in E. Lindquist, ed., *Educational Measurement* (American Council on Education, 1951).

For this reason, the remainder of the chapter will be concerned solely with the preparation and evaluation of items written in short answer, completion, multiple-choice (including true-false), and matching form. No attempt has been made to include all of the valuable hints obtainable from such references as Ebel (1950), Hawkes, Lindquist, and Mann (1936), Steckline (1956), and others. Rather, only a sample of the major types of suggestions most commonly found are mentioned.

One group of suggestions for item writing formalizes common sense principles applicable to almost any form of written communication. Most common among these are the following:

1. The question or direction should be as clear and explicit as possible.
2. Complex or awkward wording should be avoided.
3. All qualifications needed to provide a reasonable basis for response selection should be included.
4. Responses keyed as correct must be those on which competent critics agree.
5. All incorrect alternatives must be plausible to persons who lack the information or ability in question.
6. Responses that overlap or include each other should be avoided.

Another type of rule is designed to help the item writer avoid cues which might enable the examinee to obtain the correct answer even though he does not possess the appropriate information or ability. Thus:

1. All possible alternatives should be grammatically consistent with the stem sentence.
2. Correct alternatives should not be longer or shorter than the distractors in any given item.
3. Stereotyped or text-book phraseology should be avoided except where rote-memory is the trait to be measured.
4. Extreme adjectives like "always" or "never" should not be used in incorrect responses.
5. Correct answers should not appear in one particular position (for example, first, middle, last, and so forth) more frequently than any other, and patterns in the position of the correct responses should be avoided.

Other hints are useful in helping to reduce the effect of differences among the examinees in traits other than those to be measured. Of primary concern is the influence of reading ability.

Although it may be argued that the ability to read in a particular subject area is an important trait to measure in an achievement test, there are certainly some situations where it is desirable to eliminate such an influence on scores. In addition, it is usually desirable to avoid the effect of emotion and such things as response set. Typical of the item-writing suggestions of this sort are the following:

1. Trick (deliberately misleading) questions introduce irrelevant sources of difficulty and should be avoided.
2. Long and involved statements which employ many qualifying phrases should not be used.
3. Words which would have to be repeated for each response should be placed in the stem whenever possible.
4. When one exists, the responses should be placed in logical order.
5. Double negatives should always be avoided.

Finally, there are a number of rules of thumb which apply only to specific item forms. Thus:

1. At least three and preferably four response alternatives should be provided for each multiple-choice question. (Studies have shown that a fifth alternative is usually unnecessary and that items with only two alternatives, for example, true-false, are unreliable.)
2. Matching items should contain no more than ten elements on each side. Between five and eight is the preferred number.
3. Only a single, clearly indicated basis for matching should be used with each set of elements.
4. The premise and response column of matching questions should not contain the same number of elements.

ITEM ANALYSIS

Once the test items have been written, the next major step is that of trying them out in an analysis group of subjects who are representative of the population for which the total test is being prepared. To achieve a satisfactory degree of stability in the several item indices described below, it is generally recommended that around 400 subjects be used.[1] For administration to this

---

[1] Item analyses obviously can be, and often are done with fewer subjects than this. However, the test constructor who uses small analysis groups should be aware that item characteristics may shift markedly from one sample group to the next.

analysis group, the items should be prepared in a format which is as close to the final form of the test as possible. Insofar as possible, the only difference between this trial and the final testing should be in the length of time allowed. So that data will be available for every single item, all the time needed to complete the test should be granted. If this is not possible, it will be necessary to prepare several forms of the test differing only in the order in which the items are presented and arranged. Thus, different items should appear in the last portion of the test each time. Then, using additional subjects and combining the results from all forms, sufficient information can be obtained for the required analysis.

It is not difficult to suppose that if a test is composed of items, then characteristics of these items will have an influence on the test characteristics. And, as a matter of fact, it can be shown that the test mean, standard deviation, reliability, and validity which will be obtained with a particular population can all be closely estimated if the appropriate information is available for each item.

A recent review of the literature has indicated that there are at least some twenty-three different methods of item analysis. The details of describing and comparing all of these specific techniques are not important at this point. Thus, the following discussion will be confined to one of the most common of the techniques for computing item indexes and a simple graphic procedure for representing item characteristics. Both are intended to serve primarily as illustrations of the logic of item analysis.

Indexes of Item Characteristics

The three basic item characteristics needed to predict the major characteristics of a test are these:

1. *Item difficulty* (p_i): the proportion of persons answering each item correctly.
2. *A reliability index* $(r_{xi} s_i)$: taken as the point-biserial correlation between an item and the total test score, multiplied by the item standard deviation.

3. *A validity index* ($r_{yi} s_i$): taken as the point-biserial correlation between an item and a criterion score, multiplied by the item standard deviation.

The index of item difficulty certainly presents no problem. For each item, it is simply necessary to count the number of persons in the analysis group who got the item correct, and divide this by the total number of persons who have attempted the item.

To obtain the other two indexes, however, it is necessary to first compute a biserial correlation between the item response and a continuous variable. Actually the point-biserial correlation is the familiar product—moment correlation where one of the variables is allowed to take on values of only zero or one. Graphically, (see Figure 21) it is represented by the overlap of two frequency distributions on the continuous variable, one arising from scores obtained by all persons getting the item correct and the other from

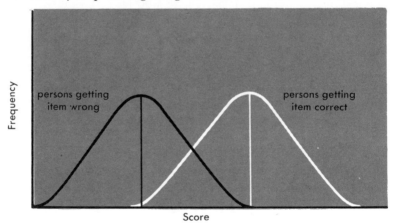

FIGURE 21: Graphic Representation of a Biserial Correlation for a Test Item

scores obtained by all persons getting the item wrong. The formula for point-biserial correlation is commonly expressed as:

$$(43) \qquad r_{xi} = \frac{(\overline{X}_R - \overline{X}_W)}{s_x} \sqrt{p_i q_i} \, ,$$

where:

$\overline{X}_R$ = mean test score of persons getting item right

$\overline{X}_W$ = mean test score of persons getting item wrong

s_x = standard deviation of the scores

p_i = proportion of the analysis group getting the item right

$q_i = 1 - p_i$.

From both the graphic representation and the formula, it can be seen that the reliability index and/or the validity index of an item will depend upon:

1. The mean difference in score on the continuous variable between those who get the item correct and those who get the item incorrect.
2. The total variation in scores on the continuous variable.
3. The item variability[2] ($s_i = \sqrt{p_i q_i}$) which in turn is a function of the proportion of persons in the group who get the item right.

Thus, to the extent to which any of the rules of thumb such as those listed in the previous section are useful, they must change one or more of these three things in the appropriate way. For example, irrelevant cues tend to make the item easier, thus reducing item variability which is at a maximum for a 50 percent difficulty, without necessarily increasing the mean difference in scores on the continuous variable. For, persons low on the total test or the criterion are just as likely (if not more likely) to depend upon such cues as those whose total or criterion scores are high. Similarly, an emotionally loaded item or an item which depends heavily on reading skills while attempting to measure something relatively independent of them will probably increase total score variance without the accompanying increase in mean difference in the trait which the instrument purports to measure.

Fortunately, it is not necessary to carry out the complete computations for the point-biserial correlation for each item. Flanagan (1936) and Fan (1952) have published tables which permit the estimation of the correlation between item response

[2] See Chapter 3, p. 72.

and a continuous variable from knowledge of the proportion of individuals in a high and low scoring group on the continuous variable who got the item correct. While both tables make use of the top 27 percent and bottom 27 percent of the total group, Fan's tables have the advantage of presenting, as well, a more accurate estimate of the proportion of the total group who got the item correct than could be obtained by simply averaging the proportions who got the item correct from the two groups.

The item difficulty index, then, may be taken as the p_i read directly out of Fan's table. The reliability index, then, is, the r_{xi} read out of either Flanagan's or Fan's table, multiplied by the quantity $p_i (1 - p_i)$ when the top and bottom groups were determined by the total test scores; and the validity index is the product of the same two quantities when the top and bottom groups are determined on the basis of a criterion score. The reason that the reliability and validity indexes as presented on page 163ff. are used, rather than the correlations r_{xi} and r_{yi} directly, is to simplify the estimate of the test-criterion correlation (that is, the estimate of ultimate validity coefficient). For, as it turns out,

$$(44) \qquad r_{xy} = \frac{\Sigma s_i r_{yi}}{\Sigma s_i r_{xi}}.$$

That is, the estimated test validity is the ratio of the average of the item validity indexes to the average of the item reliability indexes.

This also makes clear what Loevinger (1954) has called the *attenuation paradox*—that as the internal consistency of the test (as measured by the item-total test score correlation) is increased, the empirical validity of the test is decreased. This paradox, of course, holds true only as long as the increased internal consistency does not also increase the item external criterion correlation. Logically, it makes sense that a certain amount of refinement would tend to eliminate irrelevant variance, thus increasing the validity index as well as the reliability index, but that beyond a certain point, further increase in internal consistency begins to eliminate relevant variance, thereby reducing the test-criterion correlation.

Item Characteristic Curves

When an analysis group used for the tryout of test materials is sufficiently large to produce a number of persons who have obtained each of the possible scores (on a test or on a criterion), a graphic procedure provides a practical alternative to the more rigorous analysis of the item-test or item-criterion relationships just described. A plot of the proportion of correct answers given to an item by persons at each score level against that level produces a curve for that item which clearly portrays both the item difficulty and the item discrimination. Three such item characteristic curves (using fictitious data) are presented in Figure 22.

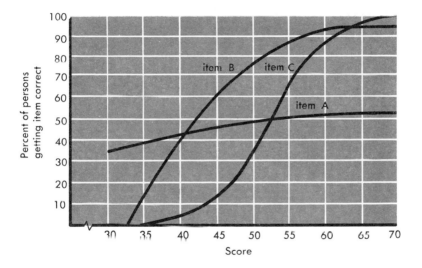

FIGURE 22: Item Characteristic Curves of Three Hypothetical Items

Source: F. Lord. Relation of test score to trait underlying the test. Educ. psychol. Measmt. Vol. 13, 1953. Figure 22 is an adaptation of Figure 2, p. 520.

From these plots it is immediately apparent that item *A* is not nearly as effective as is either *B* or *C*. A fairly substantial proportion (30 percent) of the persons who received the very lowest score on the test got this item right while only 50 percent of the persons who got the highest score did so. On the other hand, none of the persons with scores lower than 33 got item B correct while at least 90 percent of persons with scores of 60 or higher did. Item C is even more discriminating. In general, the steeper the slope of the item's characteristic curve, the more discriminating it is. An item with perfect discrimination would be represented by a vertical line, indicating that nobody who fell below the designated score got the item right while everybody with a higher score answered it correctly. In contrast, a horizontal line would result if the item were completely invalid. Such a curve would indicate that the likelihood of getting the item right is completely independent of the trait measured by the score, be it test or criterion. Negatively discriminating items, of course, would have curves which slope from upper left to lower right.

Theoretically, item difficulty can be inferred from the general position of the item characteristic curve, difficult items being represented by curves further to the right than easier ones. However, this characteristic is difficult to judge from an empirical plot without conceptually extrapolating each curve until it reaches the zero and the 100 percent points on the vertical axis. This problem can be overcome by following Tucker's (1946) suggestion that a convenient index of difficulty would be the score for which the proportion of responses is 50 percent. Thus item A and item C are readily seen to be of about the same difficulty with a value of approximately 52, and item B, with a value of 42, the easiest of the three.

It should be noted that to obtain stable estimates of the proportion of correct responses, a reasonably large number of persons is needed at each score level. In most actual situations, therefore, some score grouping will have to be done. Fortunately, even when only five or six points (as widely spread as possible) are plotted, the general characteristics of the item curve can be determined accurately enough for practical use in item selection.

ITEM SELECTION

Once the item characteristics have been determined either numerically or graphically, the question arises as to how this information should be used for the revision of items and the selection of those particular ones to be used in later tryouts and in the final test itself. This problem is not as simple as it might at first seem. It is not always possible to merely place the items in order with respect to the validity index and then, starting with the best, proceed down the list until a sufficient number has been chosen.

General Considerations

In the first place, in many instances—particularly when constructing achievement tests—it will be necessary to maintain at least some items covering all aspects or areas of the content universe as spelled out prior to the writing of the items. Thus, it may be necessary to rewrite certain items or create new ones in an area where the item validities were generally low, while discarding items of higher validity in some other content areas. In this situation it may be of help to have, as a further kind of information available, knowledge of what proportion of the high and low group has marked each of the possible distractors. This involves an item count for each alternative rather than for just the correct alternative as indicated above. This information will indicate whether all distractors are functioning (studies carried out in the armed services have indicated that seldom is it necessary to use more than three distractors along with the correct response) and may explain negative item-criterion correlations which sometimes arise.

Second, a test is often designed for use in a particular situation with a specific group, thus requiring a special level of difficulty. There is some evidence (cf Lord, 1953) that, for maximum efficiency in selection, a test should be "peaked"; that is, the average item difficulty level should match the selection ratio. Thus, for example, if the top 25 percent of persons were to be selected, the most efficient test would be that for which the average of item difficulty (proportion who get the item correct) is at 25 percent. This is true in spite of the fact that the maximum obtainable item criterion correlation occurs for items of 50 percent difficulty.

Finally, it is not possible to take the top item according to the individual validity index because the overall test validity will also be a function of the item intercorrelations. Thus, an item of high validity may not increase the test validity at all if added to a group of items with which it is highly correlated. To make the greatest contribution to total test validity, an item should be as highly correlated with the criterion as possible and still be unrelated to other items to be used. This is readily seen in Figure 23 where the extent of correlation is graphically represented by the amount of overlap. In this illustration, the order of greatest item-criterion correlation would be items two, one, three, and four. Yet, if item one is to be used, item two adds very little. The best

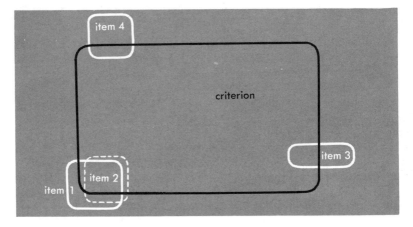

FIGURE 23: Relationship among Item-Criterion, Inter-Item, and Test-Criterion Correlation

combination of those items would be items two, three, and four even though item one has a higher correlation with the criterion than either item three or item four.

Specific Procedures

Consideration of this latter principle has led to the development of two specific approaches to the selection of items from a pool of possibilities which are worth noting.

The first, known as the method of *successive pools,* was developed by H. A. Toops (1923). For this approach, the most valid item is selected first. This item is then paired with every other one, and the most valid pair (that is, the pair contributing most to the test-criterion correlation) is chosen. This pair is then joined in turn by each remaining item until the most valid trio has been located and so on until the required number of items has been selected.

The second item selection procedure is known as Horst's (1934) method of *successive residuals.* As with Toops' procedure, the most valid (best predictor) item is chosen first. Then, that portion of the criterion not predicted by the first item is taken as the residual criterion. The next item selected is that which best predicts this residual criterion. That portion of the residual criterion not predicted by the first two items is then taken as the second residual criterion and the third item selected is the one which best predicts this new residual. The process is successively continued until a sufficient number of items has been chosen.

While logically sound, the procedures of Toops and Horst are obviously complex, requiring considerable computational time. Nonetheless, if a test is to be used regularly, it is worthwhile to take the time to do a good job. Furthermore, because the computations are repetitious, use of modern computers in this task is feasible, reducing the time and cost to reasonable proportion.

All in all, there is no completely prescribed step-by-step procedure to follow. Most test constructors, however, would adopt a procedure similar to the following:

1. Make a frequency distribution of the item validity coefficients and compare this with the sampling distribution (under the null hypothesis) for point-biserial correlation. This will insure that the observed item validities are other than chance fluctuations.
2. Examine first all of the highly *negatively* correlating items to see if they can be rewritten (or keyed) so that they will be useful positive items.
3. For items of middle validity, note the relative frequency with which each response was chosen. Eliminating distractors not chosen and replacing them with more plausible ones should raise the item validity. This is especially true of items which show a low reliability. If chance

can be eliminated from these items by removing extraneous cues or increasing the number of working distractors, they are the ones most likely to show increased validity in a second experimental tryout.

4. Items well within the chance range should probably be eliminated unless they are needed for content validity. In this case, an attempt may be made to rewrite. It is usually more effective, however, to replace such items with completely new ones.

5. The revised items should be organized into a new experimental form and again administered to one analysis group of subjects.

6. Again the appropriate item characteristics should be computed and a check of the validities made against a chance distribution.

7. Next, either Toops' or Horst's procedures should be followed to get the most valid combination of items for the length of test desired (or required to achieve a previously set minimum validity).

8. Then, the items should be classified into content areas and any vacant classification filled with some new items or the most valid items belonging to the appropriate category which have been momentarily rejected.

9. Examine the difficulty level of the items to make certain they are appropriate. Remember, for maximum discrimination throughout the range, 50 percent difficulty is best; for selection situations, the difficulty should correspond as closely as possible to the proportion of candidates to be chosen.

ORGANIZING THE TEST

The next logical step in test development is to organize the items selected into a reasonably administered format and to develop an appropriate system for scoring the test.

The preparation of the directions and the development of a specific format is largely a matter of common sense. The main factor to remember is that for adequate results the test must always be administered in exactly the same way, no matter who the person giving the test happens to be. Thus, the directions should be set up so as to instruct both the test administrator and the person who is being measured. Usually the test administrator will be required to read certain portions of the directions verbatim. Obviously, the directions must be clear and unambiguous, otherwise unreliability and possibly lower validity will result. A person who is organizing a test for the first time would do well to review carefully the format and directions of several widely known and used tests.

Some studies completed when the machine-scored tests were first being used have indicated that greater reliability is achieved if the subjects are allowed to work on one or two practice problems prior to starting on the main portion of the test. Such a practice is seldom followed today, however, since most subjects are quite familiar with machine-scored tests and once one or two items have been done, additional practice seems to be of little value.

Similarly, some early studies have indicated that the easier items should be arranged in order of difficulty, starting with the easiest and placing the most difficult near the end. This requirement seems to be of less importance with objective tests than with essay tests, and today most authorities feel that other considerations—for example, getting an adequate sample of behavior in all content areas included—should take precedent. Any unreliability which normally would result from examinees spending too much time on a difficult item while not attempting an easy item can be prevented by setting adequate time limits and by suggesting in the directions that the examinee should not spend too much time on any one item, but rather skip a difficult item and go back to it later if time permits.

A major decision with which a test constructor is faced is that of determining the length of the test. Ideally, this should be decided in terms of the number of items required to achieve maximum validity. In Chapter 3 it was pointed out that reliability is a direct function of test length, and it is not difficult to conceive of the effect of length on validity when one remembers the discussion of sampling validity. There is, of course, a point of diminishing returns beyond which the gain in reliability and, more important, validity, achieved by additional items may be considered negligible or not worth the effort. Thus, where practical considerations do not limit the time, the test length will be determined by the number of items required to achieve as high a degree of validity as possible without exceeding the point where costs in terms of time, effort, money, and patience of the examinee outweigh the additional gain. Time limits on such a test are usually taken so that approximately 90 percent of the examinees will be able to finish. The exception to this, of course, is the case of a speed test in which the time limits must be set so that no one is likely to quite finish it. In a great many, if not most, situations, however, time is of utmost practical importance. A test used in the school classroom cannot require more time than one period—or at least must be divided into parts each of which is no longer than a single class period and which can be separately administered. In many selection, clinical, or research situations where it may be possible, it simply is not reasonable to expect the examinees to spend several days or a week doing nothing but taking tests. Even with measures of typical behavior which traditionally have had no time limits, practical considerations of such things as fatigue, the tendency to fake, etc. have led most test constructors to limit the test length in some way other than might be dictated purely on the basis of ultimate maximum validity.

Thus, today, test length is often thought of in terms of time rather than number of items, and the problem is that of achieving maximum reliability and validity within the specified time limits (cf Horst, 1956 and Horst and MacEwan, 1956, 1957). Of course, a certain minimum satisfactory degree of validity must be achieved, and if the time limit allowed is so short that the required level is not reached, the test is usually divided into two or more separately timed parts. Although there may be some exceptions, it has generally been found that when a test is carefully constructed and appropriate item evaluation and selection procedures employed, a completely satisfactory degree of validity and reliability can be achieved with a relatively short test.

SCORING PROCEDURES

A second major decision which a test constructor will be required to make relates to the scoring procedures to be used. The question arises as to whether each item should contribute equally to the total score or whether some items should be counted more heavily than others. In addition, it is necessary to decide whether a score based only on the number right will be adequate or whether some sort of correction for guessing is appropriate. In each case, the decision should be based on whether or not the reliability and validity of the test is increased, limited, as always, by the point of diminishing returns and practical considerations of the time and effort involved in elaborate scoring schemes.

The Weighting of Items

The first question is usually discussed under the heading of weighting in connection with the problem of combining either test scores into a battery composite or the parts of a test into a single score. Since the logic is the same whether a series of items, or a series of parts of tests, or a series of tests are being combined, time will not be taken at this point to go into a great deal of detail in a topic more appropriately discussed in a subsequent chapter. Instead, the reader will simply be asked to accept the generalization that when a large number of variables (say, more than fifty) are combined, it will usually make very little difference in the ultimate outcome as to what weights are assigned to each measure. The application of this principle to item weighting has been verified by empirical studies a number of times. For example, many years ago Douglass and Spencer (1923) found, for a number of tests, that scores obtained with unit weights correlated .98 to .99 with the same scores obtained through the use of special item weights. Thus, since elaborate weighting schemes increase to a considerable extent the time and effort involved in deriving an individual's score, it is generally recommended that a simple unit weight per item be used.

On the other hand, when an adequate criterion measure can be obtained and the test constructor feels that the extra effort in scoring will be compensated by a substantial increase in validity, it is certainly worthwhile to try out a special weighting scheme. The usual procedure, in such a case, is to first correlate the scores obtained by unit weighting with the criterion, then to rescore the papers using the special weights and computing again the validity coefficient. If there is a significant increase in the validity estimate, then it is a matter of personal judgment as to whether the magnitude of the increase is worth the additional scoring effort which will be required.

Correcting for Guessing

The use of special scoring formulas which purport to "correct for guessing" has been extremely popular in the past. Starting with the assumption that a person who has no information about any item at all, has a 1 in K chance of guessing the answer to a question with K possible responses, a logical correction is derived. For example, assume that a test has N items and that a subject who knows S of the items makes a pure guess at the answer to the remaining $N - S$ items. If each item has K possible responses only one of which is correct, the binominal distribution where $n = N - S$ and $p = 1/K$ represents the chances of getting the different possible numbers of guessed items correct. Using the expected value (that is, the mean of the chance distribution) as the most likely number of items guessed correctly we obtain

$$(44) \qquad np = \frac{N - S}{K}.$$

Thus, on the average, the total number of right answers, R, will be the number the subject knows plus the expected number he will guess correctly. Therefore,

$$(45) \qquad R = S + \frac{N - S}{K}.$$

Solving this equation for the number of items the student actually knows (that is, for S) we obtain

$$(46) \qquad S = \frac{RK - N}{K - 1}.$$

By substituting for N, the total number of items, its equivalent, $R + W$,[3] the number of items which a subject knows becomes

$$(45) \qquad S = \frac{RK - (R + W)}{K - 1}$$

$$(46) \qquad = R - \frac{W}{K - 1}.$$

This is the most commonly used formula for correcting for guessing.

---

[3] While this seems to assume that there are no omissions, exactly the same formula will ultimately be obtained through a more complicated derivation assuming $N = R + W + O$ and the subject guesses at $N - S - O$ items.

The major difficulty with such a formula lies in the extent to which the basic assumptions underlying it correspond to actual happenings in practice. In this case, the assumption that a pure guess is made on those items not known (and not omitted) seems to be in error. Having taken a number of multiple-choice tests himself, the reader will have no difficulty in recognizing the fact that not all alternatives are equally attractive to him. Thus, on one item, he may be able to eliminate three distractors and his guess is only between the remaining two. Or, he may be able to eliminate two distractors, guessing among only three, and so on. Thus, his chances of getting an item is not always $1/K$ but, $1/(K - 1)$, $1/(K - 2)$, $1/(K - 3)$, and so forth, depending upon how many alternatives can be eliminated before the guessing takes place. Therefore, a student with partial knowledge should get far more items correct than would be anticipated on the basis of a pure guess and, S, as the number of items definitely known is overestimated even with the correction. Logically, if an examinee is to be given proper credit for partial knowledge, a simple count of the number right, without any correction, would seem most appropriate. For, the person who knows the correct response will get the item right, a person who lacks only a little knowledge and can therefore eliminate all but two possibilities has a one in two chance of getting the item correct, a person with less information has a one in three chance, and so forth. Thus, in the long run, a score directly corresponding to his knowledge or ability is obtained. A further reason why many persons in the field today do not recommend the use of formulas which attempt to correct for guessing is that the results of at least one study (cf Cronbach, 1949) have indicated that more reliable results are obtained when subjects are told not to guess and no correction is used.

There is one set of circumstances, however, in which a correction for guessing is absolutely essential. This is when an item is constructed in such a way that more than one response is correct and the subjects are told to mark as many responses for each item as they think are appropriate. Unless some correction for guessing is used with this type of item, the subject who marks the most responses will get the highest score. Ideally, the correction should be imposed only to the extent that the subject marks more responses than are expected. Such a procedure, however, complicates the scoring unduly and thus a more practical but somewhat severe penalty of using right minus wrong is commonly used.

FINAL EVALUATION

The last logical step in test development is that of making a final evaluation of the test, as revised and reorganized, on a new analysis group. Up to this point, the data gathered has been for the purpose of refining and rewriting the instrument. The test revised on the basis of this information is a new and different one and must now be tried out and evaluated exactly as it will be published and used. It is at this stage that the normative data are gathered, the reliability indexes as described earlier, computed, and the validity information is obtained.

Needless to say, the process of test development is a never ending one. As the instrument is used in the field, new data may suggest weaknesses, or our changing culture may set up conditions which demand a further revision, especially of norms and sometimes of the items themselves. Validity data should continually be accumulated, for each new use to which the test is put and for each new group with which it is used.

Ultimately a time may arrive when our knowledge of human behavior advances far enough so that the test will have lost its usefulness and will have to be discarded, but the general logic by which the next one is developed will likely remain much the same.

8

Scales and Inventories

SCALES AND INVENTORIES AS MEASURING DEVICES

MEASUREMENT HAS BEEN defined as the process of obtaining a numerical description of the extent to which a person or thing possesses some characteristic. In this broad sense measurement includes the use of many techniques other than formal testing procedures. It is the purpose of this chapter, therefore, to describe and evaluate self-report inventories, check-lists, rating scales, and certain psychometric scaling techniques, all of which can be properly referred to as measurement.

Some Exclusions

On the other hand, many of the so-called projective techniques and unstructured interview forms simply require the subject to respond to a standard set of stimuli and make no attempt to arrive at quantitative descriptions—the responses being interpreted in a purely verbal sense by the examiner. These latter approaches, therefore, will be excluded from the present discussion.

For the same reason, nominating techniques in which the subject simply lists those friends, classmates, or other acquaintances with whom he would like to associate for certain activities will not be included. Although these techniques provide the teacher, researcher, personnel worker, or other user with valuable information about the social interactions of a group, they generally do not result in a numerical description of each of the individuals and thus cannot be called measurement procedures.

Psychometric scaling procedures as described by Guilford (1954) and others all represent techniques for placing a set of stimuli on a numerical scale, seeking in every instance to reach the highest level of measurement possible under the experimental conditions imposed. Certain of the techniques, however, are almost impossible or at least extremely difficult to use with human beings as the stimuli. Thus, only those psychometric scaling procedures which are ordinarily applied to the description of human behavior have been discussed here. Readers who are interested in pursuing these special approaches further are invited to study such references as Guilford (1954), Torgerson (1958), and Edwards (1957).

General Evaluation

Rating scales and inventories (which are actually just self-rating scales and therefore need no special treatment) are among the most popular of techniques for describing human characteristics. Because of the many distorting factors which will be described in subsequent sections of this chapter, rating scales would not appear to be as rigorous as the more formal testing techniques discussed earlier. On the other hand, unstructured ratings, projective techniques, situational tests, and the like, are subject to all the faults of rating scales, plus some additional ones, and thus would seem to be far less satisfactory than those techniques presented in this chapter. Then, too, if the intent is to determine the way in which others react to the individual in question, a rating scale in one of its various forms, provides the most direct measure possible. In this situation, rating scales would seem to be valid by definition, the resulting measurements being limited only in terms of interpretive and variable errors.

Generally speaking, all the rating methods would be classified under the psychometric scaling technique called *successive intervals*. In this type of scaling, each of the stimuli under consideration is placed into one of a limited number of intervals or categories ordered along some continuum. Although the basic operation leads only to ordinal measurements, interval scales can be achieved if the user is willing to take the trouble to carry out an appropriate transformation of values. As compared with the other more elaborate psychometric scaling procedures, the successive interval approach leads to results which are highly satisfactory.

Among the many practical advantages which have been cited in favor of a rating approach, are the facts that it takes less time, it can be used with a large number of subjects, and it seems to work well even with relatively naive judges (or raters). The major logical objection to the rating scale form of the successive interval approach is that ratings are often based on only broad impressions about the person being rated and are usually recorded some time after the original observations have been made.

The problem with impressionistic judgments of broadly defined "traits," especially when recorded some time after the observations are made, is that such ratings do not often reflect actual behavior. Rating scales which do not in some way relate to relevant observable behaviors may be interesting, but are not useful either to a researcher or to a worker in an applied field.

Empirical evidence as to the general efficacy of rating scales is difficult, if not impossible, to obtain. In the first place, rating scales are often constructed and used in those situations where other measurement approaches are exceedingly difficult to apply. Thus, criterion data against which to compare the results of rating scales are often not readily available. In the second place, whether or not a particular rating scale will be valid depends (much more than is the case with a more formal testing approach) on the particular behavior observed, on the opportunity the raters have had to make the observations, and on the care with which the scale has been constructed. Nonetheless, it is instructive to note the results of some of the studies which have been executed since they suggest ways that evidence which is helpful in determining whether a particular rating scale is a useful measuring device might be gathered.

In an early study, Marsh and Perrin (1925) compared three types of five-point scales, which were used to rate a number of different characteristics, with respect to both the degree of agreement among five independent raters and the correlations between ratings and other measures of the same characteristics. Although the results for the three scale formats were similar, there were marked differences in the effectiveness of the ratings of the various characteristics. Thus, for example, rater agreement was highest for ratings of Size of Head and least for Leadership, Poise, and Control. At the same time, the correlation between the ratings of head size and actual physical measurement of this characteristic was .76 while ratings of leadership correlated .50 with the irrelevant but more readily observed characteristic of physical attractiveness. Other, more recent, studies also illustrate that ratings of specifically defined characteristics obtained on carefully developed scales can have validity, while judgements of broadly defined traits are often subject to irrelevant influences. For example, Gebhart and Hoyt (1958) found that overachievers scored significantly higher than underachievers on a self-report, forced-choice scale designed to measure achievement needs and significantly lower than underachievers on a scale (of the same instrument) designed to measure need for affiliation. On the other hand, Guilford (1959) describes an unpublished study of the ratings of a large group of military officers in which a factor analysis revealed that, no matter what the trait, the resulting ratings could be interpreted to reflect differences in ". . . expressional fluency, an ability to produce connected verbal discourse." Guilford also describes some experimental studies by Thornton (1943 and 1944) in which judgments were made with and without certain irrelevant clues. In these studies, persons, when wearing glasses, were judged to be higher in intelligence, dependability, and industriousness than when not wearing them, and people whose photographs showed them smiling were judged higher in sense of humor, kindliness, and honesty than they were when their photographs pictured a more serious face.

In conclusion, then, it would appear that because of their many practical advantages and their clear, logical superiority over less structured techniques, rating scales will continue to be one of the most widely used ways of obtaning measures of human behavior. The careful worker will, however, take the pains to see that his scale is well constructed, and the wise user of such devices will always obtain validity information on the effectiveness of the ratings in the specific situation in which they are employed by showing that the numerical ratings do, in fact, correspond to relevant and observable behavioral differences.

Types of Rating Scales

It has already been noted that all rating scales represent a form of the psychometric scaling technique called the method of *successive intervals,* where the person being rated is the stimulus to be assigned to a category along a continuum. To accomplish this task each instrument generally involves two components: a description of the behavior or behaviors to be considered (the continuum) and a set of alternative responses from which the rater is to choose (the ordered categories) for each person rated. While there is an almost endless variety of ways of expressing each of the components, and thus an infinite number of possible rating scale forms, certain types have been so commonly used and seem sufficiently distinct that they have been given special names. Each of these major types will, therefore, be briefly described.

Numerical Scales. One of the simplest scales to construct and easiest to use is the numerical rating scale. This type of instrument usually consists of several items each of which names or describes the behavior to be rated, and then offers as alternative responses a series of numbers representing points along the scale. For example, one item from a scale designed to present a description of a student's behavior in a classroom situation might be:

Which of the following best describes this student's verbal participation in class?
  (1) avoids expressing himself even when asked
  (2) will express himself only when asked
  (3) freely expresses himself on some things, but avoids comment on others
  (4) freely expresses himself on almost every topic

(5) insists on expressing himself on every topic even when discussion is not called for

It should be noted that such scales do not always provide a verbal description for every point along the scale and in some instances the numbers which may be used in the analysis of the results are not actually printed on the scale where the rater can see them. In the latter instance the scales are sometimes referred to simply as multiple-choice ratings.

The simple numerical scale does have face validity and therefore seems to be widely accepted. Nevertheless, many more sophisticated workers prefer other types of scales when the practical situation permits a more elaborate development. There is some evidence that this simple numerical format is more subject to the errors and biases which occur in ratings than are other types. This is probably due to the fact that such a format encourages evaluations and inferences beyond a simple recording of the behavior observed.

Graphic Scales. If the format of the rating scale is such that the characteristic to be rated is represented as a straight line along which are placed some verbal guides, the instrument is referred to as a graphic rating scale.

Because it appears so easy to construct, the graphic scale seems to be the most widely used of all the specific types of rating scales to be described. This is unfortunate since such quickly formulated scales usually fail to yield dependable measures. By representing the characteristic under consideration along a line, the graphic scale format, especially, invites the raters to make judgments about an underlying trait rather than to simply provide a record of what was observed.

Standard Scales. In the standard scale approach, an attempt is made to provide the rater with more than verbal cues to describe various scale points. Ideally, several samples of the objects to be rated are included, each with a given scale value which has been determined in experimental studies prior to the use of the scale. When products of human endeavor are the objects to be rated and the samples can be made readily available to the raters, this technique has much to recommend it. While the value of the final instrument would obviously depend upon the care used in establishing the scale values of the products, there is no logical or methodological reason why highly useful standard scales cannot be developed for measuring such things as handwriting, business letters, certain aspects of commercial drawing, etc.

When attempting to measure human characteristics which do not result in observable products, the use of the standard scale approach becomes more complex. It is apparent that it is not possible to have different persons available as samples for the raters to use in describing others. It is possible, however, to list the names of persons to represent the various points along the scale for each characteristic to be rated. The major difficulty, of course, arises in attempting to find a common group of persons with whom all of the raters are familiar and whose names can be used to define the desired points along the scale. While theoretically it is not necessary for all raters to be acquainted with all persons listed on such a scale, it is essential that each judge know at least one person listed at each of the major scale steps, and that the person constructing the scale have some way of establishing appropriate scale values by comparing all persons whose names will be used on a common basis.

One historically interesting attempt to develop a standard scale for use in measuring human traits is the *Man to Man* scale which Guilford (1954) attributes to W. D. Scott. According to Guilford, this scale was developed for military use and required the rater to write down the names of twelve to twenty-five persons whom he knew well. Next, the rater was required to put the names in rank order on each of five traits. For each trait, then, the first and last men on the list were used to represent the top and bottom points on the scale; the middle person was placed at a third position on the ultimate five-point scale, and the two men halfway between the extremes and the center position were taken as representing the second and fourth position on the final scale. Since this approach requires an assumption which is difficult to justify (namely, that each rater knows individuals who vary throughout the entire range on every trait to be rated), it is not generally recommended. The man to man scale, however, does illustrate an ingenious attempt to build an appropriate standard scale for use in rating human characteristics which do not result in a tangible product. Also, it might be used in conjunction with other techniques to produce a type of scale which combines the advantages of several approaches. Thus it has been suggested[1] that the actual job behavior of the so-called standard men be examined to obtain a list of critical behaviors which could then be scaled and ultimately cast into the check-list format described in the next section.

In conclusion, then, when the standard scale approach is used under appropriate circumstances, and when extreme care is taken to develop accurate scale values for the standards used, the resulting instrument is likely to be one of the best possible rating scales. Unfortunately, it is not likely that most users of ratings will be willing to put forth the effort required, and thus this approach will probably find its greatest use as a criterion for other, more practical techniques.

Check-Lists.   An approach which is widely popular because it is simple to administer and still permits wide coverage in a short time is the behavior check-list. Usually this instrument contains a long list of specific behaviors which supposedly represent important individual differences, and the rater simply checks whether the item applies. A person's position on the scale which represents the behavior index is obtained by simply summing the number of items which have been checked. On more elaborate scales, each item may have been weighted and the rating is obtained by cumulating the points given to those items which have been checked.

In addition to the practical advantages, the check-list technique avoids the problem of having naive raters make complex judgments, and, if properly developed, forces the rater to adhere to observed behaviors rather than general impressions. Ideally, in all rating procedures (as in formal tests) judgment should occur only when formulating hypotheses about what behaviors are likely to be both readily detectable and relevant to the future

[1] By Marvin D. Dunnette in personal correspondence.

situation of concern. Subsequent item analysis (similar to that used with tests) of data gathered in an actual tryout of the materials should identify those particular behavior descriptions which should be retained as items on the check-list.

The only problem with this approach is the response set of the rater which may lead him to check many or only a few characteristics for any one individual. This difficulty can be minimized, however, simply by asking each rater to check some specified number of items or by requiring that every item be marked as "applicable," "not applicable," or "don't know." Although even the latter format is still subject to some response set (in terms of the tendency to mark "don't know"), it is less likely to be resisted by raters who generally dislike being forced to list a given number of items when they may feel that fewer or more are really applicable.

Forced Choice Scales. One of the more recent innovations in the rating scale area has been the development of a forced choice technique which has been specifically designed to overcome some of the major difficulties encountered with most of the other approaches. In a forced choice rating the rater is required to consider not just one attribute, but several characteristics all at one time. Assuming that a relevant item is difficult for a rater to distinguish from one which is not predictive if both are equally favorable to the person, the format requires that only a few of several behaviors listed in each item be selected as applicable. In the original form as seen in Figure 24, two favorable and two

1 {
a. Insists upon his subordinates being precise and exact.

b. Stimulates associates to be interested in their work.

2 {
a. Allows himself to become burdened with detail.

b. Does not point out when work is poorly done.

FIGURE 24: Sample Item From a Forced-Choice Rating Scale Designed to Measure Supervisory Performance.

SOURCE: L. Huttner and R. Katzell, Developing a Yardstick of Supervisory Performance. *Personnel*, 1957, 33, 371-378, p. 373. Published by the American Management Association.

unfavorable statements were presented in each item, and the rater
was asked to select the one which was most and the one which
was least descriptive of the individual being rated. More recent
studies by Highland and Berkshire (1951) have indicated, however, that the most effective format was one in which four favorable characteristics were listed and the rater asked to select the
two which were most descriptive of the ratee.

In general, the forced choice technique does seem to tend to
overcome some of the most serious rating errors. The results,
however, are not as spectacular as the theory behind it would
imply, and there is not much evidence to suggest that what improvement is obtained is other than the result of the far more
than usual care in construction and validation of the devices.
Also, raters are sometimes sufficiently antagonistic toward this
type of format to make its use impractical. That this latter need
not be the case, however, has been demonstrated by Huttner and
Katzell (1957). These workers supplemented the conventional
forced choice approach by having the rater indicate, on a separate
scale, the extent to which the behavior checked applied to the
person rated. According to Huttner and Katzell, this modified
format " . . . seems to have encountered no noteworthy degree
of resistance from those who use it; indeed, widespread acceptance
of this procedure has been evidenced throughout company management."

Ranking Methods.   In some situations, it does not seem
reasonable (or the user is unwilling) to make the assumption
that the person preparing the scale or the rater can accurately
judge equivalent distances at various points along the scale. Under
these circumstances a ranking procedure which requires only that
the subjects who are being rated be placed in order on each trait
can be used.[2] On some occasions this system can be modified by
simply having the raters divide the subjects into large groups as
top 5 percent, next 20 percent, middle 50 percent, and so forth.
This latter approach seems useful primarily when large numbers
of persons are to be rated, and tends to approximate the multiple-
choice rating procedure described earlier.

---

[2] With appropriate scaling techniques, the pair comparison form of ranking can be converted to interval scales. (See Guilford, 1954.)

Although some writers refer to the ranking approach as a completely separate psychometric scaling technique, and thus not appropriate for discussion along with other rating procedures which are varieties of the successive category approach, ranking is used sufficiently often in judging human beings that it still seems desirable to include a description of it in this chapter. The ranking approach seems most desirable when but one rater is to describe an entire group of ratees. If several judges are ranking different sets of ratees to obtain a combined set of results for an entire group of subjects, it becomes necessary to assume that each set of ratees is essentially equivalent. If it is possible to start with a complete pool of subjects and draw equivalent samples from it, assigning each judge one sample, this assumption is not bothersome. Under the usual situation, however, where each rater ranks only the persons he happens to know, there is no guarantee that the assumption can be satisfied.

In general, the ranking approach has the advantage of forcing the judges to make definite discriminations among the ratees, and, in addition, eliminates differences from judge to judge with respect to leniency. On the other hand, if the number of subjects is very large, the ranking task becomes an extremely difficult one —though raters generally show less antagonism to rankings than they do toward forced choice scales. Another disadvantage of the ranking procedure is that the size of groups ranked must be uniform or special procedures used to correct for this when combining results. Finally, because the ordinal steps do not represent equal units of measure, it is inappropriate to use the mean as a measure of central tendency for obtaining composite ratings. Although the median might be used, problems still arise if it becomes necessary to interpolate between ranks. Guilford (1954) indicates that the simple sum of rank values will provide the best indication of an overall rank position when the results from several judges are to be combined.

Q-Sort. Another relative rating technique is the so-called Q-sort, developed by Stephenson (1953). In contrast with the ranking procedure described above, however, the judgment in this technique is among various behavior descriptions for a single individual rather than among several individuals for a given behavior. In this sense, then, the Q-sort is like the forced choice approach. The rater is given a series of cards on each of which a single statement describing the behavior is written. Following a successive category procedure, the rater is then required to sort the cards into a series of piles according to the extent to which the statements are descriptive of the person being rated. Usually, but not always, eleven piles going from most to least applicable are used and the statements have been weighted by a prior Thurstone-like (see Thurstone and Chave, 1929) scaling procedure. Each subject's score is then obtained by taking the sum of the products of the statement weight and the scale position.

When properly carried out, the Q-sort would seem to be one of the best approaches devised to obtain a comprehensive description of one individual. Because this technique does require considerable effort in the original scale preparation as well as raters who will give careful consideration to a long list of behaviors for each person to be rated, the Q-sort has not yet received the popularity it deserves. However, with modern computers, a Q-sort deck can be "distilled" in such a way that a great deal can now be accomplished with a relatively small number of items. Thus, it is possible that the Q-sort will become one of the most widely used ways of rating persons in school or on the job, as well as in research situations where it is desired to obtain comprehensive measures of changes either over a period of time or as a result of the introduction of some experimental variable.

OBTAINING SOUND RATINGS

It has been pointed out that just any rating scale, quickly devised, cannot be depended upon to provide accurate descriptions of the extent to which a person possesses some trait. As a matter of fact, a great many of the faults of rating scales can be attributed to the illusion that such devices are simple to construct. The user of rating scales, therefore, should be aware of several of the special problems which arise in the application of rating procedures, and should know some of the major techniques which have been developed to help overcome these difficulties.

Special Problems in Using Ratings

When ratings are used, errors arise which may be attributable to either the particular behavior under consideration or to the person who is doing the rating. Both will be considered in this section.

Errors Resulting from Rater Characteristics. To be sure, each individual rater will have his own unique biases and these idiosyncrasies will have an influence upon his particular ratings. This type of error, however, need be of no great concern to the careful user of rating scales. Appropriately motivated raters can be helped to overcome such specific biases, and, since they are different for each rater, they tend to cancel out when separately obtained individual ratings are pooled. The errors most bothersome are those which are constant in the sense that they seem to be similar for all or almost all raters. Failure to take appropriate measures to reduce these types of errors can lead to ratings which are of little value in spite of fairly high interrater reliability.

Perhaps the most widely observed constant error is that of *leniency*—a tendency of almost all raters in this country to be overly generous in their descriptions. Whether this arises because of a humane unwillingness to make unfavorable remarks about one's fellow man or because of an identification with the ratee such that a rater feels it is a reflection upon himself to give low ratings, scores on a rating scale of whatever format tend to pile up at the upper end of the scale. This error is so marked as to seriously reduce the discrimination power of rating scales at any place but the lower end, where even an average rating may signify a person who is quite low on the scale.

Another widely observed error is a tendency on the part of raters to obscure intraindividual differences by rating a given individual in the same way on all behaviors whether the characteristics tend to go together or not. This type of error has been detected by noting relatively high intercorrelations among ratings which, by other measures, seem to be relatively independent. Usually, this so-called *halo effect* is attributed to the fact that many raters allow an overall impression of the subject to influence their description of his specific behaviors. One of the important results of the halo error is to displace the ratings on each of a person's behaviors toward the average rating received on all of his behaviors.

Somewhat akin to the halo error are the *proximity* and *logical* errors. Proximity errors are those which arise because of a tendency for a judge to describe behaviors which appear close together on the printed rating sheet more nearly alike than they do behaviors which are physically separated by some distance. The logical error is a tendency for raters to rate a person similarly on characteristics which the rater feels should go together.

All of us tend to perceive other individuals in relationship to ourselves. This leads to a habit of raters to place others on a scale in contrast to their own characteristics. Thus, a generally optimistic individual tends to see others as more pessimistic than he is; and a generally pessimistic judge would displace the ratings toward the optimistic end of the scale. Whether this *contrast error* represents a reaction-formation or whether it simply reflects different standards held by the various judges is not clear. However, such a behavior-rater interaction effect can be serious if all of the raters happen to be persons who themselves lie at one general position on the scale.

One additional error which should be noted because it is typical of almost all raters is that referred to as the *error of central tendency*. Regardless of the descriptive phrases used, raters seem to avoid using the extreme positions on a rating scale. The effect of this error is to reduce the variability of the ratings and thus to make adequate discrimination among those rated more difficult to obtain.

In addition to those errors described above, there are several types still attributable to the rater which usually will be reflected in a lack of consistency from judge to judge (that is, a low inter-rater reliability). First, are the errors which result from the fact that a judge may have had only a limited contact with the person he is to rate, or perhaps is unwilling to take the trouble to do the kind of job that is required. The effect of lack of information (or refusal to use it) is generally to allow irrelevant and/or chance effects to influence the scale positions and thus to produce a wide variation in scores assigned to a given individual by several judges or even the same judge on two different occasions.

Even when the rater has had an opportunity to make adequate observations to know well the person he is to rate, there is a possibility of variable errors occuring. Each rater may hold a slightly different conception of the behavior under consideration or each different rater may be basing his ratings on somewhat different standards. In either case there may be marked consistency from time to time when the same judges are used, but wide differences at all times among the ratings given to the same individual by different judges.

Errors Resulting from the Behavior Selected.   Intuitively, it is perfectly reasonable to anticipate that some characteristics can be more dependably rated than others. It is not difficult to see that broadly defined general "traits" like good citizenship, kindliness, and adaptability might mean quite different things to different people; or that a person's kindliness, adaptability, and even good citizenship might vary markedly from one specific situation to the next. Similarly, it would be expected that such things as loneliness and sensitivity which refer to one's "inner" feelings and can only be inferred indirectly from certain observables would be more difficult to describe than the more overt characteristics such as talkativeness and perseverence. In fact, it might be said that traits are never really rated; that only behavior is described and scaled. The fact that some characteristics are more readily "rated" than others has been adcquately verified by a number of empirical studies of the interrater consistency with which various behaviors can be observed. Rather than attempting to compile a list of characteristics which can and cannot be rated with a reasonable degree of reliability, it is sufficient to point out that the interobserver agreement is highest for those characteristics which are specific entities rather than composites and for those characteristics which are directly descriptive of one's behavior rather than those derived indirectly by evaluation or by interpretations from different behaviors.

Techniques for the Improvement of Ratings

In spite of the many special problems outlined in the last section, ratings can be obtained which are both reliable and highly useful in a wide variety of situations. By restricting the use of ratings to particular behaviors, by following certain suggestions in the construction of the scales, by carefully selecting and training the raters, and through an appropriate analysis of the raw data gathered, the conscientious worker will be able to achieve measurements which are entirely satisfactory for most situations, both applied and research. The specific techniques by which each of these general approaches to the improvement of ratings can be carried out are described in the following sections.

Selecting the Proper Behaviors. The first rule in deciding whether to obtain ratings of a particular behavior is to eliminate those which can be measured by the more rigorous forms of testing. Next, the characteristic selected must be one which has a readily discernible and highly consistent meaning for a wide variety of judges. Any behavior which is to be appraised by means of rating scales should also be relatively specific. Highly complex behaviors are best handled by analyzing them into specific components and having the raters observe each specific behavior separately. Finally, attempts to assess future promise should be avoided in favor of ratings of past or present accomplishments.

In general, the further the characteristic is from a specific, readily observed behavior the less satisfactory the ratings will be. Any inferences to be made from the behaviors either to traits or to future performances should be left to later analysis and not required of the judges at the time of observation.

Building the Scales. The most dependable means for assuring adequate ratings is through the careful preparation of the rating scale itself. Many elaborate techniques have been devised to help to overcome some of the errors involved in using ratings. However, rating schemes which become too complex often result in sufficient rater resistance to add errors of a different type which are large enough to make the scale useless. The object, therefore, is to be able to develop the right kind of scale for the particular conditions of rater sophistication, time, information available, and ultimate use at hand.

One of the most important aspects of scale development is the selection of behavior labels which are short enough to fit on the scale yet sufficiently unambiguous to result in general uniformity of meaning for all potential raters. Usually, labels alone will not turn out to be satisfactory. Thus, it is almost always desirable to include a concise description, and, if possible, a few examples along with each behavior label. Some writers have suggested that the label and description be replaced entirely by the specific examples which a rater can simply check as present or absent. Although this will bring about the desired uniformity of meaning, such a listing makes the scale more complex, and if many behaviors are to be described, will almost always result in careless marking on the part of the raters. Therefore, it is generally recommended that short but precise descriptions be used.

Once a clear understanding of the individual behaviors has been accomplished, the next task is that of deciding how many steps should be used. It would seem reasonable, and studies by Champney and Marshall (1939) verify, that there will be an optimal number of steps above and below which it does not pay to proceed. If possible, it would seem best to determine what this number is empirically in each specific situation. Early studies by Symonds (1924) indicated that seven would be sufficient for most purposes, and that even fewer would produce as much accuracy as could be obtained when complex behaviors or naive, unmotivated raters were used. Guilford (1954) now, however, feels that seven is usually lower than optimal, and suggests that under some conditions as many as twenty-five steps should be used. Most popularly used rating scales still use somewhere between five and eleven, however.

In addition to deciding on the number of steps, it is usually necessary to provide the rater with reference points at various positions along the scales. The use of general terms like "average," "excellent," and "very poor" should be avoided, if possible, because they mean different things to different raters. The more specific the cues, the better. At the same time, extreme words are likely to be avoided by raters and therefore contribute to the central tendency error. Thus, words like "never" and "always" should not be used as cues. Champney (1941) provides an excellent list of characteristics of useful cues. It is possible to further reduce the piling up of scores on one end and to obtain some degree of uniformity of standards by indicating the percentages of a group which are likely to be found at each level.

When the individual behavior scales have been adequately developed, it is necessary to organize them into a complete rating instrument. The way in which the behaviors are listed can be of some help in reducing certain of the types of errors described earlier. Ideally, the best way to eliminate both proximity and halo errors would be to have each scale placed on a separate card and to have the judges rate one behavior, then wait a period of time sufficient to obliterate their recollection of the way in which the previous characteristic was rated before turning to the next. Because such a procedure can be followed only under the most unusual of circumstances, various compromise suggestions have been made. For example, it has been suggested that proximity errors can be considerably reduced simply by placing behaviors which are judged to logically go together as far from one another as possible in the physical makeup of the scale. Similarly, it has been suggested that halo errors can be reduced by alternating the direction of the "high" end of the trait scales. Although this latter approach would seem to reduce the halo effect, at least one writer (Guilford, 1954) has contended that such a format is so confusing to inexperienced raters that sufficient clerical errors are likely to be made to offset any advantage which such a format may have in other respects. Thus, for naive raters, it is recommended that all scales be set up with the "high" end of the scale at the top or toward the left.

Perhaps the best practical suggestion is to have each judge rate all subjects on a given behavior before he turns to the next. A format which lists each behavior on a separate page, say across the top, and places the persons to be rated following it will facilitate this approach. When trained judges are used (so that the unusual format is not disturbing), the listing of the names across the top and placing the descriptions of the various forms which the behavior can take on vertical rather than horizontal scales has the advantages of permitting longer cues to be used and of pinpointing the cues more precisely along the continuum. Both formats have the additional advantage of encouraging a more stable standard for a given judge from one ratee to the next.

Selecting and Training the Raters.   No matter how well constructed the rating scale might be, if it is misused by those doing the rating, the results will be unsatisfactory. Thus, one of the most effective ways of insuring adequate results from this approach to measurement is in the careful selection and training of those who will do the rating.

Obviously, it is impossible for a person who has had inadequate opportunity to observe the subjects to provide accurate descriptions even with the best of scales. Thus, the first rule in selecting raters is to choose only those who have or can be provided with the opportunity to make the necessary observations of the subject and to make them in pertinent situations. Next, it is important to try to secure raters who are willing to provide the necessary information without distortion. This latter task may prove somewhat difficult since it is not always possible to detect those who seem to derive pleasure out of faking the results. However, some simple common sense suggestions can be helpful in this respect. Persons who seem to delight in criticizing everybody and everything, persons who through family ties, social friendships, or employment relationships may be ego-involved in the outcome, and persons who may have to face the person rated with his ratings are not likely to be able to provide unbiased ratings no matter how conscientious they are. Finally, in the selection of raters, it would appear that the contrast error can be reduced if care is taken to use judges who themselves represent the entire range of the scale being used.

Perhaps the first task in the training of raters to use a scale appropriately is to convince them of the value of honest and accurate ratings. If this can be accomplished with properly selected judges, the greatest difficulty in obtaining good ratings will have been overcome. Next, simply pointing out the types of errors which raters are likely to make and providing some suggestions for avoiding them can be a great deal of help. For example, a simple awareness of the existence of halo errors and an understanding as to why one should rate all subjects on one trait, then all subjects on the second trait, and so on, proves extremely valuable in eliminating this bothersome error. If, in addition to just telling the raters about the errors, it is possible to have them obtain some practice with the specific instrument they are to use and on persons similar to those for whom the ratings are desired, much more can be accomplished. Practice, of course, is valuable only if knowledge of the results can be secured. Thus, it is desirable that the pilot use of the instrument be executed under supervision, and essential that the results of these practice ratings be discussed. Not only will the viewing and discussion of the results illustrate the types of errors which occur, but they will be very helpful in clarifying the meaning of the descriptions used along the scale positions and in developing a uniform standard among all the judges.

Analyzing and Using the Results.   A final opportunity to make ratings the most accurate descriptions possible under the circumstances arises from combining and analyzing the results. The reliability of ratings can be greatly improved by pooling the results from several judges who have made their ratings independently. When such a procedure is followed, the individual errors and biases tend to cancel out, and the lack of information on the part of one rater may be compensated for by the results from the others. Studies have indicated that the combining of ratings in this way has an effect similar to that of lengthening a test. In fact, the Spearman-Brown formula presented earlier can be used to predict the increase in reliability which can be obtained by pooling the results of a given number of judges.

It is important to note that the value of pooling judgments is greatest when the individual ratings have been obtained independently. Having all raters sit down together to arrive at a joint rating would seem to provide a description which is influenced greatly by the personality interactions of the judges. For example, a dominant, or a highly persuasive, or a socially prestigeful person may have far greater influence on the joint result than is desirable.

If the ratings are obtained in a situation in which it is imperative that the results be as accurate as possible without consideration of time or expense for additional analysis, further modifications can be made. Guilford (1954) for example, has developed a rationale for errors of rating and presents techniques for making adjustments to eliminate the effects of leniency, halo, and rater-trait interaction errors. Also, many of the standard psychometric techniques which are presented in more advanced books can be used to raise the level of measurement from ordinal to at least an interval scale. Thus, if sufficient care and trouble are taken, rating scales can be used to obtain highly satisfactory quantitative descriptions of many behaviors which cannot be studied by other measuring devices.

9

Multiple Measurement

ALL OF THE PRINCIPLES of testing discussed in previous chapters have been concerned with the construction, evaluation, and use of a single measuring device. Whether the instrument used measured a single unitary trait or a highly complex function which was the result of many subtraits, the result was assumed to be a single numerical report of the extent to which a person possessed the characteristic of concern. In this chapter, however, attention will be given to the examination of some additional principles of measurement which arise when several different measures are used in combination in an attempt to make a more intelligent decision than would be possible without test information.

As might be anticipated, the minute more than one score is used in combination, several special problems arise which demand a reassessment of the testing situation with respect to constant, variable, and interpretive errors of psychological measurement. Thus, consideration will first be given to the special problems of validity, reliability, and standardization which arise in multiple measurement. Next, procedures, both graphic and algebraic, for combining several measures will be described; and finally, the situation in which there are multiple criteria as well as multiple measurements will be discussed.

SPECIAL PROBLEMS

Validity of a Combination of Scores

It should be obvious that when more than one test is used at a time, a great deal more evidence in the way of validity is needed than when each test is used by itself. Not only must each test itself be valid, but there must be additional evidence that the particular combination of test results is valid for the particular use to which it is to be put. That is, we must have empirical evidence that the inferences we would like to make from the particular combination of scores we have are valid.

For example, suppose it is desired to select students for a special course in remedial reading through the use of a combination of reading scores and academic ability scores. The idea is to select students whose academic grades will likely improve following the additional instruction, as contrasted with those who might be better readers, but who will still fail out of college. One common procedure has been to simply use a reading-scholastic ability score discrepancy for such selection purposes, admitting only those who had high academic ability, but who were low in reading achievement. Usually, it has been simply assumed that since the scholastic ability test was valid and since the reading achievement test scores were valid, the difference between the two would result in a combination which was a valid selection device.

In one study, however (Helmstadter, 1958), it was discovered that such a selection procedure did not result in dividing students into two groups which differed with respect to grade-point average when controlling for scholastic ability. Thus, in this particular instance, even though the two separate tests were each valid in their own right, the combination of scores used was not valid for the stated purpose. In this instance, the solution to the problem was to use each test independently in a two-step process. First, underachievers were identified with the ability test and grades. Then, the underachievers were given the test in reading achievement to help to determine which of them might not be succeeding because of poor reading.

Reliability of Differences

The problem of variable error and reliability also requires special consideration when more than one measure or score is used. One reason is that all too often, and especially in the diagnostic uses of testing, full length tests are not combined. Rather, subtests, or other part scores are used in special combination. In many instances, then, the resulting diagnostic indices are based on short tests of 20 to 40 items as compared with total scores and common measures composed of 100 to 120 items, on which the reliability estimates are usually based. Recalling the relationship between test length and reliability discussed earlier and described by the Spearman-Brown prophecy formula, it is not difficult to imagine the tremendous loss in reliability which occurs when subtests or part scores are used. Thus, to be fully aware of the score fluctuations likely to be encountered when using a combination of scores, the reliability of each separate part must be determined as well as the reliability of the total test. As a specific example, Derner, Aborn, and Carter (1950) have reported subtest reliability for the Wechsler Intelligence Scale as low as .62, while the full scale had a reliability of .90.

Unfortunately, the fact that shorter tests are often used when combinations of measures are employed is not the only reason for concern about variable errors. The problem of reliability is also of special concern because, in many instances, score differences (rather than additive combinations) are used. Except under very unusual circumstances (and one not likely to arise in practice) the difference between two scores is less reliable than the reliability of either score alone.

This result is readily seen by looking at the formula which expresses the reliability of the difference between two measures as a function of the reliability of each and the correlation between them.

$$(45) \qquad r_{(X-Y)(X-Y)} = \frac{\dfrac{r_{XX} + r_{YY}}{2} - r_{XY}}{1 - r_{XY}},$$

where:

$r_{(X-Y)(X-Y)}$ = the reliability of the difference between score X and score Y

r_{XX} = the reliability of the X scores

r_{YY} = the reliability of the Y scores

r_{XY} = the correlation between the two test scores.

From this formula it is apparent that unless the two tests are negatively correlated, the reliability of the difference will be smaller than the reliability of the average of the two.

Just how great an effect this will be can be seen from a case in which one test correlates .60 with the second, while the reliability of one is .86 and of the other is .90. Substituting these values in the formula we obtain:

$$\frac{\dfrac{.86 + .90}{2} - .60}{1 - .60} = \frac{.28}{.40} = .70.$$

Thus, it becomes apparent that in the case of reliability, just as in the case of validity, evidence must be gathered which will evaluate the *combination* as used. It is never safe to make the assumption that just because each component meets acceptable standards, the simultaneous use of multiple measures will achieve the reliability necessary for practical application.

Comparability of Norms

The third problem which becomes especially important in using more than one test at a time is the lack of comparability of the groups used in the standardization of the different tests. Strictly speaking, only if the various measures to be used have all been standardized on the same individuals is it possible to appropriately use combinations of the scores. From a practical point of view, however, if the norm groups used with one test are comparable in the sense of having been (or able to consider to be) samples from the same population as the norm groups for the other tests, the test user is on safe grounds. One must be careful, however, to take the time to examine carefully the norm groups which are used for each test, and to assure himself that they all contain approximately the same proportions of persons from given age, sex, school grade, geographical region, etc. groups.

To illustrate the way in which failure to do this can affect inferences from test scores, consider an example, which, while perhaps exaggerated, does illustrate the point.

Suppose a high school student was having difficulty with his schoolwork and his teacher, knowing that the boy had recently been given both a reading and a scholastic ability test, hurriedly looked up his scores. Upon noting the percentile rank for reading to be 16 and that for scholastic ability to be 84, the teacher concluded that the student's difficulty was very likely due to his lack of accomplishment in reading. Suppose, however, a more careful examination of the case folder indicated that the reading test was one developed and standardized at the state university, while the general aptitude test had been standardized on draftees at an induction center in one of our southern states. It is clear that the conclusions might be quite different. For example, if the mean of the college students on whom the reading test was standardized happened to be one standard deviation above that for high school students and the adult population used in standardizing the scholastic ability test was one standard deviation below the high school mean, we would have the situation illustrated in Figure 25.

Converting the scores to a comparable group (the HS group), it is found that the correct Percentile Rank to interpret in each case is 50. Now, the high school teacher will probably attribute the scholastic difficulty to lack of motivation, home problems, etc. rather than either lack of scholastic ability or reading.

COMBINING THE RESULTS OF SEVERAL MEASURES

If one attempts to use several measures at once, he must have some way of combining the results to make a single overall estimate or single description of what the subject is like. Whether this is done explicitly with precise weights or implicitly by a

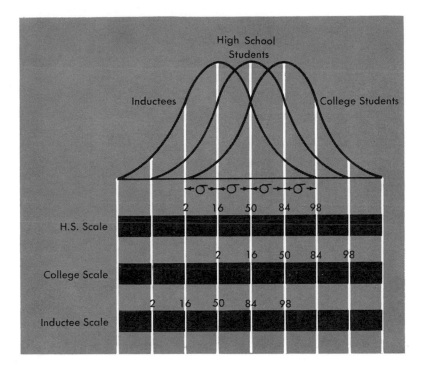

FIGURE 25: Hypothetical Scales for the Interpretation of High School Tests When Reported Norms are for a College and an Inductee Population

judgmental process, the weighting and combining *is* done, and the user of more than one test at a time should be aware of several things which may have an important influence on this combination of measures.

Graphic Combination—Profiles

One of the most common ways of representing a series of measures on the same individual is by means of a test score profile. The test profile is obtained by letting various points along the horizontal axis represent different tests, and drawing a line or bar such that the height represents the magnitude of the scores received. Sometimes the tips of the lines or bars are connected. Two typical test score profiles are shown in Figures 26 and 27.

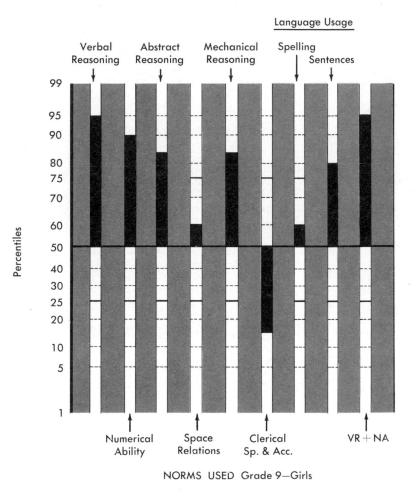

FIGURE 26: Typical Bar Graph Profile

Source: G. Bennett, H. Seashore, and A. Wesman, *A Manual for the Differential Aptitude Test*, 1959. Reproduced by permission of The Psychological Corporation. Copyright 1947, 1952, 1959.

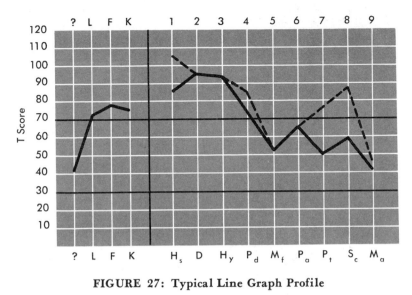

FIGURE 27: Typical Line Graph Profile

Source: *An MMPI Handbook: A Guide to Use in Clinical Practice and Research* by Grant Dahlstrom and George Schlager Welsh. University of Minnesota Press, Minneapolis. Copyright 1960 by the University of Minnesota.

If carefully used, the test score profile can be a valuable aid in visualizing the psychometric characteristics of an individual or of a group of individuals. However, as with many other ostensibly simple aids, there are some dangers which need to be avoided.

First of all, in plotting profiles, it is absolutely essential that some form of derived score be used; otherwise, a large score may signify a long test or an easy test rather than a large amount of whatever characteristic it measures. Most published forms on which profiles can be plotted provide for an automatic conversion from raw score to either percentile scores, grade scores, or standard scores.

Second, it is essential that the derived score plotted on a given test profile be obtained from the same or at least a demonstrably comparable standardization group; otherwise, the profile will lead to misinterpretations such as those illustrated in the previous section in the case of the high school student who was having scholastic difficulty. Finally, it must be noted that while the order in which the tests are listed is arbitrarily determined, once a decision has been made, the same order must be used for every single case. Otherwise, two highly similar profiles may represent extremely different patterns of ability and two persons with highly similar ability or achievement patterns may end up with test score profiles which appear extremely dissimilar.

When making judgments on the basis of test score profiles, it should be kept in mind that there are three major character-istics of profiles which need to be considered: *level, variability,* and *shape.* Profiles which differ in any one of the characteristics should not be considered similar, since they would lead to differ-ent inferences from the scores. By level is meant overall level of performance as shown by the average height of the graph. Thus, in Figure 28, profiles *A*, *B*, and *D* all represent the same level of performance, even though, in other respects, they are extremely

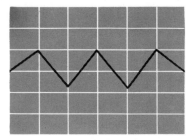

Profile A

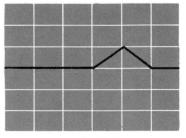

Profile B

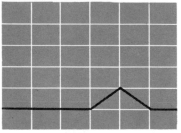

Profile C

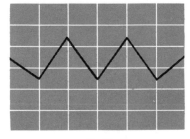

Profile D

FIGURE 28: Four Hypothetical Test Score Profiles Plotted on the Same Scale

different profiles. The term variability as applied to test score profiles refers to the extent of intraindividual differences indicated. A person with a high degree of intraindividual variability will have scores which vary considerably from one test to the next, while a person with little intraindividual variability will perform at about the same level on all tests. In Figure 28 profiles A and D show a great amount of variability, while profiles B and C show little variability. The term *shape* refers to differences between profiles which remain after level and variability have been accounted for, and represent different patterns of variation. Profiles A and D represent different patterns of ability even though they are at the same level and have the same variability; profiles B and C show the same shape (and variability) even though they differ markedly in level. There is some evidence that when users of test scores take all three characteristics into consideration, they can make fairly accurate judgments (and interpretations) of profiles, but that when one or more of the characteristics is ignored, serious misinterpretations can result.

Algebraic Combination—Weighting

Whenever the appropriate data is available and when time permits, it is generally considered better to combine the results of several measurements into a single index explicitly with numerical weights rather than judgmentally, even when aided with a test score profile. Although some writers have argued that the usual systems for weighting do not take into account the curvilinear relationships or the higher order interactions among the variables as can a judgmental process, at least one study has indicated that such complex relationships are not often found in practice. Thus, for most purposes, a simple additive combination (not necessarily unit weights) of the scores is adequate; and, if not, it is only necessary to use a more sophisticated mathematical weighting scheme, not to abandon explicit numerical combinations.

When using even a simple numerical weighting scheme (such as just adding the scores together to arrive at a total), it is essential to note, however, that there is a real difference between the apparent weights assigned to each test score and the effective contribution it makes to the total or composite test score. For example, in attempting to obtain a complete measure of reading facility, a combination of reading speed, reading comprehension, and vocabulary scores may be desired. Unfortunately, using the combination

$$6X + 3Y + Z = \text{composite score,}$$

where:

$$X = \text{comprehension}$$
$$Y = \text{speed}$$
$$Z = \text{vocabulary,}$$

will not guarantee that comprehension will have twice the importance that speed has, or that vocabulary will have an effect upon the scores only one-third that of speed. This is because the actually effective weights are dependent upon two other things besides the ostensible (or assigned or apparent) weights. In addition to the assigned weights, the contribution of the different parts is a function of the variance of the part scores and the intercorrelation among the parts.

The reasonableness of these relationships can be seen by examining an extreme case. Suppose, in the reading example cited above, that every child read at exactly the same rate. Thus, the variance of the reading speed scores would be zero. Adding reading speed scores to the comprehension and vocabulary measures would amount to adding an arbitrary constant to every total score. Thus, in no way do we have more information about the extent to which the children differ in their reading achievement than we had at the start. Thus, in this instance, the contribution of reading speed to the composite score is zero. In general, the larger the variance of the part scores, the greater contribution that part will make to the composite score.

Similarly, if there were a perfect correlation between reading speed and vocabulary scores, then the vocabulary measure would add nothing new to a composite of speed and comprehension. The effect of adding vocabulary would simply be that of increasing the apparent weight given to the reading speed scores.

If, then, the apparent weights and the effective weights are *not* the same, the question arises as to whether or not anything at all can be said about the nominal (assigned) weights and their effectiveness. Gulliksen (1950) points out the following generalizations:

1. If a large number of scores are to be combined (say fifty or more)

   OR

   if the scores being combined have high inter-correlations, it makes very little difference what set of positive weights are used.

2. If only a few scores (say less than ten) are combined

   AND

   if the average inter-correlation of the variables is less than .50, different nominal weights *will* be effective.

3. If the assigned weights are to be given appreciably different results than a simple addition of the part scores (a nominal weight of one in each case) the assigned *weights* must have a large variance.

4. If two alternative sets of weights are highly inter-correlated, then it will make little difference which is used.*

It is apparent, then, that using different weights for different items in a typical multiple-choice test, or a rating scale of reasonable length will not prove significantly valuable, but for essay exams with only a few items, or when combining a few subscores to obtain a composite score, the weights used will make a difference. If the situation does not fit either of the extremes described by Gulliksen, then a weighting scheme may or may not be of value depending upon the special circumstances involved. In this situation, it is probably best to try several weighting schemes and to note what happens empirically.

If the circumstances are such that differential weighting is worthwhile, a decision must be reached as to what weights to assign. When a reliable external criterion is available, it is best to use multiple regression weights—that is, those weights (determined by a multiple regression analysis) which will maximize the correlation between the criterion and the composite scores. When no external criterion is available, then the use of expert judgment

* H. Gulliksen, *Theory of Mental Tests* (New York: John Wiley and Sons, Inc., 1950).

as to the weight each part should have seems most defensible. To make sure, however, that these assigned weights come close to being the effective weights, it is necessary to cancel the effect of different variabilities of the part scores. For all practical purposes, this can be accomplished simply by dividing each assigned weight by the standard deviation of the scores for that part.

One other procedure which may be reasonably used to determine weights in the absence of an external criterion is that which maximizes the reliability of the composite. Whenever the validity of the composite scores can be assumed, this is an acceptable approach. However, if the assumption does not hold, a highly reliable but completely useless composite score may be obtained.

Some authors have suggested other schemes, for example, weighting in terms of the average scores on the parts, weighting in terms of the size of perfect scores, or weighting on the basis of the number of items. For the most part, however, there is no logical justification for such arbitrary approaches. Use of a system of automatically determined weights merely to avoid judgment is *not* a defensible procedure.

MULTIPLE CRITERIA

The last major topic of concern in multiple measurement is the situation in which not only several predictor measures are involved, but several criterion measures as well. This situation arises in problems of vocational or academic choice where a person is interested in his likely success in many occupations or fields of study; and it arises in military or industrial placement problems where the task is to accomplish maximal overall efficiency of operation by arriving at the best overall fitting of personnel to jobs (which may not be the best for every single individual).

In the research literature, this type of problem is generally discussed under the heading of *differential* and/or of *comparative* prediction. In differential prediction an attempt is made to determine *relatively* likely level of performance of a person among several tasks. For example, Will Mr. *A* do better in art than in business? (or how much better?): In comparative prediction the goal is to predict absolute level of performance in each of several tasks. Thus, for example, even though Mr. *A* may do *better* in art than in business, he may not do sufficiently well in either area to succeed.

Although there are many variants of the solution to this problem of multiple measures and multiple criteria, there seem to be only four basic approaches. These will be referred to as the *specific validity*, the *multiple cut-off*, the *multiple regression*, and the *multiple discriminant function* approaches. The remainder of the chapter will be concerned with describing the differences among these basic approaches and pointing out the advantages and disadvantages of each.

Specific Validity

This first approach, while most commonly used of all, hardly deserves the name technique. Actually, it refers to what must be done in the absence of data directed specifically to comparative prediction. Nevertheless, some authors find a rationale behind it. The argument runs something like this:

Validity is specific. There is no "validity of a test," there are only empirical "validities" describing the usefulness of the test in numerous situations. Out of the mass of data, generalizations emerge regarding the test's effectiveness. Validation is a never-ending process. The test user himself must evaluate and integrate all the data available to him. As the counsellor accumulates experience, the separate test scores take on increased meaning as measurements of human abilities.

Although one might agree with all of these statements taken separately, simply because they are bunched together, "en masse," they do not provide a very good argument for failing to get data designed specifically to answer the question at hand. What this philosophy leads to (as one writer has put it) is a horrendous mass of validity data through which the counsellor must plow, and which he must digest and skillfully use to somehow build up an accurate construct or picture of what the individual is really like. Then, from this picture, the test user makes his predictions. From the evidence on actuarial versus clinical prediction gathered by Meehl (1954) (see Chapter 1) it should be apparent that this is not the ideal approach—though a possible one when the appropriate data is not available.

Multiple Cut-Off Approach

The second general approach is that used by the U.S. Employment Service in connection with its General Aptitude Test Battery. Actually, this method provides only a rough guide as to the individual's probability of success in various occupations. What it does do is to indicate whether or not an applicant meets the minimum qualifications for various job families.

Typically, what happens is this. The entire battery is given to inexperienced workers applying for the job in question. Hiring is done without benefit of the scores. Then, after the workers are well beyond the training stage of their work, they are rated on their job performance.

Next, a thorough job analysis is made, and correlations are computed between the test scores and the performance on the ratings. From these results, "Key" aptitudes are selected on the basis of the following considerations as described by Dvorak (1953):

1. Higher mean (standard) score relative to the population and relative to mean scores on the other tests. The assumption here is that persons successful on the job will have a high score on those aptitudes which are important.
2. A *low* S.D. relative to that for the general population and for other tests. The assumption here is that successful persons will be relatively homogeneous in aptitudes important for that job. That is, if an aptitude is really important, those having low and medium scores will not be successful. Thus, among those remaining on the job, the range of scores will be small.
3. A correlation between job performance and the aptitude score which is significant at or beyond the 1 per cent level, that is, the test has to have empirical validity for the job.
4. Corroboration evidence from the job analysis that the aptitude is a necessary one. This latter is important to eliminate as "Key" aptitudes those which workers have in common different from others but are still not important to the job. For example, it was found in one study that mechanics get a high score on a test of carelessness. Carelessness is not, however, an essential requirement to be a good mechanic—as shown by the job analysis.*

* B. Dvorak, in "Conference on Using Multi-Factor Aptitude Tests in Education and Vocational Counseling and Prediction."

Once the "Key" aptitudes have been selected, norms are established in terms of minimum requirements of each aptitude for the job in question. These cutting scores are set mathematically at the point which provides the maximum differentiation between the good and the poor workers. Generally, though not always, this score turns out to be around 1 S.D. below the mean of the entire distribution of scores based upon persons employed in the job (that is, the good and poor workers combined, but *not* including scores for people in general).

Finally, these cutting scores are checked on a new sample of workers in the particular occupation. Then, in a counselling situation, an applicant is considered to have the requisite aptitudes for the specific jobs *if and only if* he exceeds the critical qualifying score for each of the key aptitudes for that job. Thus, falling down on any one of these disqualifies him.

This lengthy description of the GATB validation will convince the reader that the answer to the problem of comparative prediction is not a simple one. It requires a great deal of painstakingly gathered data. As far as it goes, however, this technique probably provides the best kind of evidence now available for comparative prediction. What is needed to solve the problem more completely is a set of critical scores not only for a minimum level of success in each occupation, but for each of several degrees of success within the occupation. That is, it would be desirable to have different sets of cutting scores for successful, above average successful, and highly successful. Until this is done, however, the process will remain that of eliminating from among the jobs which an applicant or counsellee is considering, those in which he definitely would not succeed.

Multiple Discriminant Function

The third basic approach to the problem of comparative prediction employs a statistical technique which combines the results of a whole series of measurements in such a way as to optimally predict to which one of several groups or classes of people an individual belongs (just as the multiple regression approach to be discussed next enables us to combine a series of measurements in such a way as to best predict some criterion score). At first glance this technique appears to be ideal. A whole series of measures and a set of occupational groups are available. The task is to assign an individual, on the basis of these measures, to one of the groups. While, under certain circumstances, this procedure is one of the most satisfactory, there are a number of disadvantages which make it less useful than often supposed.

To begin with, it might be noted that the Multiple Discriminant Function is the statistical solution to the problem of matching profiles. In a sense, what the discriminant function does is to mathematically compare an individual profile with a set of group profiles and to indicate which group profile the individual one comes "closest" to matching. Note that in profile matching the only criterion is whether person A (with respect to the aptitudes measured) is more like successful people in occupation X than he is like successful people in occupation Y and Z. With this kind of evidence alone, there is no information as to whether those aptitudes which best distinguish among groups are essential for success, and there is no evidence, once an individual has been classified, as to the extent to which he is likely to be successful. It is only *assumed* that if an individual is in an occupation with people like himself, he will be successful. Under these circumstances there is considerable possibility of making an error which is so carefully avoided with the GATB multiple cutoff approach by means of the job analysis, namely, assigning a person to the occupation of mechanics simply because, like other mechanics, he was careless. While an assumption of the similarity-success relationship may be valid when concern is with interest and/or job satisfaction as a measure of success, it seems far less reasonable when referring to aptitudes and job performance.

There is, however, a saving factor to the procedure of assigning persons to occupational groups purely on the basis of matching. Through the process of natural selection in job success, and in recent years through occupational guidance work, people do better than chance in getting into an appropriate field of work. Thus, using the similarity approach, it is possible to do some good. On the other hand, this technique does not help people to be placed in any more appropriate jobs than are the people in the criterion groups. That is, it merely perpetuates the success and the mistakes that people *now* make in getting placed.

There is also another weakness of this process which is very bothersome. This becomes obvious when it is remembered that the group profile is based upon what the average person in the occupational group is like. Thus, a person who deviates from the average by having high aptitude in all the measures will show the same degree of dissimilarity as a person low in all the aptitudes. For example, the best engineer of the whole group may be just as far from the average of the group as the worst engineer. And, with the multiple discriminant function, only similarity is considered. Thus, there is no way of knowing whether a deviation of a given person is in a desirable direction for success or in an undesirable direction, or in a side direction which makes no difference at all.

On the positive side, the multiple discriminant function provides us with the best possible answer to the classification problem when no continuous criterion measure of the degree of success is available. Thus, if the only criterion data available is grouping by occupations, by academic areas, by socioeconomic levels, by pass-fail, and so forth, then the multiple discriminant function provides the appropriate technique to use.

Multiple Regression

The final approach to the problem of comparative prediction is one which probably gives the most direct answer to the question, but which requires a number of assumptions that cannot always be met in practice. This is the multiple regression technique, by means of which it is possible to predict, from a set of measures, either differences between criterion scores or the separate criterion scores directly. When the prediction is of differences between a pair of criterion scores, the result is an answer to the question as to which of two occupational groups an individual belongs; when the prediction is of the criterion scores separately, an estimate of the extent to which the individual is likely to be successful in the particular occupation is obtained.

Regardless of which of the two is done, the form of the prediction equation will be as follows:

$$(46) \qquad Y_j = a_j + b_{j1}X_1 + b_{j2}X_2 + \ldots + b_{jk}X_k,$$

where Y_j represents a criterion of success in a particular occupation (occupation j) or difference between criterion scores in a pair of occupations, and the X_1, X_2, and so forth represent aptitude test scores. The $a_j, b_{j1},$ and so forth are the regression weights which will be different for each criterion and which are determined in such a way as to mathematically minimize the error of prediction. By considering this prediction equation, we can determine some of the limitations of the method. In the first place, a linear relationship between test scores and criterion is assumed. Whether this assumption holds can be readily detected in the case where all regression weights but one are seen (as in the familiar case where there is but one predictor and one criterion), but not so easily when more than one measure is involved.

Although, as noted in the discussion of weighting, curvilinear relationships do not appear too often, they do occur in some situations. For example, in some clerical and production line jobs, either a *low* or a *high* scholastic ability might indicate poor on-the-job performance. As seen in Figure 29, the effect of a

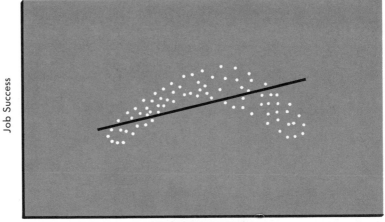

Scholastic Aptitude

FIGURE 29: Possible Relationship Between Scholastic Aptitude and Performance on a Production Line Job

curvilinear relationship on a correlation is to reduce it. Thus, it is possible to give only a small weight or to eliminate entirely a predictor which would be very useful if linearity had not been assumed.

While assuming linearity when it does not exist might not be a very serious error since all that happens is that the prediction is not made as accurately as it otherwise might be, failure to meet a second assumption can have serious consequences. The second assumption made is that exceptionally high ability in one area can compensate for low ability in a second. Suppose, for a particular criterion, the prediction equation was

$$Y - 5X_1 + 10X_2 + 7X_3.$$

Consider two individuals who receive the following set of scores:

	X_1	X_2	X_3
Person A	10	5	0
Person B	7	3	5 .

For both persons, $Y = 100$. That is, both persons would be predicted to have the same degree of success. Yet, person A has not even a measurable minimum of ability measured by X_3. If the aptitude X_3 is important for the job, and surely it is or it would not be in the equation at all (for it would have a zero weight), person A is almost certain to fail. He received a high prediction of success only because he has far better than average ability in aptitudes X_1 and X_2. This is the kind of error which the multiple cut-off approach, described earlier, was specifically designed to avoid.

There is a third difficulty with the multiple regression approach which is not apparent from the prediction equation. This involves the comparability of the samples from which the regression weights for the different occupational criteria have been developed. To get at a prediction of the difference between two criteria, it is necessary to have the correlation between the criterion scores. Since a series of paired scores is needed to compute a correlation, this means that it is necessary to have a score on both criteria for a number of subjects. In an academic situation, where the criteria are, say, grades in English, grades in Math, grades in Chemistry, etc. this is no problem. *But,* in a job situation, this kind of data is seldom available. Not very many people have been both mechanics and beauticians or both clerks and carpenters. Thus, there is no way of obtaining the pairs of criterion measures needed to make prediction of differences between criterion scores.

Even when the goal is only to make predictions of the absolute level of success in one occupation and to compare it with those in another, the groups on which the validity coefficients are based should not be radically different. If they are, it is quite possible to get a restriction of range on important variables through natural selection. The effect of restriction on range is the same as that of curvilinearity—except more serious. The chances are that only a small weight, perhaps even a zero one, will be given to the most important factors.

In summary, there are four basic approaches to comparative prediction: it is possible to look at all the data, to arrive at a clinical impression of what the person is like, and to make a prediction; it is possible to use a set of multiple cut-off scores to eliminate those occupations for which the person is not qualified; it is possible to compare the individual, on a series of aptitude measures, with others now successful in the field, recommending that he become a member of the group he most resembles; or it is possible to combine test scores to reach an optimum prediction of each of the criteria noting the extent to which an individual is likely to be successful on each. Perhaps, in a practical situation, all four approaches might be used in the following manner:

1. Eliminate occupations for which there is definitely no aptitude (multiple cut-off).
2. Match up the individual with successful people in each of several occupations on the basis of interest and personality variables (discriminant function).
3. Use the multiple regression technique to make absolute prediction of success for those occupations which in Step 2 seemed to be likely possibilities.

If no really appropriate data is available, then the only possibility is to study as many specific validity coefficients as can be found and to make a clinical judgment.

10

Overview

FROM RETROSPECT TO PROSPECT

THE MEASUREMENT OF behavioral characteristics has come a long way from the simple sensory-motor performances studied as mental traits in the early laboratories of Galton and Cattell; and even from the single, global index of the "more complex" traits which Binet in France and Terman in this country made so famous. In their stead we find, today, complex systems of selection and decision theory (see Cronbach and Gleser, 1957), elaborate schemata for the classification of traits both cognitive and noncognitive (see Guilford, 1957, 1959), entire books written in the language of mathematics on a single topic such as item analysis (see Solomon, 1961) or on the interpretation of a single test (see Hathaway and Meehl, 1951), and gigantic electronic test data processing installations such as that developed by Lindquist at the State University of Iowa.

At the same time that the concepts, the techniques, and the procedures of measurement have become more complex, the application of testing has extended from the laboratory to the schools, to the armed services, to the hospitals, to the business office, and even to the Sunday supplement, until now there is hardly a person whose life is not at one time or another, influenced by a test score. One of the consequences of this two-way expansion is a consumer of tests who, all too often, is prone to throw up his hands in horror, frightened by the technology involved, afraid that, somehow, all of this knowledge will lead to less rather than more humane treatment of each person as a unique individual. But those who seek simple devices for the description of man's characteristics and who wish to apply them without taking the time to understand the concepts involved, must remember that each person is truly a unique and complex individual and that it is not so strange, therefore, that to study him as such requires complicated ideas, complicated instruments, and complicated procedures.

SUMMARY OF CURRENT PRINCIPLES

The state of our knowledge today, less than eighty years after the first clear-cut concepts in the measurement of other than physical and physiological human traits made their appearance, is such that no single volume, nor any one individual, can present all the topics and all the pieces of detailed information which have been gathered and reported in the literature. On the other hand, the basic concepts, even though complex, are not too many for everyone to learn. Each has been spelled out in some detail with appropriate examples in the preceding chapters. Here, so that they stand out clearly and so that the relationship among them becomes more apparent, the major principles and ideas will simply be restated.

The Logic of Testing

In its broadest sense, measurement can be thought of as the process of obtaining numerical descriptions of the extent to which a person (or thing) possesses some characteristic. Thus defined, several different levels of measurement are discernible: the *nominal* level, in which numbers are used simply as labels to define different classes of things; the *ordinal* level, in which the objects measured can be put in a rank order from highest to lowest; an *interval* level in which it can be assumed that the distance between units on the scale is the same throughout the range of measurement involved; and finally, a *ratio* level in which a value of zero is meaningful in an absolute (as contrasted with relative) sense. Only when measurements are at the highest level are all of the ordinary operations of arithmetic legitimate. Since measures of behavioral characteristics often reach only the ordinal level, various derived scores must be obtained from the raw numerical report of performance before interpretations can be appropriately made.

The so-called mental traits which are measured at the various levels just described are best thought of as hypothetical constructs invented by psychologists to explain certain behavioral relationships which have been observed. As such, the exact nature of traits such as intelligence, mechanical ability, artistic aptitude, and so forth, cannot be specified. Thus, when making use of tests for measuring individuals with respect to these traits, it is essential to fully understand the particular construct under consideration as well as the way in which the numerical description is obtained. No test, scale, or other device can be thought of as yielding an absolutely true measure of intelligence, aptitude, knowledge, interest, attitude, or personality. Rather, these instruments should be considered tools for providing useful information on the basis of which it is possible to describe, diagnose, and predict human behavior.

In a logical sense, the descriptive and diagnostic use of tests can be subsumed under the heading of prediction. The purpose of accurate description, if it is to involve more than entertainment, is to make better predictions; and diagnosis is simply an elaborate form of prediction involving the anticipated consequences of suggested therapies or other contemplated actions. To know the logical steps by which predictions are made from tests, then, is to understand the rationale of all of testing. Actually, there are two logics of prediction, an *actuarial* (or statistical) and a *clinical*. In the statistical approach, which can be used for individual as well as group prediction, it is first necessary to classify persons (or situations) into groups and to note what happens to the people in the various categories. Then, when a new person comes along, he is similarly classified and the prediction is made that what has happened in the past to others so classified, will also happen to him. In the clinical approach, a hypothesis is formulated (and reformulated on the basis of each new piece of information which is gathered) as to what the individual under consideration is really like. Then, on the basis of this "structural dynamic" hypothesis, and of knowledge about the way human beings behave, a prediction is made as to the specific behavior of the person in some particular situation. The empirical evidence gathered so far to compare the two approaches suggests that the statistical approach reaches or exceeds the accuracy of prediction which can be accomplished by the clinical method. Of course, as more and more is learned about human behavior, this can change.

The Evaluation of Tests

Beyond the common sense considerations of the purposes of the test in terms of both the trait and the individual measured and of the feasibility of the test in terms of such things as its cost, the length of time it takes, the ease of scoring, and whether two forms are available, there are four major technical criteria by which a test is evaluated. Each such criterion is related to a type of error which can be made when interpreting test scores.

Interpretive Errors. In the measurement of behavioral characteristics, unlike the usual case in physical measurement, there is no absolute zero point. Neither can it be assumed that a unit on the scale represents the same degree of difference throughout the range of measurement. Thus, the simple raw score report of an individual performance cannot be interpreted directly and is meaningful only when related to the performance of some group of individuals. If there is a misunderstanding either as to exactly with what group an individual score is compared or as to precisely how the comparison is made, the result is an interpretive error.

In testing, interpretive errors are minimized by a process called *standardization*. Standardization involves first, the administration of a test to some well-defined group of persons and a retention of careful records of performance. Then, a specific system for converting a raw score to some sort of derived score which can be interpreted directly is worked out and published as a table of "norms." Thus, the performance of an individual can be compared with the performance of a group of persons to which he belongs (or with that of a group to which he hopes to belong) by means of age scores, grade scores, percentile ranks, standard scores, or expectancy tables.

Variable Errors. Certain chance happenings occur during the process of measuring which lead a person to obtain a slightly different score on one measurement occasion from that which he would on some other. Since these chance errors vary from person to person on a given occasion and from one time to the next for a given person measured for the same trait, they are referred to as variable errors. The extent to which variable errors are present in any measurement procedure is estimated by means of some index of reliability.

Most common among the procedures devised to estimate the reliability of a measuring device are a test-retest correlation coefficient, which defines as variable error any time to time fluctuation; a parallel form reliability, which defines as an error both time to time and form to form fluctuations; split-half reliability, which calls error only fluctuations from one half of the test to the next; and a Kuder-Richardson reliability which defines error in terms of inconsistency of performance from item to item. In general, the parallel form reliability is preferred because it provides a conservative estimate—an index which is not likely to be higher than the true reliability.

Test reliability is affected by test length, the heterogeneity of the group upon which the estimate is based, and the degree to which speed is an important component of the total score. The longer the test, the more heterogeneous the group, and the greater the speed component, the more reliable the instrument will appear.

Personal Errors. Personal errors refer to inconsistencies in the scoring of an instrument either by one person who scores the test on two separate occasions or among several different persons scoring the same instrument. Because personal errors represent a particular type of variable error, no new index is needed to assess an instrument in this respect. However, a measure which is relatively free from this type of error is referred to as *objective*. Other things being equal, the greater the objectivity of an instrument, the greater its reliability will be.

Constant Errors. Because the measurement of behavioral characteristics is indirect, it is never possible to be completely certain that a test measures that precise characteristic for which it was designed. Thus, an error can be made in using tests which is the same for every person to which the instrument is applied and the same every time it is used. These errors are called *constant* errors and information that is gathered to determine exactly what kind of inferences can be made from the test scores is referred to as *validity evidence*. Validity is by far the most important criterion by which a test may be judged, for an objective, reliable, and well standardized instrument can still be completely useless unless the kinds of inferences which can legitimately be made from the test score are known.

Validity information may be classified into three basic types according to whether the data gathered are concerned primarily with the test-taking behavior, with the relationship between test performance and some second behavior, or with establishing the instrument as an adequate measure of a hypothetical construct.

Validity evidence gathered by examining test-taking behavior is referred to as *content* validity and includes *face* validity, which involves a simple judgment as to whether the content is adequate; *logical* validity, in which care is taken to determine whether the test behavior is a representative sample of the behavior in question; and *factorial* validity in which the relationships among many test-taking behaviors are examined to determine the extent to which certain factors contribute to the total test scores.

Data showing the relationship between test and some later (criterion) behavior is called *empirical* validity. Although empirical validity can be interpreted in terms of the accuracy of predicting an individual's criterion score, a more common procedure today is to determine the extent to which selection decisions are improved by the use of the test.

Evidence that goes beyond just describing a relationship between scores on a particular test and some criterion performance and which seems to establish the test as a measure of some hypothesized trait which may affect performance in a variety of ways in many different kinds of situations, represents *construct* validity. Much more complex than other types of information, construct validity requires that the test user be familiar with the theory and evidence about the trait in question as well as the instrument itself and can involve such diverse evidences as group differences, change in performance as a result of experimental manipulation of certain variables, multitrait-multimethod matrices of correlations, internal consistency information, and studies of the test-taking process.

The Construction of Tests and Scales

It is not surprising that the quality of any measuring device depends upon the way in which it was constructed. Yet, all too often it is assumed that a test or scale quickly assembled the night before it is to be used will provide adequate measurement information. Such is seldom the case.

The first and most essential step in the construction of any device designed to measure behavioral characteristics is the careful and specific description of both the behavior to be examined and the context in which the behavior will (or should) occur. Once the characteristic has been adequately defined, the actual writing of the item for either a scale or a test is a matter of casting the content into a particular format according to rules of thumb derived from much trial and error experience in the construction of useful instruments. It should never be assumed, however, that just because an item looks adequate, it will serve the purpose intended. Each item or descriptive statement for a scale must be tried out to determine whether those who respond (or are described) in one way do, in fact, behave differently from those who are described or respond in some other way. Once a set of such discriminating items or discriminating descriptive statements have been assembled, they must be organized in such a way as to minimize the "overlapping" of information and to facilitate scoring and marking.

Multiple Measurement

If several different measures are to be used in combination, a few additional concepts and principles must be kept in mind. First, there are several special problems which arise. For one thing, it cannot be assumed that simply because each single test score is in itself a valid measure, any combination of these scores will also be valid. For another, it should be noted that the reliability of any difference in scores is likely to be less than the average of the reliabilities of the individual scores themselves. Finally, since the measurement of behavioral characteristics is always relative, a score combination cannot result in valid inferences unless the individual components derive their meaning from comparable norm groups.

Whether the results of several measures are combined visually by means of a test score profile, or algebraically, as in a regression equation, some system of weighting comes into play. Unfortunately, the obviously assigned weights do not entirely determine the influence of the individual component on the total score. The actual or effective weights of the separate measures vary directly with their nominal size and with the variance of the scores involved, and inversely with their intercorrelation with the other measures. There is some evidence indicating that when a relatively large number of measures are combined, the differential weighting of the individual components will not usually have a great deal of effect on the total score; but that when only a few different measures are combined, assigned weights which vary to a considerable degree are likely to have a marked effect on the combined score.

Sometimes it is desirable to make inferences from one or more test scores about behavior in several different criterion situations. When working with multiple criteria in such a comparative prediction situation, several alternative procedures are available to the user of tests. It is possible to examine a large number of specific validity evidences, to formulate a general impression of the person in question, and to make a prediction; it is possible to determine a set of cut-off scores and to successively describe the level of an individual's performance in each situation; it is possible to use a discriminant function to compare the individual with those successful in the various situations and to determine which group he most closely resembles; and it is possible to use multiple regression to obtain an optimal prediction of the likely success on each individual criterion. In a practical situation, some combination of these four approaches might be used so as to capitalize on the advantages and minimize the limitations of each alone.

THE CRITICS OF MEASUREMENT

It is not surprising, when a field as technical as that of psychometrics becomes so widely applied in a way that has such a tremendous influence on the lives of those involved, to find a number of well-meaning and highly capable, but unknowledgeable, persons offering criticisms which sometimes present a distorted picture of the place and value of psychological measurement. No specialist in the field of measurement would contend that the measures now available come anywhere near providing a complete and highly precise description of an individual's behavioral characteristics. Rather, tests, inventories, and scales are seen as devices with varying degrees of usefulness for providing information on the basis of which more intelligent decisions can be made.

When carefully extricated from the emotional overtones in which they are all too often shrouded, most current criticisms of testing amount to statements that the accuracy of tests is not perfect, that many important attributes are not yet measured, that the use of tests is a cold, machine-like process, and that the results of tests are sometimes misused.

Critics who point out that the accuracy of tests is not perfect always can cite a case or two in which the inference drawn from measurement was incorrect. Usually, the story is about Johnny or Susie who was discouraged from entering a particular occupation or field of study, but who made a tremendous success anyway. The inference which is intended is that since test scores do not produce completely perfect results, their use should be abandoned. But to say that tests are not perfect (who would disagree with this?) is quite a different thing from saying that they are not useful. Seldom does the critic provide the reader with an alternative to the use of the test score. Apparently, Johnny and Susie are to remain in a position of suspended animation until somebody invents a way of gathering information which will enable them to make decisions without error. If another way of obtaining information is suggested, it often involves a procedure which is known to be far less accurate than the test. Thus, in addition to (or at least instead of) Johnny and Susie, there will be Roger, and Mary, and Dick, and Harry, and Ruth, and many others who will be incorrectly advised. No, test scores are not perfect. But, as long as it is possible to make fewer errors with tests than without them, and until something which can be shown to be better comes along, their continued use will be beneficial to all concerned.

Few students of human behavior would claim that all important characteristics can be assessed with present instruments. Most would feel that the surface has just begun to be scratched, and many, many attributes thought to be of considerable importance have thus far eluded the behavior scientist who seeks ways to describe individuals in quantitative terms. The fact that our concepts are not yet clear nor our measures even reasonably adequate in such areas as social intelligence, creativity, and appreciative reactions does not mean, however, that tests of scholastic ability, of achievement, or of interests, attitudes, and certain personality characteristics should be avoided. These latter characteristics are important, too, and their measurement provides us with some valuable information about the individual.

The argument that tests should be abandoned because the use of a test score selection or prediction system seems cold and machine-like would appear to represent an inappropriate application of humanistic values. Surely, everyone would feel that the most humane process is that which results in the fewest serious errors in making decisions. Thus, those who seem to fear the use of numbers and automatic prediction systems when working with human beings are assuming either that a procedure which involves human estimation will always be more accurate than one which depends upon instruments, or that somehow human value judgments have not been involved when a numerical prediction system is set up.

Neither of these two assumptions is valid. Those who continually admonish "Never use test scores alone" seldom take the trouble to determine whether the additional information which they are recommending will, in fact, improve the situation. Unfortunately, the additional data sometimes reflects human biases and errors, and an implicit combination and use of the information available which is processed inside the human skull rather than through a rigorous, external analysis often fails to capitalize upon empirically valid relationships. The result is, therefore, often deleterious rather than beneficial to the individual involved.

Rather than eliminating value judgments, an automatic prediction system often provides the only means by which human values can be fully implemented. A human being must be able to decide what it means to be successful, what kind of person should get a scholarship, and whether selecting a person who will fail or passing over someone who would have succeeded is the most serious error. Once the value judgment has been made, however, numerical description and analytic prediction will usually provide the greatest assurance that the implications of these value judgments are accurately carried out.

Tests, like every other tool which man has invented, can be misused. There are those who forget, or fail to understand, the probabilistic nature of inferences from test scores and feel that once the results of the measurement of behavioral characteristics are reported, one's destiny is determined. But this does not mean that we should abolish tests any more than the fact that some persons maim or kill others with the automobile means that we should eliminate the car as a form of transportation. Rather, the problem is one of education, and, perhaps, restricting the use of the tool to those who are willing to take the trouble to understand it and use it in a way which will be beneficial rather than harmful to those concerned.

IN CONCLUSION

Those who know and understand the nature of the measurement of behavioral characteristics and who faithfully apply the concepts and principles set forth in this book, need not be dismayed when they read or hear criticisms such as those outlined above. History makes clear the fact that no amount of well-intentioned but ignorant criticism and no amount of resistance to complex concepts will prevent our knowledge from expanding nor keep the application of measurement from spreading to those areas in which it can make a contribution toward enhancing the welfare of each person as an individual human being.

For those who have an interest in studying and working with human beings, for those who are willing and diligent enough to examine complex concepts both through verbal and mathematical analysis, and for those who can find creative solutions to seemingly impossible problems, there are thrilling prospects in store in the field of psychometrics.

References

APA Committee on Psychological Tests. Technical recommendations for psychological tests and diagnostic techniques: preliminary proposal. *Amer. Psychol.*, 1952, 7, 461–476.

APA Committee on Psychological Tests. Technical recommendations for psychological tests and diagnostic techniques. *Psychol. Bull. Supplemt.*, 1954, 51, 2, Part 2, 1–38.

BARNES, E. Response bias and the MMPI. *J. consult. Psychol.*, 1956, 20, 371–374.

BROEN, W. and WIRT, R. Varieties of response sets. *J. consult. Psychol.*, 1958, 22, 237–240.

CAMPBELL, D. and FISKE, D. Convergent and Discriminant Validation by the multitrait-multimethod matrix. *Psychol. Bull.*, 1959, 56, 81–105.

CATTELL, J. M. Mental tests and measurements, *Mind*, 1890, 15, 373–380.

CATTELL, R. Psychological measurement: ipsative, normative and interactive. *Psychol. Rev.*, 1944, 51, 292–303.

CHAMPHEY, H. The measurement of parent behavior. *Child Develpm.*, 1941, 12, 131–166.

CHAMPHEY, H. and MARSHALL, H. Optimal refinement of the rating scale. *J. appl. Psychol.*, 1939, 23, 323–331.

CRONBACH, L. *Essentials of psychological testing.* New York: Harper & Row, 1949.

CRONBACH, L. *Essentials of psychological testing* (2nd ed.) New York: Harper & Row, 1960.

CRONBACH, L. Response sets and test validity. *Educ. psychol. measmt.*, 1946, 6, 475–494.

CRONBACH, L. and GLESER, G. *Psychological tests and personnel decisions.* Urbana: University of Illinois Press, 1957. 165 pp.

CRONBACH, L. and MEEHL, P. Construct validity in psychological tests. *Psychol. Bull.*, 1955, 52, 281–302.

233

CURETON, E. A recipe for a cookbook. *Psychol. Bull.*, 1957, 54, 494–497.

DERNER, G., ABORN, M., and CARTER, A. The Reliability of the Wechsler-Bellevue subtest and scales. *J. consult. Psychol.*, 1950, 14, 172–179.

DOUGLASS, H. and SPENCER, P. Is it necessary to weight exercises in standardized tests. *J. educ. Psychol.*, 1923, 14, 109–112.

DVORAK, B. Occupational prediction by means of multi-factor tests. *Proceedings: Conference on using multi-factor aptitude tests in educational and vocational counseling and prediction.* Berkley: University of California, 1953.

EBEL, R. Writing the test item. Chap. 7 *in* E. Lindquist (Ed.), *Educational measurement,* Washington: Amer. Council on Educ., 1950. 819 pp.

EDWARDS, A. *Techniques of attitude scale construction.* New York: Appleton-Century-Crofts, 1957. 256 pp.

EYSENCK, H. Criterion-analysis — an application of the hypothetical deductive method in factor analysis. *Psychol. Rev.*, 1950, 57, 38–53.

FAN, C. *Item analysis table.* Princeton, N.J.: Educational Testing Service, 1952.

FLANAGAN, JOHN C. A table of the values of the product-moment coefficient of correlation in a normal-bivariate population corresponding to a given proportion of success. 1936.

FLANAGAN, J. Critical requirements: a new approach to employee evaluation. *Personnel Psychol.*, 1949, 2, 419–425.

FRENCH, J. The description of aptitude and achievement tests in terms of rotated factors. *Psychometric Monogr.*, 1951, No. 5. Chicago: University of Chicago Press. 278 pp.

FRENCH, J. *The description of personality measurements in terms of rotated factors.* Princeton, N.J.: Educational Testing Service, 1953.

GEBHART, G. and HOYT, D. Personality needs of under and over achievers. *J. appl. Psychol.*, 1958, 42, 125–128.

GUILFORD, J. *Psychometric methods* (2nd ed.) New York: McGraw-Hill, 1954.

GUILFORD, J. *A revised structure of the intellect.* Reports from the Psychological Laboratory, No. 19. Los Angeles: University of Southern California, 1957. 27 pp.

GUILFORD, J. *Personality.* New York: McGraw-Hill, 1959. 562 pp.

GULLIKSEN, H. *Theory of mental tests.* John Wiley & Sons, 1950.

GUTTMAN, L. A basis for analyzing test reliability. *Psychometrika,* 1945, 10, 255–282.

HARMAN, H. *Modern factor analysis.* Chicago: University of Chicago Press, 1960. 469 pp.

HATHAWAY, S. and MEEHL, P. *An atlas for the clinical use of the MMPI.* Minneapolis: University of Minnesota Press, 1951. 799 pp.

HAWKES, H., LINDQUIST, E., and MANN, C. *The construction and use of achievement exams: A manual for secondary school teachers.* Cambridge: The Riverside Press, 1936. 497 pp.

HELMSTADTER, G. Procedures for obtaining separate set and content components of a test score. *Psychometrika,* 1957, 22, 381–393.

HELMSTADTER, G. The selection of students for the reading and study skills course. *Research Memo 57–3.* Fort Collins, Col.: Colorado State University, 1957.

HIGHLAND, R. and BERKSHIRE, J. A methodological study of forced-choice performance ratings. V *Res. Bull.* 51–9 HRRC. San Antonio, Texas, 1951.

HORST, P. Item analysis by the method of successive residuals. *J. exp. Educ.,* 1934, 2, 254–263.

HORST, P. Optimal test length for maximum differential prediction. *Psychometrika,* 1956, 21, 51–56.

HORST, P. and MACEWAN, C. Optimal test length for maximum absolute prediction. *Psychometrika,* 1956, 21, 51–66.

HORST, P. and MACEWAN, C. Optimal test length for multiple prediction: the general case. *Psychometrika,* 1957, 22, 311–324.

HOYT, C. Test reliability estimated by analysis of variance. *Psychometrika,* 1941, 6, 153–160.

HUTTNER, L. and KATZELL, R. Developing a yardstick of supervisory performance. *Personnel,* 1957, 33, 371–378.

KEATS, J. *A statistical theory of objective test scores.* Melbourne, Australia: Australian Council for Educational Research, 1951.

KELLEY, T. *Interpretation of educational measurements.* Yonkers, N.Y.: World Book, 1927.

KUDER, G. and RICHARDSON, M. The theory of estimation of test reliability. *Psychometrika,* 1937, 2, 151–160.

LOEVINGER, J. The attenuation paradox in test theory. *Psychol. Bull.,* 1954, 51, 493–504.

LOEVINGER, J. Theory and techniques of assessment. *Annual Review of Psychology,* 1959, 287–318.

LORD, F. Optimum level of item difficulty. *Research Memo,* Princeton, N.J.: Education Testing Service, 1953.

LORD, F. The standard errors of various test statistics when the test items are sampled. *Research Bull.,* Princeton, N.J.: Education Testing Service, 1953. 53–20.

LUCAS, C. Analysis of the relative movement test by a method of individual interviews. *Bur. Naval Personnel Research Report* Contract Nonr-694, 00 N R 151–13 ETS, March, 1953.

MARSH, S. and PERRIN, F. An experimental study of the rating scale technique. *J. abnorm. and soc. Psychol.*, 1925, 19, 383–399.

MEEHL, P. *Clinical vs statistical prediction.* Minneapolis: University of Minnesota Press, 1954.

MEEHL, P. and ROSEN, A. Antecedent probability and the efficiency of psychometric signs, patterns, or cutting scores. *Psychol. Bull.*, 1955, 52, 194–195.

METFESSEL, N. and SAX, G. Systematic biases in the keying of correct responses on certain standardized tests. *Educ. psychol. Measmt.*, 1958, 18, 787–790.

MOSIER, C. Symposium: the need and means of cross-validation. I. problems and designs of cross-validation. *Educ. psychol. Measmt.*, 1951, 11, 5–11.

MURSELL, J. *Psychological Testing.* New York: David McKay, 1947. 449 pp.

SARBIN, T. The logic of prediction in psychology. *Psychol. Rev.*, 1944, 51, 210–228.

SOLOMON, H. (Ed.) *Item analysis and prediction.* Stanford, Calif.: Stanford University Press, 1961. 310 pp.

STALNAKER, J. The essay type of examination. In E. Lindquist (Ed.) *Educ. Measmt.* Washington, D.C.: American Council on Education, 1950.

STECKLINE, J. *Bulletins on classroom testing.* Minneapolis: Bureau of Institutional Research, University of Minnesota.

STEPHENSON, W. *The study of behavior: Q-technique and its methodology.* Chicago: University of Chicago Press, 1953. 376 pp.

STEVENS, S. Mathematics, measurement and psychophysics. Chap. 1 *in* S. Stevens (Ed.) *Handbook of experimental psychology,* 1951, 1436 pp.

SYMONDS, P. On the loss of reliability in ratings due to coarseness of the scale. *J. exp. Psychol.*, 1924, 7, 456–461.

TAYLOR, H. and RUSSELL, J. The relationship of validity coefficients to the practical effectiveness of tests in selection: discussion and tables. *J. appl. Psychol.* 1939, 23, 565–578.

THORNTON, G. The effect upon judgments of personality traits of varying a single factor in a photograph. *J. soc. Psychol.*, 1943, 18, 127–148.

THORNTON, G. The effect of wearing glasses upon judgments of personality traits of persons seen briefly. *J. appl. Psychol.*, 1944, 28, 203–207.

THURSTONE, L. and CHAVE, E. *The measurement of attitude.* Chicago: University of Chicago Press, 1929.

TOOPS, H. Test for vocational guidance of children thirteen to sixteen. *Contributions to Educ.,* No. 136. New York: Teachers College, Columbia University, 1923. 137–153.

TORGERSON, W. *Theory and methods of scaling.* New York: John Wiley & Sons, 1958. 460 pp.

TUCKER, L. Maximum validity of a test with equivalent items. *Psychometrika,* 11, 1946, 1–13.

WEBSTER, H. Correcting personality scales for response sets or suppression effects. *Psychol. Bull.,* 1958, 55, 62–64.

WILKES, S. Sample criteria for testing equality of means, equality of variances and equality of co-variances in a normal multivariate distribution. *The ann. math. Stat.,* 1946, 17, 257–281.

WISSLER, C. The correlation of mental and physical tests. *Psychol. Rev. monogr. suppl.,* 1901, 3, No. 6.

Name Index

239

Subject Index